PELICAN BOOKS

THE ENERGY QUESTION

Gerald Foley was born in Ireland in 1936. He studied engineering at University College, Cork, and at Leeds University. He worked as a professional engineer for twelve years. From 1971 to 1978 he taught at the Architectural Association School of Architecture in London, becoming Director of the Post-Graduate Energy Programme. In the past decade his work has increasingly been focused on the developing world. He has travelled widely and has worked as an energy consultant to the government of Tanzania, as well as for the World Bank, EEC, FAO, the International Fund for Agricultural Development, the Beijer Institute of the Royal Swedish Academy of Sciences, the International Institute for Environment and Development and other international organizations. His publications include *Nuclear or Not: Choices for Our Energy Future* (joint editor), 1978; *A Low Energy Strategy for the United Kingdom* (co-author), 1979; the report of the World Coal Study *Coal Bridge to the Future* (technical editor), 1980; *Energy and the Transition from Rural Subsistence* (co-editor), 1982; as well as an extensive series of reports, technical studies and academic papers covering various aspects of energy in the industrial and developing worlds. He is currently Director of Policy Research at the Panos Institute, an international organization concerned with research and the dissemination of information on environment and development issues. He lives in London.

GERALD FOLEY

The Energy Question

Third Edition

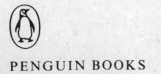

PENGUIN BOOKS

To Lanna, Katie, and Conor

PENGUIN BOOKS

Published by the Penguin Group
27 Wrights Lane, London W8 5TZ, England
Viking Penguin Inc., 40 West 23rd Street, New York, New York 10010, USA
Penguin Books Australia Ltd, Ringwood, Victoria, Australia
Penguin Books Canada Ltd, 2801 John Street, Markham, Ontario, Canada L3R 1B4
Penguin Books (NZ) Ltd, 182–190 Wairau Road, Auckland 10, New Zealand

Penguin Books Ltd, Registered Offices: Harmondsworth, Middlesex, England

First published in Pelican Books 1976
Second edition 1981
Third edition 1987
Reprinted in Penguin Books 1989
10 9 8 7 6 5 4 3 2 1

Made and printed in Great Britain by
Richard Clay Ltd, Bungay, Suffolk
Filmset in Lasercomp Times

The laws expressing the relations between energy and matter are not solely of importance in pure science. They necessarily come first . . . in the whole record of human experience, and they control, in the last resort, the rise or fall of political systems, the freedom or bondage of nations, the movements of commerce and industry, the origin of wealth and poverty and the general physical welfare of the race. If this has been too imperfectly recognized in the past, there is no excuse, now that these physical laws have become incorporated into everyday habits of thought, for neglecting to consider them first in questions relating to the future – FREDERICK SODDY, *Matter and Energy*, 1912

Contents

List of Figures and Tables

Figures

Tables

x   *List of Figures and Tables*

Acknowledgements

My greatest debt of gratitude is to Charlotte Nassim, who collaborated with me on the first two editions of this book. I would also thank Gerald Leach, who suggested the book in the first place and has been a valued friend and colleague over the past fifteen years.

The many people who helped in the preparation of the previous editions have already been gratefully acknowledged. In the six years since the last edition was published, I have been helped and influenced by many people. I owe a great deal to Ariane van Buren, with whom I worked on a number of energy projects. Geoff Barnard has been a staunch collaborator in a series of studies and publications on energy in the developing world. And I owe a great deal to Jon Tinker and my colleagues in the Panos Institute, who have been a continued source of help and encouragement. I would also like to thank Mike Prior and Mr Eric Ruttley for their help with this edition. My wife, Lanna, as always, has cheerfully borne the burden of my obsessions; without her support nothing would have been possible.

No one except myself should be blamed for any deficiencies in the content or style of the book.

G.F.

Preface to the Third Edition

The second edition of this book was published in 1981. While it was being prepared, the gloomy prognostications of the early 1970s appeared to be coming true. Oil prices had doubled again in 1979 and there were confident predictions of it reaching $100 a barrel before the turn of the century.

Advocates of nuclear power were vigorously promoting it as a means of breaking the economic stranglehold of the Organization of Petroleum Exporting Countries (OPEC); this provoked an ever more determined hostility on the part of those opposed to it. The coal industry was quietly confident of its potential to fill the energy 'gap'.

Now the price of oil is more or less back to where it was at the end of the 1960s. The once all-powerful OPEC has become a group of squabbling oil producers, each desperately trying to keep afloat economically in a world which is suddenly awash with oil. On the nuclear side, the tragedy at Chernobyl has shown that, despite all the assurances of the experts, terrible nuclear accidents can take place. In complete contrast with the 1970s, the industry is in a chastened and defensive mood. The coal industry, worldwide, is in a state of financial crisis because of the failure of markets to grow as anticipated.

Looking back, it is also apparent how much the general sensibility about energy and technology have changed in the past five years. It is no longer necessary to sound warnings against over-optimism about the potential of new energy technologies; most of them have almost completely dropped out of sight. There is no need to rail about the need for increased energy conservation in buildings and industry or more economical engines for cars;

everyone is now in favour of them, and enormous improvements have been made and more are on the way.

The terms of the energy debate have thus changed in a number of major respects. But the subject remains as interesting and important as ever. Without secure and adequate energy supplies the modern world would totally disintegrate.

The objectives of this edition remain those of the first two: to provide background and current information, and a guide to what is most significant. It has been very substantially rewritten to reflect the greatly changed energy world of the late 1980s, and to explain how and why this has come about. A new section has been added in which the very different energy systems and problems of the developing world are discussed.

G.F.
1987

Notes on Units and Conversions

No widely used system of units covers the full range of topics discussed in this book, and any attempt to impose one would be both pedantic and confusing. The following conventions have, rather arbitrarily, been chosen for use in the text; tables of detailed conversion factors have been included in the Appendix.

Metric System

This has been used throughout with the exception of oil-industry statistics, which obstinately follow rules of their own. The small difference between Imperial tons and metric tonnes has generally been ignored.

Numbers

Powers-of-ten notation has been used for very large and very small numbers. A million is thus 1.0×10^6 and a millionth is 1.0×10^{-6}. International English-speaking usage has been followed for the terms billion, which is taken as a thousand million, 1.0×10^9, and trillion, which is 1.0×10^{12}.

Energy Units

Système International d'Unités (S I) energy units have been slowly creeping into more popular use in recent years, but are still unfamiliar to many people. The kilowatt-hour (kWh) – the use of which does not have to be confined to electricity – is therefore retained as the general energy unit most commonly used throughout the book. One kilowatt-hour is equal to 3·6 megajoules (MJ).

Large quantities of energy have generally been expressed as tonnes of oil equivalent (toe), or million tonnes of oil equivalent (mtoe). In some cases, tonnes of coal equivalent (tce) have been used. One tonne of oil equivalent is equal to 1·5 tonnes of coal equivalent.

The output of power stations follows conventional practice and is usually expressed in megawatts (MW); very large power outputs are expressed in gigawatts (GW). One gigawatt is equal to 1000 megawatts.

Oil-industry Statistics

The oil industry almost invariably expresses quantities of petroleum products in barrels. The barrel is a measure of volume and the number of barrels per tonne varies in accordance with the density of the product – from 6·7 barrels per tonne in the case of heavy crude oil, up to 8·5 barrels per tonne in the case of motor spirit. The commonly accepted average figure of 7·3 barrels per tonne has been used for crude oil and petroleum products in general. One barrel per day is thus equivalent to 50 tonnes per year.

Energy Equivalents and Statistical Inconsistencies

The factors used to convert different fuels to oil or coal equivalents vary widely. Caution is therefore required when making detailed comparisons between statistics from different sources. No attempt has been made to 'correct' or harmonize the various sources used in this book. To do so would simply introduce further distortions and inconsistencies in statistics which are often accurate only to within 5–10 per cent.

When dealing with electricity produced by nuclear or hydro stations, the usual convention, which is followed in this book, is to express it in terms of the oil or coal which would have been required to produce it in a modern power station.

Some 'Energy Signposts'

The following approximate figures may help readers to obtain a sense of the comparative magnitude of various energy-using processes:

A single-bar electric fire uses a kilowatt-hour every hour.

The daily intake of food energy of a well-nourished western adult male is about 3 kilowatt-hours; the maximum daily output of work of a manual worker is about 0·5 kilowatt-hours. The work output of a horse in an eight-hour day is about 6 kilowatt-hours.

A litre of petrol contains about 10 kilowatt-hours.

A tonne of coal contains about 8000 kilowatt-hours.

A typical large modern coal-fired power station (of 1000 megawatts) produces a million kilowatt-hours every hour and consumes about 400 tonnes of coal while doing so.

The United Kingdom consumes about 200 million tonnes of oil equivalent every year.

The world uses about 7·4 billion tonnes of oil equivalent every year.

The total amount of solar energy intercepted by the earth every hour is about $1·7 \times 10^{14}$ kilowatt-hours, more than twice the total annual energy consumption of the world.

Introduction

Energy is one of the most familiar concepts. People may talk of the energy of a lively child, of the sun, of the waves or of the wind. They recognize that energy is stored in a spinning flywheel, in the wound spring of a watch or in the plutonium core of an atomic bomb.

William Blake said, 'Energy is Eternal Delight.' The author of an academic work on thermodynamics cautiously ventured, 'Energy may be thought of as a capacity for doing work.' And Einstein pointed out that energy is equal to mass multiplied by the velocity of light squared.

Energy is all these and more. It is described in a variety of ways and none defines it fully, though each reveals one of its aspects. Energy is heat, light, electricity and a capacity to do work. More fundamentally, it is that which each of these has in common with the others. And energy is matter. It is this last which enables it to be said that energy is everything, the ultimate, irreducible essence of the universe.

But considering universal truths is useful only up to a point. Looking at everything can prevent one seeing anything, particularly the practical. And energy is emphatically a practical concern. Energy grows food and keeps people alive. It transports them, fuels machines and sustains economic systems. The fossil fuels – coal, oil and natural gas – are the basis of modern industrial society. When energy supplies are in question, all that depends on them is also in question; not only the way of life but life itself.

A chilly air of reality intrudes itself very quickly into any discussion about energy. Food and warmth, transport and jobs, standards of living and future prospects, all depend on society's ability to continue supplying itself with the energy it has grown to need. It must do this without disrupting the great natural energy systems of the earth on which the heat balance and climate depend, and without destroying the living web of the biosphere of which human society is itself a part. And it must look beyond these immediate concerns to the inevitable decline in the availability of the fossil fuels and the need to find a substitute for them if industrial civilization is to survive.

For most of human history the majority of people have had nothing but the energy of their own leg muscles to transport themselves. In the medieval city all the necessities of daily life had to be located within walking distance of everyone. Shops, markets, workplaces and dwellings were clustered together with a minimum wastage of space. Furthermore, the slow pace of animal carts and beasts driven along unmetalled roads limited the area of hinterland from which a city might draw its food supplies.

Up to as late as 1830, the London villages, now more familiar as the names of stations on the Underground were being supplied with food carried in on carts or driven on foot from the fields around them. The size of a town and its supportable population was, even then, governed by such factors as how far one could make a cow or a goose walk, and the length of time food would remain edible as it was being transported.

Now the abundant energy of petroleum has removed most of these limitations. Food can be carried hundreds of miles by road or rail in a single day. Ships make the rich food-producing areas of the world accessible to everyone. Refrigerated storage eliminates the problem of decay. A country with money to spend can obtain all the food it needs to feed its people at any level of nutrition they care to adopt. A measure of the change which has occurred can be obtained by a simple comparison: a tonne of oil contains an amount of energy equivalent to the hourly work output of a herd of no less than 17 000 horses. A couple of modern trucks are more effective than the whole transport system of even the largest cities of 150 years ago.

Victorian Britain was not just a pyrotechnical display of mechanical and scientific inventiveness, commercial skill and opportunism, imperial ambition and military prowess. It was also a twenty-fold increase in the consumption of coal. America's ability to put a man on the moon sprang not just from the skill of its scientists and technologists; it was also a product of a society which at that time was consuming a total of thirteen times as much energy as Britain was at the height of its imperial power just before the First World War.

The gulf between a highly developed and a subsistence economy does not exist because the researcher examining samples of moon rock is an inherently superior human being to the hill shepherd. It depends almost entirely on the relative availability of energy within their two societies. Like some great hovercraft, industrial society is lifted and maintained above concern with the elemental necessities of life by a prodigious expenditure of energy. Without this energy supply, the sophisticated skills of the industrial world are merely a burden in the struggle for survival. The theme of this book is the relationship between energy use and the evolution, present functioning and potential future of human society.

The first part examines energy systems. Human existence depends upon a delicate balance between the earth's absorption and reflection of solar energy. The distribution of the deserts and fertile areas, ice-bound tundra and temperate zones, even the relative areas of land and ocean, depends on the solar-energy-driven circulatory systems of the winds, rains and ocean currents.

The history of humanity's emergence from the ecological niche appropriate to a medium-size omnivorous mammal to its present position as the earth's dominant species is one of increasing skill at harnessing and manipulating energy. Each step in this evolution has been marked by an extension of the ability to control the flows and accumulated energy resources available in the surrounding world.

But energy has been more than just the fuel for humanity's material advance: it has been a major unifying principle in the development of an understanding of the universe. The fundamental principles of heat, light, sound, electricity, magnetism and radio were elucidated in the extraordinary scientific work of the seventeenth to nineteenth centuries. Energy was the common ground on which these independent disciplines could be joined and mutually reinforced. The twentieth century brought Einstein and a revolutionary proposition about matter and energy.

The second part of the book looks at the energy resources on which humanity depends. Coal, oil and natural gas are the basis of industrial society, but they are disappearing at a rate millions of times faster than they were formed. The question of how long these resources can last is vitally important to the future of the human race.

There has been a great deal of discussion about possible alternatives to these fuels. A decade ago, vast sums of money were being poured into schemes for extracting the oil trapped in tar sands and the world's vast resources of oil shales. Many people are optimistic about obtaining energy from the sun, wind, tides, waves, the earth's internal heat and the temperature gradients of the oceans, or of turning plant material into liquid or gaseous fuels. Hydro power already contributes significantly to the world's energy supplies and could be expanded. There are the benefits and increasingly obvious dangers of nuclear power. On the horizon there is the mirage or reality of nuclear fusion.

It is not just a question of the absolute magnitude of these resources. The practical availability of energy is limited by social, geographical, political, technical and economic constraints. It must be possible to deliver it to customers in a form they can use and at a price they can afford. And this must be done without endangering the biosphere and environmental systems on which society's continued existence depends.

The third part deals with energy in the developing world. This focuses particularly on the 2 billion people who rely mainly upon wood for their basic energy needs. Many are now facing the prospect of the depletion of this renewable energy resource on which they depend. A major element in the task facing the developing countries, ironically, is to devise a way of enabling them to tap into the non-renewable energy systems of the industrial world. Only by doing so can they participate in the search for a sustainable solution to the problem of meeting humanity's long-term energy needs.

The final part is called 'Choosing the Energy Future'. There is no reliable method of predicting what is going to happen. The most dismal predictions are a challenge to use the vast resources of human ingenuity to ensure they do not come true. Much has been learned about energy in the past ten years. It provides a basis for an informed debate on the energy that future society wishes to create for itself.

Part One

Energy and Society

No one today is ignorant of the part played by energy, not only in science, but in industry, politics and the whole science of human welfare. From the cradle to the grave everyone is dependent on Nature for an absolutely continuous supply of energy in one or other of its numerous forms. When the supplies are ample there is prosperity, expansion and development. When they are not, there is want. Often, it is true, energy appears to play a very subsidiary and indirect part in the development, just as, no doubt, the supply of wind might be looked upon as playing a very secondary role in the music of an organ. The fact remains that, if the supply of energy failed, modern civilization would come to an end as abruptly as does the music of an organ deprived of wind – FREDERICK SODDY, *Matter and Energy*, 1912

1

The Earth's Energy Systems

In the sun-centred myths of many early religions, people acknowledged the supremacy of the sun-god who controlled night, day,
the seasons and the elements. Later, science, astronomy and the
telescope got rid of the magic and poetry. But for the human
race, the sun is still supreme. All living creatures depend on it.
It provides the energy without which nothing could live or
grow.

The energy of the sun originates in its core, where the temperature is about 12 000 000°C. Under these conditions matter
exists in the form of a plasma in which atoms are stripped of
their electrons. In the solar plasma, elements are transmuted as
the nuclei of light atoms fuse together to form heavier elements.
This is nuclear fusion. In the process some mass is transformed
into energy in accordance with Einstein's equation $E = mc^2$
(energy is equal to mass multiplied by the velocity of light
squared). The sun is losing mass at the astonishing rate of six
million tonnes a second.

The energy released by the sun's nuclear fusion is in the form
of electromagnetic radiation. This is a generic description of all
types of radiant energy. It includes visible light, X-rays, wireless
and television waves, ultraviolet and infra-red rays, each of which
differs in its wavelength from the others. They range from the
millionths of a centimetre of the shortest gamma rays, through
to the hundreds of metres of long-wave radio.

In the core of the sun the radiant energy is mainly in the form
of gamma rays. At the surface, 500 000 kilometres away, the
radiation is no longer concentrated at the extreme short end of
the spectrum but has been spread and shifted along it. The

temperature is about 5800°C. A large proportion of the energy is emitted in the form of light – those wavelengths which are visible to the human eye. With distance from the sun, the intensity of radiation diminishes; it falls off in proportion to the square of its distance. At the outer limits of the solar system the sun's radiation has diminished almost to the point of vanishing; it is far too low to support life in any of its terrestrial forms.

The Global Energy Balance

At the edge of the earth's atmosphere the intensity of radiation is 1·4 kilowatts per square metre; it is referred to as the solar flux, or the solar constant. The earth's outline intercepts energy at the rate of about $1·7 \times 10^{14}$ kilowatts, which is approximately 100 000 times the total generating capacity of all the world's electricity generating stations.

Yet in spite of this inundation of energy, the earth's temperature remains remarkably constant. The inflow of energy must therefore be balanced by an equal outflow. An equally important factor as far as the earth's living creatures are concerned is the difference between the amounts of energy reflected and absorbed. The earth and its atmosphere absorb about 70 per cent of the energy reaching it from the sun. If it absorbed more, the temperature would be higher; if it absorbed less, the temperature would be lower. This is because the amount of energy an object radiates is related to its temperature: the higher the temperature, the greater the rate at which energy is lost. If the earth begins to absorb more of the sun's energy, its temperature will rise until the rate at which it is radiating energy balances the energy inflow. The converse is true if the amount of energy being absorbed is reduced. In either case, life which evolved under the previous temperature conditions may find the new situation intolerable. There are strong incentives for the human race to do nothing which would upset the present division between the amounts of solar energy absorbed and reflected.

A great deal of human activity could well have an effect on this. Energy is reflected from clouds and atmospheric particles as well as from the surfaces of land and water. An ice-covered continent, a jungle and an ocean all reflect differently. Changes in the vegetational cover, large-scale discoloration of the seas and variations in the composition or dust content of the atmosphere can all alter the balance between absorbed and reflected energy.

Over the past couple of hundred years and most particularly in the present century, human activity has changed the texture and colour of the landscape: it has poured dusts and gases into the atmosphere; it has created palls of smoke, steam and smog; it has changed the colour of large areas of seas and oceans. Some of these effects reinforce each other; others act in opposite directions. The results of this global experiment are completely unpredictable in the present state of knowledge. But so far the equilibrium which has permitted human life to exist has been maintained.

As it passes through the earth's atmosphere, the energy from the sun is absorbed in a variety of ways. The role played by the ozone layer, which occurs about 25 kilometres above the surface of the earth, is another of those quirks of nature which has permitted the evolution of terrestrial life in its present forms. Ozone is a molecular form of oxygen with three atoms instead of the usual two. It is important here because it absorbs ultraviolet light, which is dangerous to life even in moderate doses; in laboratories it is often used as a sterilizing agent. If the full intensity of the ultraviolet light in the sun's radiation were to reach the earth's surface, most life would be eliminated.

The ultraviolet component accounts for about 5 per cent of the sun's radiation. In the ozone layer a complicated process occurs in which 'ordinary' oxygen and ozone interact with ultraviolet radiation and prevent most of it reaching the surface. The small amount which does penetrate can, however, be thanked for holiday suntans. When exposed to small doses of ultraviolet radiation, the skin produces a protective pigment. Even in the comparatively slight exposures necessary to produce a skin tan, however, ultraviolet radiation is to be treated warily. The fact that it causes malignant skin cancer is making many people revise their attitude to sunbathing.

It is thus important that the ozone layer should continue to remain effective. One of the most serious objections to supersonic air travel is that the exhaust emissions from aircraft like Concorde appear to have damaging effects upon the ozone layer and its action as a life-preserving filter. There are also worries about the fluorocarbon gases released from aerosol containers; these gases are believed to ascend into the ozone layer and damage it. As always, there are plenty of people who feel there is no cause for alarm, but it is an issue on which the human race cannot afford to be optimistic – and wrong.

Solar radiation is also absorbed by water droplets, dust particles and carbon dioxide. Some wavelengths are more heavily absorbed than others. Figure 1 shows a typical distribution of solar energy at the earth's surface in comparison with the outer edge of the atmosphere. The ultraviolet is almost completely absorbed, as are some of the infra-red wavelengths. The diagram shows clear sky conditions. Downwind from a cement works on a cloudy day in November, the solar energy distribution at ground level would show a near-zero intensity for all wavelengths.

The total radiation reaching the earth's surface is called the 'insolation'; it is about half the total solar flux. In clear weather about half the insolation is in the visible band of the spectrum, with the rest being in the form of infra-red radiation. All the radiation, whether visible or infra-red, which is not reflected from an object causes its temperature to rise. In daylight, therefore, the earth and the objects upon it become warmer; at night they lose their heat and become colder.

When objects give off heat, they do so in the form of infra-red radiation. This can be 'seen' by using a scanner which is sensitive to it, as is done in many forms of missile detection and night-sight systems. All objects have an 'emission spectrum' which is determined by the temperature they have reached. At low temperatures the emission spectrum will be confined to the infra-red; it will be possible to feel but not to see the radiation. As the temperature rises, the wavelengths of the emitted radiation shorten and the object, say a piece of iron, starts to glow. The mean global surface temperature at present is about 13°C.

Carbon dioxide is another component of the atmosphere which contributes to the regulation of the global heat balance in an important way. It is transparent to visible light, but it absorbs infra-red radiation. Solar radiation in the visible spectrum therefore passes unimpeded by the carbon dioxide content of the atmosphere on its inward path to the earth's surface. When it is

Figure 1. Distribution of solar energy intensity along the electromagnetic spectrum

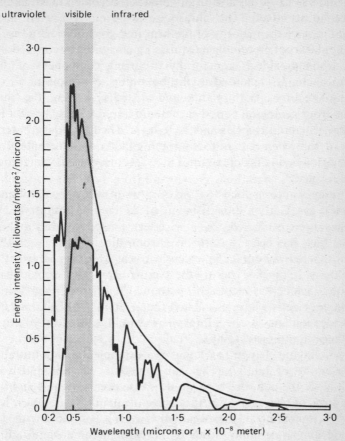

Note: Top curve shows intensities at the edge of the atmosphere. Lower curve shows typical 'clear-sky' distribution at ground level. Visible spectrum is shown shaded.

re-radiated in the form of infra-red radiation, however, it is absorbed.

A somewhat similar effect occurs with a greenhouse. Glass transmits visible light, but absorbs infra-red. When the greenhouse is warmed by sunlight, some of the heat is trapped inside by the glass and it remains warmer than its surroundings. The similarity between this and the effect of atmospheric carbon dioxide has led to discussion of what has become known as the 'greenhouse effect'. The phrase is, however, somewhat misleading, since the majority of the heat in a greenhouse is a result of the glass roof preventing it from being dissipated by convection.

Carbon dioxide is a naturally occurring component of the atmosphere. It is emitted in the breathing, or 'respiration', of living creatures, both plants and animals. During the carboniferous geological period carbon dioxide levels are thought to have been about twice as high as today's. The temperatures were considerably higher than today's and conditions were better for plant growth and the creation of the vast forests from which coal was formed.

Present concerns focus on the burning of wood, coal, oil and natural gas. Carbon dioxide is one of the combustion products. It has been estimated that the effect of the combustion of these fuels has been to raise the carbon dioxide content of the atmosphere by about 0·25 per cent per year over the past twenty-five years. In the past century the average atmospheric content of carbon dioxide has increased by about 15 per cent.

Some scientists have calculated that a doubling of the carbon dioxide content of the atmosphere would cause the average temperature to increase by 2°. This could be sufficient to trigger major climatic changes, affecting, for example, the amount and distribution of rainfall. The fear sometimes expressed that a melting of the polar ice-caps would cause ocean levels to rise by hundreds of metres is unjustified since the major part of these ice masses is floating in the ocean; but even a 3–5-metre rise, as would almost certainly occur if the earth became significantly warmer, would have devastating effects on the world's major ports and coastal cities.

The consequences of a major shift in climatic patterns are incalculable. The earth is inhabitable because of a very delicate balance between enormous flows of energy; there is no way of predicting how they would settle into a new equilibrium if they were disrupted. The deadly danger is that the production capacity of the world's great food-growing regions would be destroyed before alternatives could be established. It is one of the reasons why the carbon dioxide question is seen by many as the most important issue facing the human race as it makes its decisions about energy.

Rains, Winds, Ocean Currents and Tides

The solar energy absorbed by the atmosphere does not merely determine its temperature. It is also the power source which drives the evaporation and precipitation cycle, the winds, waves and ocean currents, and the photosynthetic processes of the biosphere. The distribution of the solar flux between these systems is shown in Figure 2.

By far the largest of these systems is the evaporation and precipitation, or hydrological, cycle. About 23 per cent of the total solar energy intercepted by the earth goes into driving this vast engine. Most of it is used to turn water into water vapour. Once this has happened, the winds transport the water vapour until it finally condenses and returns to earth as rain or snow.

The working of this cycle is complex. It is also variable in its timing. Water may condense and fall back immediately into the

Figure 2. Distribution of solar flux between the earth's energy systems

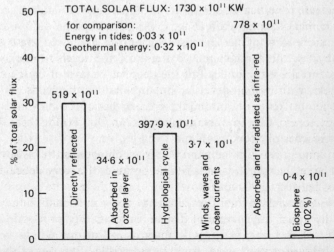

Source: M. King Hubbert, 'The Energy Resources of the Earth', *Scientific American*, September 1971.

ocean from which it has evaporated. It may travel in a regular seasonal pattern, bringing the monsoon rains with a regularity predictable within a period of a few days. It may produce the vagaries of a northern European summer.

Once the water is on the ground, there are further variations possible. It may fall on the uplands of a continent and travel thousands of miles before it reaches the ocean again. It may become locked in a glacier or a polar ice-cap and remain there for hundreds of thousands of years. It may become trapped as ground water, or interact with minerals in the earth's crust and be released only on a timescale measured by the emergence and disappearance of land masses. In each case the process is the same: when water is lifted from the ocean by evaporation, energy is absorbed; and when it returns to the ocean, all that energy has been released and the energy account has been balanced.

The wind systems of the earth also owe their energy to the sun. They are minor in comparison with the hydrological system; they absorb only about 0·2 per cent of the solar insolation. They occur because of the variation in solar radiation over the surface of the earth. Warm air rises at the equator and draws in cooler air from the areas to the north and south. The air from the equator, having lost its heat, descends at about latitude 30°, setting in motion a similar vertical circulatory system between 30° and 60°, and a further system between 60° and the polar regions.

When the effects of the earth's rotation are added to these vertical cycles, the fundamental patterns of the earth's major wind systems are established. But the detailed behaviour of the atmosphere, with its high-level jet-stream winds with speeds of over 500 kilometres per hour and the great eddies of the cyclones and anticyclones, is far from being understood. Only where there are great reaches of open ocean and freedom from the distorting effects of land masses do the wind patterns conform to the basic model. The regular ocean winds blowing towards the equator are usually called the trade winds.

The wind systems, in their turn, drive the ocean currents. These profoundly affect the climate of different regions of the world. The Gulf Stream brings warmth northwards to Europe. Without it, the climate of Britain and Ireland would be like that of northern Canada locked in its snowbound winters. The Humboldt current, in contrast, brings cold water up along the west coast of South America. Its upwelling from the deep ocean depths creates an area of ocean rich in minerals which supports an unparalleled abundance of marine life. It is because of this current that penguins are found on the Galapagos Islands almost on the equator.

The winds also determine where the rain falls, and hence the difference between deserts and fertile land. Minor shifts in the wind patterns over west Africa, for example, make the crucial difference between a rainy season which lasts long enough for people to grow the millet and sorghum on which they will be able to survive the year, and a drought which brings all their efforts to nothing.

All of this makes it clear why those huge schemes to remodel vast regions of the earth by damming the Bering Straits or diverting the great rivers of the USSR, which were talked of with such enthusiasm up to a couple of decades ago, are now viewed with such alarm by climatologists. A measure of how thinking has changed is given by this extract from a book in the late 1950s:

We could use nuclear energy to pump the warm waters of the Pacific into the Arctic Ocean . . . the result would be a new Gulf Stream warming up northern Canada and Siberia, making them as habitable as northern Norway is today thanks to the existing Gulf Stream . . . the creation of two enormous seas in the midst of Africa to change the whole climate and ecology of that continent . . . the jungle and desert areas could thus be turned into pleasant and fertile land for settlement and farming in a process taking thirty to fifty years.[1]

Such schemes would introduce a new element into the intricately meshed energy systems of the earth. To predict the results is impossible. But the range of possible effects is clear. They could alter the timing of the rainy seasons; could reduce or increase the polar ice-caps; they could make deserts of now fertile land. The risks are immense, and the benefits far from certain.

Last among the earth's energy systems is the tidal system. The amount of energy involved is surprisingly small. It is only 1 per cent that of the winds. It comes not from the sun's radiation, but from the gravitational forces and motions of the sun and moon in relation to the earth, with the moon's effect being dominant.

Tidal energy is obtained at the expense of a slight slowing down of the earth's rotation – about 0·001 seconds per rotation per century.

The Biosphere

The term 'biosphere' is used to define the zone encircling the earth in which life exists. Its outer limit is the upper atmosphere where occasional bacteria and spores of fungi are blown by the winds. Its inner limit is the dark, sparsely inhabited water of the ocean depths. Only a tiny proportion of the earth's life inhabits these extremes. Most of the living creatures of the biosphere are found within a few tens of metres of the surface of the land and in the upper regions of the lakes and seas.

The energy-capturing process on which all these creatures depend is called photosynthesis, which literally means 'putting light together'. Green plants on land and algae in water are able to use light from the blue and red bands of the visible spectrum to break down carbon dioxide and water and recombine the constituents to form the complex molecules of living tissue. The total energy budget of the biosphere is a tiny proportion, just 0·02 per cent, of the total solar flux.

The photosynthesizing organisms are the basis of life for all other living creatures. They are the only forms of life which can exist without eating other creatures, and they are sometimes called 'autotrophic', or self-nourishing. The rest are called 'heterotrophic'; they are nourished by others. Heterotrophic creatures include bacteria, grazing insects and animals, fish and flesh-eating animals, and humans. Fungi too are heterotrophic because they can grow without light, taking their energy from decaying vegetable matter – in this, a mushroom is more like an animal than a plant.

In the long-running debate about the origins of life on earth, most opinion still holds that it started in the 'primeval soup' of the oceans some 3·0–3·5 billion years ago. It had protection there from the ultraviolet wavelengths in the sun's radiation. In developing, life created the conditions for its own wider colonization of the earth. Oxygen is one of the products of photosynthesis. As life spread in the oceans, oxygen accumulated in the atmosphere, the ozone layer began to play its protective role and colonization of the land became possible. Land-based life probably began between 300 and 400 million years ago.

Photosynthesis needs quite a precise combination of circumstances before it can occur. The temperature must be neither too high nor too low. Few photosynthetic organisms can survive sustained temperatures above 40°C or below zero. Most photosynthetic activity takes place within the narrow temperature range 10–35°C. There are also other requirements. There has to be a supply of the basic materials, water and carbon dioxide. Nitrogen is also needed. It is a major constituent of the atmosphere (78 per cent), but plants and algae cannot use it in a gaseous form. Before they can assimilate it, it has to be 'fixed' in a compound such as ammonia. Nitrogen is fixed naturally by bacteria which live on the roots of certain plants, most notably those of the pea family, whose fruit is in the form of pods or legumes. These leguminous plants include beans, peas and alfalfa, as well as trees such as the acacia and leucaena. Artificial fertilizers use nitrogen fixed by artificial processes which consume considerable amounts of energy.

Other major requirements of plant and algal life are potassium, phosphorous, calcium, magnesium, iron and sulphur. These are called 'macro-nutrients'. Smaller quantities of the micro-nutrients, or 'trace elements', are also needed: these include manganese, copper, zinc, boron, sodium, molybdenum, vanadium, chlorine and cobalt.

Over most of the earth the optimum conditions for growth do not occur. In the polar regions and above the snow-line on mountain ranges it is too cold for plants to grow. Water is almost completely absent in the deserts. Many soils are lacking one or more of the nutrients essential to plant life. Most of the oceans have only a meagre supply of nutrients; they too are deserts in their own way. At the other extreme, there may be an excess of some substance which inhibits life. Pollution may be no more than too much of a good thing. Farming is essentially concerned with ensuring that, as far as possible, the optimum supply of nutrients and the right conditions for growth are provided for selected photosynthesizing organisms.

The photosynthetic reaction is complex. Substances such as

chlorophyll, fructose, glucose and phosphoglyceric acid are involved as plant tissue is built. Some of the energy of the sunlight becomes locked into the chemical bonds of these substances, to be released again as they are broken down in the living processes of the organism.

Most of the energy absorbed by a photosynthesizing organism is used to maintain its vital functions. A living creature has to use energy to take in nutrients, move them to where they are required, combine them into the substances it needs, control its temperature, adjust itself to light and shade, and repair itself when damaged. On a summer day a beech tree, for example, may emit through its leaves up to five times their weight in water, and this must be replaced if the tree is not to wilt. The production of just five tonnes of dry weight of a crop can require that some 2000 tonnes of water are drawn from the soil.

The amount of organic material formed by a photosynthesizing organism during the hours of daylight is called its gross photosynthetic production. During the various chemical processes involved in photosynthesis, oxygen is produced. At night some of the material formed during the day is broken down by the organism and is used for its repair and self-maintenance. While this is taking place, there is a release of carbon dioxide. This is called 'respiration', a term which usually means breathing, but is used by scientists as a general term for the breaking down of organic compounds within a living creature and the emission of carbon dioxide.

The efficiency with which the photosynthesizing creatures of the biosphere convert solar energy to plant tissue is in general low. Under optimum conditions a couple of per cent of the visible radiation may be used, but more usually it is only a small fraction of this. The total production of organic matter in the whole biosphere is about 160 billion tonnes of dry weight per year. Since the energy stored in each tonne is about 4000 kilowatt-hours, this represents a rate of utilization of the full visible spectrum of about 0·2 per cent. About a third of the production occurs in the seas and oceans; the rest takes place on land.

Photosynthesis is basically the same on land or in water. Without a proper combination of nutrients, climate and sunlight it cannot take place. But there are also important differences. On land the nutrients are in the soil and are absorbed through the roots of the plants. When plants die, their constituents are returned to the soil and become available for new growth, provided they are not carried away by water flows, winds, grazing animals or human intervention. But in deep water the position is much more difficult for living creatures. Photosynthesis can occur only in the top layer of the water, where there is enough sunlight. In muddy water this may be only a few centimetres; in the clear oceans it may be a couple of hundred metres. The nutrient supply is also critical: when an organism exhausts the nutrients in its vicinity, it must have the supply replenished, move to another area or die.

In places where the ocean currents well upwards and bring sediments back to the surface, the nutrient supply is continually replenished and marine life can thrive; an example is the Humboldt current off the west coast of South America. On the continental shelves and in the shallow seas, too, there is a steady supply of nutrients brought down by the rivers; this is why they are such rich fishing grounds. Cutting off the supply of nutrients by, for instance, damming a river will reduce the amount of marine life. This happened in the Mediterranean off the coast of Egypt, where the sardine catch was heavily reduced after the construction of the Aswan Dam.

In deep, still water remote from land the amount of living matter which can be supported is small. The sediments at the bottom may be rich in the required nutrients, but because there is no light no photosynthesis can occur. Since there is no mechanism for bringing the nutrients up to the surface, the only supply comes from the drift of water from richer areas. The organic production of the oceans averages about 0·1 grams of dry weight per square metre per day. In comparison, the production under good conditions on land can be 200 times as much.

Solar energy, once fixed in organic tissue by photosynthesis, can be used by other creatures of the biosphere. The heterotrophic creatures which feed on it are called primary consumers: they are the grazing creatures, the herbivores, and include caterpillars, whales, cows, deer and those vegetarian humans who exclude eggs, milk and cheese from their diets.

Secondary consumers, or carnivores, eat herbivores. They in

their turn may also be eaten by other carnivores. Such a succession of consumers is called a 'food chain'. Some creatures are, of course, not fixed in one exclusive position on the chain. Cats eat seed-eating birds as well as those which feed exclusively on insects; they may even tackle an owl which feeds upon small herbivores and carnivores. The human diet has probably the widest range of all.

Only a small proportion of the energy available to a creature is converted into its tissue. Under reasonable conditions this may be about 10 per cent in the case of a growing creature; the rest is consumed in the daily activities of moving, eating, breathing and so on. A full-grown animal which is not putting on weight uses the whole of its food intake for self-maintenance. This means that the further along a food chain a creature is positioned, the lower its numbers must be.

The yield of grain from an area of land may be sufficient to support, say, 100 people. Assume that, instead of being fed directly to people, it is fed instead to cattle which are able to convert 10 per cent of it to meat and milk. The number of humans who can be supported is now only ten. If lions were imported to feed on the cattle and their flesh were the sole human food, the population which could be supported would be only one.

Of course, this simplifies greatly. It ignores dietary considerations, the role of proteins as opposed to carbohydrates, the use the body makes of different kinds of fats and so on. But the basic point is valid: the closer a creature is to the primary energy source – solar energy – the greater its numbers can be. This is why the eagles, owls and hawks are so much rarer than the birds on which they prey, and why the polar bear is such a lonely hunter. In the sea with its longer food chains, the predators at the end of the chain are rare even by these standards.

The results of an analysis of the energy flows in an actual living system are shown in Table 1. They are taken from Howard T. Odum's study of Silver Springs, a stream in Florida with vegetation covering the bottom and with numerous species of herbivores and carnivores. The net photosynthesis is only 0·5 per cent of the total insolation. Of this, about 17 per cent is converted to flesh by the herbivores, and about 4·5 per cent of this is in turn converted by the carnivores which prey on them. By the time the solar energy has reached this last step in the chain, 99·996 per cent of the original solar energy has been lost.

Table 1. Simplified flow of energy through a natural eco-system

	kilowatt-hours/metre^2/year
Insolation	1977·10
Absorbed by plants	476·83
Photosynthesized (gross production)	24·20
Photosynthesis less respiration (net production)	10·27
Intake by herbivores	3·92
Net production by herbivores	1·72
Intake by carnivores	0·45
Net production by carnivores	0·08

Source: Howard T. Odum, analysis of Silver Springs, Florida, quoted in David M. Gates, 'The Flow of Energy in the Biosphere', *Scientific American*, September 1971.

There is also a range of creatures in the biosphere whose function is to process the complex compounds of dead organic matter and break them down into their simple original components, thus releasing them for use once again by the photosynthesizers. These are the decomposers, the bacteria of decay, worms, and other creatures which participate in the process of decomposition of dead organisms. Through their action the cycle of the biosphere is completed, and in a closed system there is neither gain nor loss of material. The materials flow in a closed loop and this ensures the continuity of the system. If the loop is opened, the material passes out of the system and it can no longer sustain itself.

Human food production is one such opening of the loop. It removes nutrients from the land and rarely returns them. In this it is akin to mining the land. The food production process can be sustained only by using fertilizers to replace the nutrients taken from the soil. When the American Forest Institute advertises that 'unlike coal or oil – wood is renewable so we need never run out', it omits this crucial point. Wood can be used as an industrial raw material or a fuel, but if it is to be cropped on a continual basis the forest soils, just like those of the farmer, must have their fertility renewed.

The natural cyclic return of nutrients in natural systems must not be confused with the energy flow. Energy is not recycled. It flows through the system, entering it as solar energy and leaving it as waste heat. Each step in which the stored energy of one creature is converted into the food of the next along the food chain wastes a large proportion of the energy involved. When the final work of the decomposers has been done and the organic material has been reduced to its mineral constituents again, the energy flow is complete. All the captured energy has been dissipated.

But throughout the earth's geological history there have been some quirks of behaviour. At times some of the organic matter escaped the decomposers. It became locked into sedimentary rocks of the earth's crust before it had been completely broken down or recycled. It turned into coal, oil and natural gas. In this way large amounts of solar energy were stored in the world's coal and petroleum deposits. They were later to play a crucial part in the escape of the human race from the niche in the biosphere for which its natural physique seemed to have ordained it.

2

Harnessing Energy:
The Pre-industrial Stage

The biosphere is sometimes portrayed as a region of harmony and peace. This is misleading. It is not a realm of friendly collaboration but of balance: the balance of opposing forces. The equilibrium is between the consumers and the consumed, both having a total common commitment to survival. Inefficiency or weakness or inability to adapt to changing conditions is punished by extinction. From the dinosaurs down, a multitude of species has been eliminated for the one crime the biosphere does not forgive: inability to stand the tests of competition and adaptability.

Early humans were among the creatures involved in this unrelenting struggle. They belonged to a group of related ape-like animals, medium-sized carnivores, not as common as monkeys but more common than horses. During the early Stone Age (up to about 300 000 years ago) the human population was probably not more than about 100 000 and was confined to the African continent. They lived as hunters and gatherers, obtaining their food requirements by foraging and scavenging, and by killing other creatures slow or careless enough to allow themselves to be caught. Their limitations of size, speed, strength and agility confined them to a minor role in the biosphere.

The creature which is less efficient than another in collecting or digesting its food is making less than it might of the available energy. If times become harder, it will be at a competitive disadvantage with another creature more efficient in utilizing the same food source and it will be displaced. Over the millions of years of evolution living creatures have therefore tended to reach an optimum efficiency in food collection and conversion for their particular position in the biosphere.

However, this optimum efficiency is a compromise, not necessarily a maximum. Any creature so efficient in food gathering that it eliminated its food supply could not survive more than one season. There must always be sufficient left over to produce next year's crop, or flock, of food. Nature's survivors are those which achieve the necessary balance. They are economical and efficient in the collection and utilization of their food; but they do not deplete the resources on which they depend.

Creatures generally become efficient by specialization. The birdlife of a wood illustrates the point. On the ground are the worm and snail eaters; treecreepers feed on the grubs and insects in the crevices of the bark; woodpeckers dig into the bark; seed and bud eaters are found at the outer ends of the branches; fly catchers hunt between the trees; predators and carrion eaters prowl through the whole system. This refinement of methods of food collection is countered by specialization in self-defence. The lower life forms ensure their continuance by a profligacy in seeding or procreation; the higher forms use camouflage, fleetness, protective armour or well-equipped ferocity.

This development of capacities peculiar to itself defines the ecological niche which a creature makes its own. For some creatures this niche may be as rigidly defined as the stomach of a cow or the leaves of a particular tree; for others, such as a carnivore or carrion eater, the range will be much greater. But those physical characteristics which make a creature the most effective in pursuit of its own food usually bar it from making use of other foods, so that with increased specialization comes vulnerability to scarcities or change.

Humanity alone emerged from the niche to which its physical characteristics would have confined it. Where other creatures reacted to competitive pressures by increased specialization of their bodily forms and functions, humans used their intelligence to make weapons and tools. A sharp stone, wielded by the hand, concentrates energy at its edge or point and can be used to split or bore. A stone-tipped spear makes a human as deadly as a lion or as swift as a cheetah. A woven net hung across a game path makes a trap as subtle as that of a spider. A raft of logs lashed together gives the hunting range of a crocodile or a water bird. As the human food catch improved and the choice of prey was extended, so were the chances of survival and of increasing the species. And this was achieved without the need for specialized body characteristics. In developing these primitive devices, humanity was outwitting the biosphere, managing to have its cake and eat it. The long tongue of the ant-eater makes it a very effective gatherer of ants but it prevents it eating nuts. The long spear of the early hunter enormously increased his food-collecting power but in no way reduced his versatility.

The other crucial advantage humans acquired over their fellow creatures was culture. This has been neatly defined as the 'non-genetic transmission of experience'. With its development the human race was no longer dependent for its advancement on the chance occurrence of favourable genetic mutations, which is the slow way the rest of nature adapts. For humans the experience of one generation was immediately available to the next, and not only the knowledge but also an accumulation of capital in the form of weapons, tools and artefacts. If there is a natural order in which each creature has a place determined by its physical characteristics, humans were perpetrating a gigantic fraud. By physical nature the human being was a land-based, slowish, weak, not particularly agile omnivore. But here they were rapidly extending their range and poaching into those areas hitherto reserved for the specialized animals of land, air and water.

The domestication of fire was a gigantic step forward. It probably began 400 000 to 500 000 years ago. Excavations in the Choutoukien Cave, near Peking, have shown that some 400 000 years ago fire was used by *Homo erectus*, the early human forebear who lived there. It is likely that this early use of fire was for warmth and for protection against animals.

At some later point cooking became common, though clear evidence of when it began and its development is scant in the archaeological record. The remains of plant foodstuffs rapidly decompose and leave no trace; the same is true of the fleshy parts of meat. Only the bones are sometimes preserved, because of their high mineral content, as may be the stones and ashes from the fire. Such evidence as there is suggests that cooking began to become widespread in the middle or early part of the Upper Palaeolithic period, about 100 000 years ago.

The effect of this was to extend the range of foods on which humans could rely. It also rendered food more digestible and nutritious. And by providing a counter to cold, fire widened the territorial domain they could conquer and inhabit. The control of fire thus played a crucial part in the spread of the human race.

Up to 100 000 years ago the zone of human habitation had been almost entirely restricted to south of the line of freezing winter temperatures. This colonized area expanded and contracted with the successive retreat and advance of the glaciers during the Pleistocene era. The development of clothing by Neanderthal man and the regular use of dwellings heated by fire was the breakthrough which permitted the barriers imposed by climate to be finally breached. Some 75 000 years ago the cave dwellers of the Dordogne, who used fur clothing and cooking hearths, were able to survive the cold winters of the time as the glaciers advanced yet again. About 35 000 years ago humans of fully modern type were pushing their zone of habitation up even into eastern Siberia and north of the Arctic circle. At the end of the last ice age, 10 000 years ago, human hunters had spread to all the continents, and the extinction of major animal species such as the woolly mammoth and the mastodon was virtually complete.

Most of the basic methods of cooking were developed relatively early. Spit-roasting was carried out by threading pieces of meat on a stick and cooking them over the embers of a fire. Baking was done by wrapping a piece of food completely in soft clay and placing it in the fire. The abundance of fragments of baked clay among the debris of Palaeolithic hearths reveals the prevalence of this technique.

Boiling food seems to predate the emergence of pottery or metal cooking pots by a long time. Some societies used stone cooking pots permanently situated in the middle of the hearth; others seem to have placed hot stones into water in containers of wood, bark or skin. The use of a bag made of animal skin, or the stomach, as a container in which water could be directly boiled over the fire is more surprising. By the end of the Upper Palaeolithic, around 13 000 B C, leather-working techniques were well developed and cooking bags made from animal skins were commonly used.

The warming of global temperatures which brought the long series of ice ages to an end took place some 10 000 years ago. Vegetation once again began to cover the northern areas and huge herds of reindeer grazed across them, providing ample stocks of meat for the hunters who pursued them. But with the improved climate the deciduous trees which could not survive in the former cold conditions began to invade the areas occupied by grass and by the hardier birch and pine forests. These new trees created dense, shady forests which gradually eliminated the rich grazing areas on which the reindeer herds relied.

The climatic change and its consequences created both the opportunity and the necessity for the next great human advance. The emergence of farming not only introduced fundamental changes into the human diet, it also changed the way in which society organized, housed, clothed and supplied itself with the necessities and comforts of life. The earliest manifestations of neolithic farming, stock rearing and early village culture are generally placed in the Fertile Crescent in the Near East around 10 000 to 12 000 years ago. In comparison with what had happened before, human progress was now astonishingly rapid. By the eighth millennium B C Jericho was an established settlement with stone and mud buildings and evident links with other places. Farming was spreading rapidly eastwards into India and northwards into Europe.

Agriculture is essentially a means of harnessing the process of photosynthesis for human purposes. It begins with the selection and cultivation of plants. But there is much more that can be done. The available solar energy is often wasted because there is not enough water, or because the nutrient supply is deficient. Irrigation and the application of manure, compost or lime are remedies for these deficiencies, and by using them humanity further increases its capture of solar energy.

The selection of seeds for crops changes the characteristics of plants. Instead of adapting to enhance their own chance of survival, they are directed into evolutionary paths which serve humanity's interests: these crops do not survive untended in the wild. In diverting water, in supplying fertilizers, in selective cultivation, humanity gains energy for itself. In general, it is at the expense of creatures which would have thrived if the natural balance had been left undisturbed.

The domestication of animals also widens control over natural energy flows. Just as fire enabled the human race to tap the energy of the forests, the use of animals opened another storehouse of otherwise inaccessible energy. Every blade of grass converts solar energy, but is useless to humanity: it cannot be eaten, nor is it a particularly good fuel. But if cattle are put to graze on it, animal milk or meat for food, animal hide for clothes or to cover a dwelling, animal bones or tusks as weapons or tools, animal dung to burn, animal muscle power to plough fields, haul loads, dig irrigation trenches, raise water, all become available. True, the efficiency of conversion of solar energy to flesh or work is low, but the area of grassland is large. With the domestication of animals the grasslands of the world became energy gatherers – vast natural solar collectors.

The use of human beings as domestic animals was also a feature of the rise of early civilizations. The slaves worked for a master and received no pay. But they consumed energy in the form of food. In this they were the same as animals – though the problem of their maintenance and control were often more difficult. Both the slave and the domesticated animal were precursors of the mechanical engine; they were a means of turning the energy of food, or fuel, into the work their owners required of them.

By 2000 BC village and urban settlements were common and the pace of change was increasing. World population was reaching 100 million. With its growing ability to harness energy and provide itself with reliable food supplies humanity was finding itself with time to think and organize. Civilization and the founding of states and cities occurred when the increased efficiency of agriculture enabled society to exempt an increasing number of people from the daily toil of collecting food. They became the priests, craftsmen, politicians, thinkers, warriors, builders, designers. On the foundation of the energy supplied by the farming community they moulded dynasties in China and Babylon, planned pyramids and plotted the movements of the stars. Other means of harnessing and concentrating energy began to be discovered.

The waterwheel appeared around 100 BC in the West, though it was reputedly in use centuries earlier in China. The energy it tapped still came from the sun which had lifted the water in the mill-stream from the oceans, but the inefficiencies of photosynthesis and biological energy conversion were eliminated. A moderate-sized watermill could provide perhaps 10 kilowatts, an energy supply far beyond anything previously obtainable in such a concentrated form. The energy costs of constructing and maintaining the mill were trivial compared with those of feeding animals or human slaves. Once it was constructed, the waterwheel was a source of free energy for years or decades. The windmill, known in the Arab world several centuries earlier, was brought to northern Europe in the eleventh century. It rapidly acquired a place beside the watermill as a major provider of energy in the medieval economy. The new availability of energy enabled the pace of social and technical development to quicken.

By the fifteenth century Europe had so advanced in control of its own environment that it could look beyond this and embark on voyages of 'discovery' to new parts of the earth whose people were 'primitive natives', scarcely to be regarded as human. When conflicts occurred, the indigenous people were rapidly swept aside by the European superiority in weaponry, mobility and training in the abstract and practical arts of warfare. Backed by the big energy-consuming economies of their own countries, the explorers were more than a match for the hunter–gatherers, subsistence farmers and fishermen they encountered. Even the sophisticated societies of South and Central America were no match for the concentrated weaponry and fire power of their Spanish invaders.

Of course, there was nothing equitable about the distribution of energy within the late-medieval and feudal societies of Europe. Many people lived lives of real slavery and for the average person life was little better. The concentration of energy was in the hands of the minority. Energy and power are related in the technical sense in that power is defined as the rate of energy flow; access to energy also provides economic and political power over others. The mill owner was often an economic despot in his own community.

Nowhere had the energy-harnessing capability of pre-industrial society reached a higher level than in Britain. A truculent and powerful country, it had pushed the capture of natural energy flows about as far as seemed possible. Windmills and waterwheels were built in their thousands. Charcoal makers cut swathes through the forests as they felled trees to make fuel for smelting and working iron, lead, tin and copper, for glass making, and a variety of other purposes. As a result, objects now taken completely for granted became commonly available for the first time. Chains, nails and iron hand-implements were produced in ever-increasing numbers from small workshops. Scythes, sickles and knives of increasingly high quality were produced by the growing cutlery industry in Sheffield and elsewhere. Iron replaced wood in the blades of ploughs and the bearings and hubs of cartwheels, thus increasing the effectiveness of draught animals.

Fears of a shortage of wood in England led to a commission to inquire into the destruction of woodland caused by iron-making in the weald of Sussex in 1548. But neither its recommendations nor a succession of Acts of Parliament such as that of 1558 in the first years of Queen Elizabeth's reign called 'An Act that Timber shall not be felled to make Coals for Burning of Iron' were able to prevent the continued depletion of wood resources.

The wood shortages affecting the iron industry in England led to the Irish woods being exploited. From about 1600 onwards ore was shipped across to Ireland for smelting. The woodland destruction was immense and became a theme for lament in Irish poetry. The Welsh and Scottish forests were also devastated to provide fuel for English ironmasters.

By the end of the eighteenth century it seemed as if a limit had been reached. The population of England had reached 8 million people, a density of 66 persons per square kilometre. In comparison, the population density of a hunter–gatherer society in similar climatic conditions is about 1 person per square kilometre and that of an early agricultural community about 10 persons per square kilometre.

3

The Industrial Revolution to the Oil Age

In 1798 Malthus published his famous essay 'On the Principle of Population'.[2] Britain was in trouble: its population was rising rapidly and its agriculture showed few signs of being able to keep pace with the growing demand for food. The poor were on the verge of starvation.

Malthus thought the problem of growing and distributing enough food for the increasing population under the conditions then prevailing was impossible of solution. The land was still mainly controlled by the gentry. The cities were, for the majority of their inhabitants, filthy, overcrowded, disease-ridden agglomerations of human misery. He wrote that 'the perpetual tendency in the race of man to increase beyond the means of subsistence is one of the general laws of animated nature which we have no reason to expect will change'. And if humanity failed to recognize this fact, he warned that 'we shall not only exhaust our strength in fruitless exertions and remain at as great a distance from the summit of our wishes, but we shall be perpetually crushed by the recoil of this rock of Sisyphus'.

One of Malthus's aims in his essay was to refute the optimism of Condorcet and Godwin. Writing after the French Revolution, they saw humanity proceeding steadily into a boundless era of peace, justice and plenty. Malthus's view of the future was a brutal and gloomy one. He used the paltry statistics available to him to support his case in a thoroughly modern way. He contrasted the compound, or exponential, growth of population with what he believed was the simple, or linear, growth possible in agricultural production. The arithmetic is naive; the conclusions drawn are at times blatantly tendentious. Nevertheless, the dark shadow of Malthus's vision of population outstripping the resources on which it depends has never been completely dispelled. That there are limits to resources is obvious; where these limits are is the question that remains unanswered.

To Malthus, famine in Britain was not a remote future possibility, it was an immediate threat. The recoil of the rock of Sisyphus was a danger requiring urgent action. In this he was to be proved completely wrong. He failed to see that in the workshops of the inventors, toolmakers and ironwrights of the seventeenth and eighteenth centuries the way had already been prepared for the construction of an energy-consuming social and industrial system which would belittle humanity's earlier accomplishments and provide a means of escape from the closing trap of hunger.

The crucial breakthrough had been almost a century earlier. In 1709 Abraham Darby had developed a method of using coke for iron smelting. This broke the dependence on wood which had existed since the discovery of iron smelting by the Hittites about 1400 BC. But Darby's discovery took some time to make its impact. Because of the limitations of the available designs of blast furnace, the quality of the iron made with coke was poor and brittle and it could be used only for casting. Moreover, there were limits to the amount of coal which could be obtained in the traditional ways. It was simple to dig coal from a surface outcrop and even to follow this some way underground. But when the seam dipped below the natural water level, mining depended on continual heavy pumping – a task generally beyond human and animal muscle power.

In 1708 Thomas Newcomen had built his first beam engine. This used the expansion of steam in a cylinder to drive a piston which was then sucked back by the partial vacuum when the steam condensed. It was slow, cumbersome, dangerous and by modern standards had a horrendously poor energy efficiency of about 0·8 per cent, but answered precisely to the need for pumping power. By 1765 there were a hundred of these engines working in the Tyne and Wear coalfields. Soon the beam engine gave way to the much more efficient rotary engine developed by Boulton and Watt. Steam was also harnessed to make an effective blast furnace. The way was now open to the exploitation of the massive reserves of England's coalfields.

By the time Malthus was writing, therefore, the country was already beginning to experience an upward swing in agricultural and industrial productivity unprecedented in human history. Marshlands were being drained and soils improved. Eighteenth-century developments such as Hargreave's spinning jenny, Arkwright's spinning frame, Wedgwood's potteries and Roebuck's ironworks and ordnance factories had already provided a technical foundation for the Victorian revolution in energy use. In the nineteenth century a host of new inventors and entrepreneurs responded to the growing availability of energy and the opportunities it created for industrial progress – and making money.

Stephenson's locomotive introduced an era of prodigious railway building. Telford, Brunel and McAdam, with their associates and disciples, bursting with inventiveness and determination, constructed a network of roads, railways, viaducts and bridges which could carry food and manufactured goods to all parts of the country. Agricultural productivity had been transformed as the discoveries of the German chemist Liebig about the role of nitrogen and other elements in soil fertility led to the establishment of the artificial fertilizer industry. The emergence of factory capitalism was described, analysed and excoriated by Marx and Engels.

The population increased enormously during the nineteenth century, from 11 million in 1800 up to 38 million in 1900. There was also a massive shift of people away from the countryside to the towns. In the year 1700 about 80 per cent of the population obtained a living from the land. By 1800 this had fallen to around 50 per cent, and in 1900 it was down to 9 per cent. Table 2 shows some comparative data from other countries from 1850 to 1950 and reveals how far the process of industrialization had advanced in Britain by the middle of the nineteenth century.

Malthusian pessimism had certainly not been vindicated by events. The fear of famine had completely disappeared. For the majority of the population an almost complete divorce from the biosphere had taken place and food had become something obtained not from the earth but from a shop. Coal had made it

Table 2. Percentage of active population employed in agriculture – selected countries, 1850, 1900, 1950

	about 1850	about 1900	about 1950
AFRICA:			
Algeria	—	—	81
Egypt	—	70	65
South Africa	—	60	33
AMERICA:			
Canada	—	42	20
USA	65	38	13
ASIA:			
Japan	—	71	48
India	—	—	74
EUROPE:			
Belgium	50	57	12
France	52	42	30
Germany	—	35	24
Great Britain	22	9	5
Ireland	48	45	40
Netherlands	44	31	20
Spain	70	68	50
Sweden	65	54	21
USSR	90	85	56

Source: Quoted in Carlo M. Cipolla, *The Economic History of World Populations*, Penguin, 1970.

possible for the country to feed itself on the produce of foreign farms. H. G. Wells wrote:

The sober Englishman at the close of the nineteenth century could sit at his breakfast table, decide between tea from Ceylon or coffee from Brazil, devour an egg from France with some Danish ham, or eat a New Zealand chop, wind up his breakfast with a West Indian banana, glance at the latest telegrams from all over the world, scrutinize the prices current of his geographically distributed investments in South Africa, Japan and Egypt and tell the two children he had begotten (in the place of his father's eight) that he thought the world had changed very little.[3]

Coal had made all this material progress possible. In 1800 the total annual coal production in Britain was about 10 million tonnes. By 1850 this had climbed to 60 million tonnes, and by 1900 it had reached 228 million tonnes. More coal was consumed in the two years 1899 and 1900 than in the whole century between

1700 and 1800. In 1900 coal exports were no less than 58 million tonnes.

As a fuel for an industrial economy coal had immense advantages over any other major energy source known at the time. The biosphere is slow in converting solar energy: a tree takes twenty or thirty years to grow to a usable size. The total dry-matter production of a temperate forest is about 11 tonnes per hectare per year, of which perhaps 50–70 per cent might be usable as fuel if cutting and gathering were carefully carried out. To harvest the equivalent of 225 million tonnes of coal in the form of timber would therefore require about 600 000 square kilometres of forest: the total area of England, Scotland and Wales is about 223 000 square kilometres. Ignoring all the practical difficulties of cutting and transporting the timber as well as the energy costs of forest maintenance and fertilizer inputs, Britain was simply not big enough to produce the energy it was consuming by any cultivation of the biosphere.

Coal supplied in a concentrated, portable form the energy of hundreds of thousands of square kilometres of forest. With a productivity of over 200 tonnes per man per annum in 1900 each coal-miner was producing the energy equivalent of about sixty hectares of forest. The comparison with other energy sources is equally devastating. A reasonably large sail windmill is capable of producing about 30 kilowatts under favourable conditions and might work for 2500 hours in a year. Over thirty such windmills would be required to produce the equivalent energy-output of a single coal-miner.

During the nineteenth century the rate of growth in energy consumption in Britain exceeded the rate of population growth by a factor of nearly five. Coal consumption per head in 1800 was under a tonne a year; by 1900 it had grown to nearly four and a half tonnes.

Karl Marx noted that the main beneficiaries of the increased energy flow were the bourgeois. He wrote that

the extraordinary productiveness of modern industry, accompanied as it is by a more extensive exploitation of labour power in all other spheres of production, allows of the unproductive employment of a larger and larger part of the working class, and the consequent reproduction on a constantly extending scale, of the ancient domestic slaves under the name of a 'servant class', including men-servants, women-servants, lackeys etc.[4]

And certainly the sweating kitchen staff of the large houses, enslaved winter and summer by those gigantic coal-devouring ranges, would have been hard put to see the liberatory effects of so much energy consumption. The copious availability of energy had made the Industrial Revolution and the development of Victorian Britain possible, but it had not determined the precise path of social development. The newly created wealth could have been distributed in many different and better ways.

The Industrial Revolution was not, of course, confined to Britain. But it came later elsewhere. America and Europe avoided some of Britain's worst horrors and were able to benefit from the technological progress already made. The early locomotives and steam engines had efficiencies of no more than a few per cent – if they were well made and working properly. Later developments were much more efficient. In other words, they provided more useful work for the same consumption of energy. European and American industry was not handicapped by accumulated equipment of low efficiency, and their pace of development could therefore be more rapid. Industry around the great coalfields of the Ruhr and the Saar, of Belgium and Alsace-Lorraine, grew quickly and began to compete very effectively indeed with that of Britain. The British iron and steel industry, for instance, which in 1850 dominated the world, had only a 10 per cent share of world production by the beginning of the First World War.

By then yet another energy revolution was well under way. Like coal, oil had been known and used for thousands of years. Seepages at ground level were common enough to make it a reasonably well-known commodity – but in quantities more appropriate to gourds and flasks than supertankers. It was sometimes encountered in drilling for brine, and as the brine well had then to be abandoned, oil was regarded as an unmitigated nuisance. An account of one such occurrence in Kentucky in 1829, however, shows that it could at least provide good spectator sport. The brine well

vomited forth many barrels of pure oil . . . 25 to 30 feet above the rock . . . About two miles below the point at which it touched the river it was set on fire by a boy and the sight was grand beyond description. An old gentleman who witnessed it says he has seen several cities on fire but that he never beheld anything like the flames which rose from the bosom of the Cumberland to touch the very clouds.[5]

Commercial drilling for oil began in 1859. Edwin Drake, a former railway conductor turned entrepreneur, with the self-bestowed rank of 'Colonel', used a percussion rig to drill a bore hole in Pennsylvania which struck oil at a depth of sixty-nine feet. Drake earned his place in history, though he died in poverty on a small pension provided by the oil industry. The oil boom had begun and within a year 175 further wells had been drilled in the same area.

Coal was superior to wood as an energy source, and oil in its turn was superior to coal. Writing in 1915 in Britain, Professor Herbert Stanley Jevons, a leading authority on the coal industry, discussed the advantages of oil. It was, he said, more easily stored and handled; it was cleaner; its use eliminated dirty and dangerous jobs such as those of stokers on ships; and having a 50 per cent higher calorific value than coal, it enabled the paying cargo of ships to be increased. It could be used 'in the invention of Dr Rudolph Diesel, whose internal combustion engine contained several new and ingenious features', and which was 'three and a half to four times as efficient as the steam engine'.[6] Professor Jevons was right, and there were yet more advantages, the most important being the ease with which oil could be obtained. Spindletop, the famous Texas oilwell, blew out as a 'gusher' in 1901, at a rate of over 100 000 barrels a day. This was the energy equivalent of the work of 37 000 miners, simply running to waste. Oil was much cheaper than water: at Spindletop oil cost 3 cents a barrel and water 5 cents a glass.

Production and consumption of oil rose rapidly and by the turn of the century American oil production had reached 9 million tons a year. When Jevons was writing, it had reached about 40 million tons a year. No one believed that production could continue at this rate, let alone continue to expand. Jevons wrote of the 'scare writings of people of vivid imagination who see in recent engineering progress "the dawn of the oil age" ' and re-assured his coal-industry readers that 'the extensive general adoption of mineral oil as a power producer for all purposes is a very unlikely contingency for, as far as our present knowledge extends, the supply of oil is strictly limited' and the USA, which produced most of the world's oil, had 'probably reached its zenith' of production.

Yet despite the incredulity of both experts and non-experts, new and rich oilfields were discovered in increasing numbers. Production doubled every eight or nine years. Apart from a brief period in the early 1900s when Russian production was actually greater, America remained the largest producer. Up to the 1950s it was still producing, and consuming, well over half the world's oil. While other countries still retained the distinctive characteristics they had evolved during the coal-based Industrial Revolution, America was leading the way in the development of the social and industrial patterns of the oil-based high-energy society.

The most obvious feature of this society is its mobility. Only in the wild imaginings of fairy tales about magic carpets and witches' broomsticks had society ever before liberated itself from the tyranny of time and space. For most of human existence the pace of people's movement had been limited to five or six miles an hour and that for short distances. The bicycle, of course, had been a vehicle of social revolution, liberating at least some of the Victorians – as *The Complete Cyclist* said in 1897, '. . . women, even young girls, ride alone or attended only by some casual man friend for miles together through deserted country roads'.[7] The train too had been a miracle in its own time. But now instant mobility came within the reach of everyone; the Ford Model T annihilated distance. America created the first mobile society.

American cities, designed around the car and for the car, began to spread across the countryside over distances impossible to cover on foot. Superhighways were built. Patterns of social behaviour, shopping, entertainment, family life and courtship were fashioned around the new mobility and thus created a continuing and growing need for it. By the eve of the Second World War there were nearly 30 million cars in the USA, one for every four people in the country.

In the twentieth-century development of American society the energy constraint was completely absent. From the 1890s onwards the United States was glutted with energy. Up to the late

1960s the oil industry's constant problem was its potential for over-production which kept the market weak and the price extremely low. The parallels with the position in which OPEC finds itself today are obvious.

During the 1930s the over-supply in the American market was so great that the industry agreed to introduce a system of production regulation called 'proration'. Under its rules, owners of oil wells were allowed to produce only what it was calculated the market could bear without lowering prices. Allowed production was often down to as low as 2 per cent, or even less, of the installed production capacity of some oilfields. One writer [5] referred to the introduction of proration as 'the beginning of the conservation era'; he was referring to the conservation of the price level, not the quantities of oil consumed. There was no question of advocating restrictions in use. On the contrary, since the problem was a surfeit of oil, efforts were constantly directed to finding ways of increasing consumption.

In this the Americans were extremely successful. The huge private cars produced in their millions in the factories of Detroit were grotesquely overpowered for the mundane task of carrying their owners to work or to the drugstore for a packet of cigarettes. Central heating, air-conditioning, skyscrapers, houses packed with mechanical and electrical devices, a huge consumption of food, clothes and material goods, in all these ways and more, American society developed ways of using energy undreamt of before. The change in just fifty years was astonishing.

The USA created a model of society which it exported around the world. Hollywood films, in particular, were a potent advertisement for the luxuries of mobility and high-energy living. The lead was eagerly followed by those countries which could afford to do so. If post-war reconstruction in Europe was not quite on the same scale as America, it had the American example very much in mind.

The process continues. Car ownership is still growing throughout the countries of the industrial world. The USA now has 130 million cars, one for every two people in the country. Central heating, refrigerators, freezers, dish washers, the energy-using luxuries of a couple of decades ago, are becoming the standard necessities of today. The rich and middle-class enclaves in the

Table 3. Consumption of energy by countries and world regions, 1985

	Oil	Natural gas	Coal	Hydro-electric	Nuclear energy	Total
NORTH AMERICA						
USA	724·1	444·5	443·3	82·9	104·6	1799·4
Canada	67·7	50·4	30·6	63·9	14·0	226·6
WESTERN EUROPE						
Austria	9·8	4·6	3·6	7·5	—	25·5
Belgium & Luxembourg	20·2	8·4	10·9	0·1	7·4	47·0
Denmark	10·8	0·6	7·1	—	—	18·5
Finland	10·8	0·8	3·4	3·1	4·5	22·6
France	83·9	23·3	24·1	12·9	45·1	189·3
Greece	12·0	0·1	6·0	0·9	—	19·0
Iceland	0·5	—	—	1·1	—	1·6
Republic of Ireland	3·8	1·7	2·7	0·2	—	8·4
Italy	85·0	27·3	15·5	11·1	1·8	140·7
Netherlands	29·1	33·0	7·0	—	0·9	70·0
Norway	8·8	—	0·6	22·8	—	32·2
Portugal	8·2	—	0·5	3·3	—	12·0
Spain	44·0	2·3	18·7	7·4	6·3	78·7
Sweden	16·9	0·1	2·5	11·1	10·0	40·6
Switzerland	12·3	1·0	0·4	8·4	5·5	27·6
Turkey	18·9	—	10·6	3·7	—	33·2
United Kingdom	77·8	47·9	61·9	1·3	13·0	201·9
West Germany	114·0	41·4	79·3	4·1	28·5	267·3
AUSTRALASIA						
Australia	27·0	12·5	35·2	4·0	—	78·7
New Zealand	3·8	3·2	0·9	4·8	—	12·7
JAPAN	201·3	36·0	72·6	21·8	33·6	365·3
Cyprus/Gibraltar/Malta	1·8	—	0·2	—	—	2·0
Latin America	209·5	69·9	25·0	75·2	1·3	380·9
Middle East	98·8	40·2	2·2	2·8	—	144·0
Africa	82·8	25·9	67·8	17·6	1·0	195·1
South Asia *	53·4	17·5	105·0	19·1	1·1	196·1
South East Asia †	112·8	17·6	38·2	6·3	11·4	186·3
CENTRALLY PLANNED ECONOMIES (CPES)						
China	87·6	11·5	509·4	25·8	—	634·3
USSR	447·7	477·2	361·9	53·5	36.0	1376·3
Others	124·3	92·9	330·7	21·5	11·1	580·5
TOTAL WORLD	2809·4	1491·8	2277·8	498·2	337·1	7414·3

* Afghanistan, Bangladesh, Burma, India, Nepal, Pakistan, Sri Lanka.
† Brunei, Hong Kong, Indonesia, Malaysia, Philippines, Singapore, South Korea, Taiwan, Thailand, Papua New Guinea.
Note: See Appendix for conversion factors.
Source: BP Statistical Review of World Energy, 1986.

cities of the developing world are no different; but there the contrast with a low-energy way of life is clearly visible in the teeming slums and shanty towns beside them.

Table 3 shows the worldwide distribution of energy consumption in 1985. Despite the shocks of the 1970s, the total continues to mount. It is 30 per cent higher than it was in 1973. Almost everywhere, oil continues to be the dominant fuel. It is the energy source which has given the twentieth-century world some of its most particular characteristics, amply justifying the designation of this present phase in human development as the 'oil age'.

4

A Unifying Principle

The previous chapters have shown how it is possible to trace the thread of energy through the social and economic history of the human race. Energy can also be seen as a unifying principle in the history of scientific thought.

Heraclitus, the Greek philosopher who lived around 500 BC, asserted that the universe was in a state of constant flux; he believed that its unifying principle was fire. Democritus, a hundred years later, maintained that all phenomena could be explained in terms of the motion of the indivisible atoms of which they were made. Neither, of course, could produce any experimental evidence for their theories. Their speculations remained undeveloped and were later obscured by the work of Plato and Aristotle.

The modern view of the universe, in which the concept of energy can be used to link the whole range of observed phenomena, can be traced directly to the work of Isaac Newton in the late seventeenth century. Using Kepler's work on the movements of the planets as his starting point, he was able to formulate his theory of universal gravitation. His Laws of Motion made it possible for the first time to quantify the interaction of physical objects and opened the way to an understanding of the fact that energy is neither created nor destroyed.

In Newtonian, or classical, mechanics, energy is defined as the capacity to do work – work is said to be done when an object is moved or altered. 'Work' in common usage is useful activity, but the technical definition is indiscriminate and says nothing about the usefulness of the action. A man sweeping leaves into a pile is doing work; but so is the wind in scattering them again. In the

British system of units which was developed during the early Industrial Revolution, and is still used in some areas of engineering, the unit of work is the foot-pound: the amount of work done when a weight of one pound is raised a distance of one foot.

A weight of one pound raised a distance of one foot can be said to 'possess' an energy of one foot-pound. Placed on a balance or lever, it is able, in descending, to raise another weight of one pound through a distance of one foot. In this way an energy transfer takes place: the first weight 'gives' its energy to the second. Objects which, because of their position, are capable of doing work on other bodies are said to possess 'potential' energy.

Anything which is moving can be made to do work in coming to rest. By measuring the amount of work objects do in being brought to rest it is possible to establish the relationship between speed, mass* and energy. It is found that the energy of a moving body, its 'kinetic' energy, is directly proportional to its mass and proportional to the square of its speed. A moving two-tonne car will therefore have twice the energy of a one-tonne car moving at the same speed. But doubling the speed of a vehicle quadruples its energy: a crash at 100 kilometres per hour involves four times the energy of a crash at 50 kilometres per hour.

With these concepts of work and energy, it is possible to unify a wide range of phenomena. A flowing river, a tightened bowstring, a spring wound in a clock, water stored behind a dam, and a horse, to take some random examples, are all capable of doing work. This work can be measured and expressed in precise quantitative units, such as foot-pounds.

It also became obvious to engineers and scientists that the energy of motion was closely related to heat and that a theoretical account of work was incomplete without a statement of this relationship. The friction of two unlubricated metal surfaces could produce enough heat to fuse them. Large quantities of water were needed to take away the heat produced in the boring

---

* The use of the word mass in everyday language is quite different from its scientific use. Mass can be thought of as a measure of the amount of matter in a body. Weight on the other hand is the gravitational force acting on a mass. On the moon, for example, the weight of a body is a sixth that on earth. Weightlessness can be survived, but anyone experiencing 'masslessness' is beyond recall.

of a cannon. There was plenty of evidence for the connection between heat and work, but the credit for formalizing it into a scientific proposition goes to James Prescott Joule, an English brewery owner who spent his life in scientific research. He determined the mechanical equivalent of heat in a classic experiment in 1843. In this experiment, a heavily insulated container of water with a rotating paddle inside it is connected by a string to a weight over a pulley. The weight is allowed to move downwards, causing the paddle to rotate and thus agitating the water. At the end of the experiment, when the weight has reached the bottom of its travel and the water is still again, it is found that the temperature of the water has gone up. From this Joule was able to measure the amount of heat produced by a known amount of work. He found that it took 772·5 foot-pounds to raise the temperature of 1 pound of water through 1°F. Accurate modern measurements have corrected this figure to 778·16 foot-pounds, which is within 1 per cent of Joule's value and a tribute to his experimental skills. This quantity of energy is known as Joule's mechanical equivalent of heat. It is also called a British thermal unit (Btu).

But the concept of energy could be extended far beyond this. In 1831 Faraday had shown that an electric current could be generated by moving a magnet near a conducting wire, thus relating mechanical work and electrical energy. And Joule himself had shown that the rate of heat production when a current flowed in a wire was proportional to the square of the current times the resistance of the wire. James Clerk Maxwell's electromagnetic theory of light, which was one of the major achievements of the late nineteenth century, subsequently brought together the theories of electricity, magnetism and light in a simple mathematical formulation. In the words of Professor J. D. Bernal: 'The electromagnetic theory was a crowning achievement which realized the dream of Faraday that all the forces of Nature should be shown to be related . . .'[8]

Now there was a common factor, energy, quantifiable in all the phenomena with which science was concerned, from the invisible waves of electromagnetic radiation to the motion of the planets. Even the metabolism of living creatures could be measured within the same system. Priestley had discovered oxygen in 1774 and shown how it was 'consumed' in burning – and in breathing. Later, Lavoisier, the great French scientist who died on the guillotine in 1794, was able to quantify the metabolic behaviour of living creatures, showing that they behaved just like a fire, 'burning' the materials they absorb as food by combining them with oxygen and releasing their energy in the form of heat.

As the nineteenth century reached its end it seemed that the frontiers of science had finally been delineated; only the details remained to be filled in. The Newtonian concept of the universe had been vindicated. Science rested securely on the twin principles of the conservation of matter and the conservation of energy. The quest for the philosopher's stone which would transmute the base elements into gold had long been abandoned. The elements had been identified and allocated their fixed place, in accordance with their properties, in the scheme of the universe. It was fundamental to the theory of chemistry that at the end of a chemical reaction it should be possible to account for all the elements which had entered into it. In other words, matter was neither created nor destroyed. Similarly, energy was neither created nor lost. In an ideal closed system the total quantity of energy before and after an event was the same. Its distribution between different parts of the system might change and it might appear in different forms, but the total amount could not vary.

Then in 1895 Röntgen discovered X-rays. He found that, when he was using a cathode tube, invisible rays capable of penetrating solid objects were escaping from the apparatus. The excitement of the discovery led to a rush of experiments elsewhere. Within months Becquerel had discovered the radioactivity of uranium. The Curies went on to discover radium and describe its properties. Rutherford, working at McGill University in Montreal with the chemist Soddy, did pioneering work in elucidating the nature of the mysterious phenomenon of radioactivity. From the fever of scientific investigation two conclusions emerged which undermined the existing foundations of science: elements were changing from one into another, and energy was apparently being generated spontaneously out of nothing.

Einstein later resolved many of the paradoxes by showing that an even more comprehensive synthesis of existing scientific theories was possible. According to his special theory of relativity, mass and energy were equivalent. The relationship could be expressed in quantitative terms: $E = mc^2$, energy is equal to mass multiplied by the velocity of light squared. The release of energy observed in radioactivity was the result of a genuine transmutation of the elements and a conversion of some of their mass into energy. With this Einstein was able to transcend the Newtonian concept of the physical universe and make it part of a wider understanding of the nature of physical reality.

Table 4 gives some impression of the unifying power of the concept of energy. Units commonly used in the separate disciplines of electricity, atomic physics, dietetics and engineering can not only be expressed in terms of each other, but can all be expressed in units of mass.

Table 4. Equivalents of various energy units

	joule	electronvolt	kilocalorie	kilowatt-hour	kilogram mass
joule	1	$6 \cdot 242 \times 10^{18}$	$2 \cdot 389 \times 10^{-4}$	$2 \cdot 778 \times 10^{-7}$	$1 \cdot 113 \times 10^{-17}$
electronvolt	$1 \cdot 602 \times 10^{-19}$	1	$3 \cdot 828 \times 10^{-23}$	$4 \cdot 450 \times 10^{-26}$	$1 \cdot 783 \times 10^{-36}$
kilocalorie	$4 \cdot 186 \times 10^3$	$2 \cdot 613 \times 10^{22}$	1	$1 \cdot 163 \times 10^{-3}$	$4 \cdot 658 \times 10^{-14}$
kilowatt-hour	$3 \cdot 600 \times 10^6$	$2 \cdot 247 \times 10^{25}$	$8 \cdot 598 \times 10^2$	1	$4 \cdot 007 \times 10^{-11}$
kilogram mass	$8 \cdot 988 \times 10^{16}$	$5 \cdot 610 \times 10^{35}$	$2 \cdot 147 \times 10^{13}$	$2 \cdot 497 \times 10^{10}$	1

The proliferation of energy units is, in fact, a cause of considerable inconvenience. An attempt has been made to simplify scientific measurements by devising a common system of units for all the scientific disciplines, the Système International d'Unités (SI), which, it is hoped, will be eventually adopted throughout the world. This system was initiated at the Eleventh General Conference of Weights and Measures in 1960. Its standard units of mass and length are the kilogram and the metre. Temperature is measured in degrees Celsius ($^{\circ}$C); these are the same as degrees centigrade. The SI units are usually named after famous scientists of the past: Celsius was an eighteenth-century Swedish astronomer who proposed the centigrade scale. Absolute temperatures are expressed in Kelvin (K) and are measured from absolute zero, which is taken as $-273 \cdot 15^{\circ}$C, the temperature at which an ideal gas has zero volume and pressure. The Kelvin is identical with the degree Celsius. The freezing point of pure water at atmospheric pressure is thus 0°C or 273·15K.

The concept of 'power' deserves special mention because it is so often misunderstood. In scientific language power is the *rate* at which energy is expended or work is done. When James Watt was selling his steam engines he described their capacity for work in familiar terms. A 1-horsepower engine was capable of working at the same rate as a good horse. He defined this as 33 000 foot-pounds per minute, which was the rate at which he found a horse could raise a weight suspended over a pulley. The *amount* of work done is the rate multiplied by the time. In one hour the standard horse, therefore, does 1 980 000 foot-pounds of work or 1 horsepower-hour.

The SI unit of power is the watt, a very much smaller unit than the horsepower (1 watt = 0·00134 horsepower). The unit of energy derived from it is the joule (J), a rate of work of 1 watt maintained for 1 second (not to be confused with Joule's mechanical equivalent of heat). This is also a very small unit and the kilojoule (kJ, 1000 joules) or megajoule (MJ, 1 000 000 joules) are more commonly used. A megajoule is about 0·37 of a horsepower-hour. The kilowatt-hour (kWh), however, is much more familiar: it is a rate of work of a thousand watts maintained for an hour. The kilowatt-hour is the 'unit' of electricity, the amount used in an hour by the normal single-bar electric fire. It is about 1·33 horsepower-hours.

The First Law of Thermodynamics states that energy is neither created nor destroyed. Strictly speaking, it is therefore incorrect to say that energy is 'consumed'. When it passes through an energy-using system it is merely *transformed*. When a power station burns coal to generate electricity all the energy released can be accounted for: in the cooling water, the exhaust gases released up the chimney, the heat losses from the machines and the transmission wires, the heat emitted from the machines and appliances at the point of use, and any energy stored in the final product – the electricity – could, for instance, be used to charge a battery or bring a kettle of water to the boil. None of the energy is lost or destroyed.

But there is a sense in which energy is 'consumed'. A great number of energy-using processes are not reversible. The universe is, in fact, running down. The sun is getting older and colder; the stars are burning out. All the energy can be accounted for but not recaptured for reuse. Whenever energy is used some of it is lost and flows towards the 'heat-sink' of outer space. There it adds infinitesimally to the random movement of atoms more thinly dispersed than any vacuum that science has yet managed to create. This is the end of energy: the ultimate graveyard from which no calorie or electronvolt can ever return. Lord Kelvin was the first to introduce the concept of the 'heat death' of the universe when all its energy has become uniformly distributed as low-grade heat.

The Second Law of Thermodynamics, formulated by Clausius in about 1850, states: 'No process is possible whose sole effect is the removal of heat from a reservoir at one temperature and the absorption of an equal quantity of heat by a reservoir at a higher temperature.' In other words, heat does not move spontaneously from a colder object to a warmer one. Expressed in such careful language, the Second Law seems almost a truism, but in its application it is of fundamental importance to engineering. All energy-using processes are subject to this limitation. A pot of boiling water can be used to warm a bathtub of cold water, but a bathtub of warm water will not bring the pot to the boil.

The efficiency of a system using energy is defined as the amount of useful energy produced as a proportion of the total energy input. The operating efficiency of a modern power station is about 35 per cent; in other words, 35 per cent of the energy used in its boilers is made available in the form of electricity. A working animal or a well-trained athlete can turn about 25 per cent of their food-energy intake into the work of pulling a plough or running a race.

It can be shown that the efficiency of a heat engine – that is, a device which converts heat into work – is proportional to the temperature drop which takes place within the system.* Most heat engines rely on steam or the combustion of a petroleum fuel for their energy input. The initial temperature of this 'working fluid' is therefore the key to the efficiency of the device, since the

* For a theoretical heat engine, the efficiency is given by the formula $(T_1 - T_2)/T_1$, where T_1 is the initial temperature of the working fluid and T_2 its final temperature expressed in K.

exit temperature will normally be close to that of the surrounding air, and cannot be below it.

This means that with low-temperature heat sources the efficiency of a device will be low. If, for example, solar energy were used to bring water up to a temperature of 70°C and this were used in a heat engine to drive a pump, the theoretical efficiency would be only about 13 per cent, and in practice would be a maximum of 4–5 per cent. In order to deliver a useful amount of power it would have to be extremely large, and hence expensive. In modern power stations the steam temperatures are close to the limits tolerable for machines made with reasonably available materials. Their theoretical efficiencies are 65–70 per cent, with maximum operating efficiencies of about 40 per cent.

An important practical conclusion to be drawn from this is the desirability of what is called 'thermodynamic matching'. It does not, for example, make thermodynamic sense to use natural gas to produce electricity at an efficiency of 30 per cent and then use this for space heating. If the gas were burned in a central heating boiler, it could produce the heat at an efficiency of 60–70 per cent and save half the energy.

Clausius also introduced the term 'entropy', which had a popular vogue in many of the energy-resource and 'ecological' discussions of the 1970s. It was widely misused and misunderstood, which is not surprising given that in the words of one thermodynamics textbook: 'The concept of entropy presents a difficulty because it does not represent anything tangible, or anything which has an immediate physical significance.'[9] Engineers use it as part of the mathematics of thermodynamics. In the operation of a heat engine, energy passes from a high-temperature to a low-temperature state; in the process it loses a proportion of its capacity to perform useful work. This can be expressed as an increase in its entropy, which therefore represents the energy which is no longer available for doing work in the system.

Part Two

Resources

Civilization as it is at present, even on the purely physical side, is not a continuous self-supporting movement ... It becomes possible only after an age-long accumulation of energy, by the supplementing of income out of capital. Its appetite increases by what it feeds on. It reaps what it has not sown and exhausts, so far, without replenishing. Its raw material is energy and its product is knowledge. The only knowledge which will justify its existence and postpone the day of reckoning is the knowledge that will replenish rather than diminish its limited resources – FREDERICK SODDY, *Matter and Energy*, 1912

5

Coal

Coal is a combustible sedimentary rock formed from the remains of plant life. It occurs in recoverable amounts in many areas, though the majority of the world's large coalfields are in the northern hemisphere. It is by far the most plentiful of the earth's fossil fuels.

As it was formed from land-based plants, coal dates back no further than the middle of the Palaeozoic era, about 350 million years ago. The earliest coals belong to the Devonian geological system, but the most prolific period of coal formation was the Carboniferous (345–280 million years ago), when most of the world's hard and bituminous coals were laid down. Later deposits in the Cretaceous and Tertiary systems formed the lignites and brown coals. Most peat deposits have been formed during the last million years.

In the coal-forming ages the climate was hot and humid and the carbon dioxide level in the atmosphere is believed to have been considerably higher than it is now. These conditions favoured rapid forest growth, and dead vegetation accumulated in the swamps, disappearing under silts and other deposits when land levels sank. Organic matter also accumulated when dead vegetation was carried from the forests by rivers and floods and deposited in lakes and estuaries. This process can still be observed in the deltas of very big river systems like the Mississippi and the Amazon.

Over the long stretches of time during which the coal deposits were laid down, there were many major changes in the configuration of the world's lakes, seas and landmasses. In geologically active areas the land might rise and sink many times, allowing

only relatively thin seams of vegetable matter to settle, interspersed with a variety of other sediments, whereas in less disrupted areas the vegetable seams were very much thicker.

The process by which a deposit of vegetable matter changes to
peat, then through brown coal and lignite to increasingly hard
bituminous coal and finally anthracite, is referred to by the in-
elegant name of 'coalification'. The 'ranking' of a coal depends
on how far it has progressed along the coalification scale. The
major determining conditions in coalification are the temperature
and pressure. Since both increase with depth, the high-ranking
coals are usually those formed from the older deposits and found
at greater depths, though geological upheavals can, of course,
bring once deeply buried deposits close to the surface.

The original vegetable-matter deposits from which coal has
been formed consisted principally of carbon, oxygen and hydrogen products. In the process of coalification chemical and
physical changes take place; one of the by-products is methane
(CH_4), or natural gas. Hydrogen and oxygen are lost from the
deposit at a higher rate than carbon, which means that as the
coalification proceeds, the concentration of carbon increases.
High-quality anthracite is almost pure carbon.

Apart from the degree of coalification, the physical characteristics of different coals are also determined by the types of
vegetation making up the original deposits, by the kind of silts
washed into the swamps in which they decayed, and by the degree
to which decay had proceeded before the deposit was sealed.
Table 5 shows typical compositions for a number of differently
ranked British coals; the composition of wood is also shown for
comparison.

The properties of different coals define their possible uses. A
lot depends, for example, on the amount of sulphur in a coal. A
high sulphur content will cause severe pollution problems and it
may also preclude the use of such a coal in some processes. Coke,
which is used for steel-making, can be made only from a coal
which agglutinates or 'cakes' satisfactorily when heated.

Other characteristics of coals which may limit their uses are
calorific value, ash content and the amount of clinker formed in
combustion. Near the bottom of the coalification scale are the
soft brown coals or lignites. These can contain up to 70 per cent

Table 5. Analysis of UK coals

| | Dry ash-free basis | | | | | | |
| | (Percentages by weight) | | | | | Calorific value | |
	Carbon	Hydro-gen	Oxygen	Nitro-gen	Sulphur	Btu/lb	kWh/kg
Wood	49·8	6·2	43·4	0·3	0·3	8 400	5·32
Leicestershire (non-caking)	78·6	5·2	11·7	1·6	2·8	13 990	8·87
Yorkshire (medium caking)	84·8	5·2	7·6	1·7	0·7	15 090	9·56
Durham coking coal	88·5	5·0	4·1	1·6	0·8	15 630	9·91
South Wales dry-steam coal	90·5	3·9	1·4	1·5	0·7	15 610	9·89
South Wales anthracite	93·5	3·5	1·0	1·2	0·8	15 590	9·88

moisture. They disintegrate rapidly in air and are liable to ignite spontaneously when exposed during mining. They are of low calorific value, a half to a third that of good-quality bituminous coal. Their major use is as fuel for power stations. Coal should not be thought of as a uniform fuel capable of being used indiscriminately in any combustion process; rather, it is a wide range of different fuels, each suitable for particular uses.

Before coal can be used it has to be extracted from the earth. In some areas which have had a turbulent geological history, the seams may be so warped, fractured and faulted that coal is for practical purposes unrecoverable. Lower-ranking coals are often found in thick seams reasonably close to the surface, but those of higher rank are mostly found in seam thicknesses of 3 metres or less – though in some exceptional areas the thickness may exceed 10 metres. The minimum workable thickness is about 30 centimetres. Below a depth of about 1200 metres, high temperatures, increased pressures and geological hazards, as well as the sheer distance of haulage to the top, rule out the working of all but the richest deposits.

Even under favourable conditions, underground coal extraction is difficult and a coal-mine is a dangerous place. The pressure of the overburden is about 2 tonnes per square metre per metre of depth. A means of supporting the roof of the workings has to be used to allow the coal to be extracted. In the 'long wall' method of mining, which is that mainly used in Europe, the eventual collapse of the roof is accepted. Only the area at the cutting face is supported. As the cutting machines which operate across the whole horizontal width of the coal seam move forward, the roof supports, which are themselves sophisticated, automatically controlled and powered pieces of machinery, also move forward. This leaves the excavated area completely unsupported and the roof slowly falls in, generally resulting in subsidence of the ground above the mine. In the 'room and pillar' method of mining, pillars of coal are left in position to support the roof. The investment in mining machinery and roof supports is less and the method is simpler; it also obviates the problem of ground subsidence. The penalty is that up to half the extractable coal must be left behind.

The list of mining dangers and problems is a long one; under the pressure of the overburden the mine remains in a constant state of movement. The side walls of the tunnels creep inwards and the floor bulges upwards. Newly exposed coal can suddenly release gases which were trapped and compressed within it. Methane, or firedamp, forms an explosive mixture with air, and so can the coal-dust itself. Ground water is another hazard which must be kept under control by constant pumping; and if there are unsuspected weaknesses in the rock, it can burst into the workings with catastrophic effect. In the struggle against the primeval elements – earth, fire and water – coal is hard won. Mechanization helps but does not eliminate the problems. Machines can be used only where conditions are tolerable for the men controlling them, and they cannot follow coal into the crevices of irregular rock structures.

Open-cast or surface mining is by its nature less hazardous and more efficient in recovery. Most open-cast mining is for the lower-ranking lignites and brown coals which are usually found close to the surface and sometimes in very thick layers. One deposit in Victoria, Australia, has a seam over 225 metres thick. In the same coalfield, and in parts of the USA seams of over 30 metres are found. The scale of operations is often stupendous. In the rich US fields the overburden may be up to 70 metres thick: this is removed by excavating machines which simply rip up the clays and soft rocks and dump them aside. Explosives take care of harder rocks, which are blown up by the hectare. Huge draglines, diggers and bucket-wheel excavators shift hundreds of thousands of tonnes of material every day. Large-scale strip-mining is one of the most destructive of human activities unless rigorous control of operations is maintained and followed by careful rehabilitation of the land. In certain countries, such as the UK, this is now done with some success. But elsewhere, and the USA in particular, where environmental controls have been adopted belatedly, strip-mining has often left a landscape damaged beyond possibility of repair.

Resources and Reserves

Considerable confusion has been caused by the terms 'resources' and 'reserves'. An attempt to produce generally acceptable definitions was made at the World Energy Conference in 1977. 'Geological resources' were defined as coal occurrences which may acquire some economic value in the future – in other words, it is possible to imagine them being mined some day. Coal reserves, on the other hand, were defined as coal occurrences which are exploitable with present technology and under present economic conditions. As technology improves and the price of competing fuels increases, resources will therefore tend to move into the category of reserves.

The early importance of coal as a primary fuel for an industrial economy has meant that it has been under detailed study for a long time. The first attempt to produce an estimate of world reserves was made in 1913 at the Twelfth International Geological Conference in Toronto. The tentative conclusion reached was that there was a total of 7.397×10^{12} tonnes of coal in seams not less than 30 centimetres thick at depths of up to 1200 metres and in seams not less than 60 centimetres thick at depths between 1200 and 1800 metres.

Since then a great deal more has been learned about the earth's geology and its coal resources, though very large uncertainties still remain. Discrepancies, often amounting to many billions of tonnes, are a feature of the various estimates of world coal resources, and even those of individual countries. One reason for this is the cost of detailed exploration. As long as a coal-mining country has confirmed figures for reserves sufficient to supply its

Table 6. World coal resources and reserves by coal type – industrial market economies and centrally planned countries (tonnes coal equivalent × 10⁹)

	Geological resources				Technically and economically recoverable reserves			
	Hard coal		Brown coal		Hard coal		Brown coal	
Market economies		%		%		%		%
Australia	213·8	2·8	48·4	2·0	18·1	3·7	9·2	6·4
Canada	96·2	1·3	19·1	0·8	8·7	1·8	0·7	0·5
France	2·3	—	—	—	0·4	0·1	—	—
Germany (FR)	230·3	3·0	16·5	0·7	23·9	4·9	10·5	7·3
Japan	8·6	0·1	—	—	1·0	0·2	—	—
Netherlands	2·9	—	—	—	1·4	0·3	—	—
South Africa	57·6	0·8	—	—	26·9	5·5	—	—
Spain	1·8	—	0·5	—	0·3	0·1	0·2	0·1
United Kingdom	163·6	2·1	—	—	45·0	9·1	—	—
USA	1190·0	15·4	1380·4	57·5	113·2	23·0	64·4	44·7
Others	0·7	—	1·7	—	0·2	—	0·6	0·5
TOTAL	1967·7	25·5	1466·7	61·0	239·1	48·7	85·6	59·5
Centrally planned economies								
Bulgaria	—	—	2·6	0·1	—	—	2·2	1·5
China (PR)	1424·7	18·4	13·4	0·6	98·8	20·1	not available	
Czechoslovakia	11·6	0·2	5·9	0·2	2·5	0·5	2·3	1·6
Germany (DR)	—	—	9·2	0·4	0·1	—	7·6	5·3
Hungary	0·7	—	2·8	0·1	0·2	—	0·7	0·5
Korea (DPR)	2·0	—	—	—	0·3	0·1	0·2	0·1
Poland	121·0	1·6	4·5	0·2	20·0	4·1	1·0	0·7
Romania	0·6	—	1·3	—	—	—	0·4	0·3
USSR	3993·0	51·7	867·0	36·1	82·9	16·8	27·0	18·8
Others	0·2	—	—	—	0·1	—	—	—
TOTAL	5553·8	71·9	906·7	37·7	204·9	41·6	41·4	28·8
TOTAL MARKET AND CENTRALLY PLANNED	7521·5	97·4	2373·4	98·7	444·0	90·3	127·0	88·3

coal industry for several decades ahead, it has little incentive to make heavy investments in further detailed exploration.

Tables 6 and 7 give details of geological resources and technically and economically recoverable reserves for all countries presently known to possess exploitable coal deposits. It is noticeable how widespread is the occurrence of coal throughout the

Table 7. World coal resources and reserves by coal type – developing countries (tonnes coal equivalent × 10⁹)

	Geological resources				Technically and economically recoverable reserves			
	Hard coal	%	Brown coal	%	Hard coal	%	Brown coal	%
Botswana	100·0	1·3	—	—	3.5	0·7	—	—
Mozambique	0,4	—	—	—	—	—	—	—
Nigeria	—	—	0·2	—	—	—	—	—
Zimbabwe	7·1	0·1	—	—	0·8	0·2	—	—
Swaziland	5·0	0·1	—	—	1·8	0·4	—	—
Zambia	0·2	—	—	—	—	—	—	—
Others	2·4	—	—	—	1·0	0·2	—	—
TOTAL AFRICA	115·1	1·5	0.2	—	7·1	1·5	—	—
Bangladesh	1·6	—	—	—	0·5	0·1	—	—
India	55·6	0·7	1·2	0·1	33·3	6·8	0·3	0·3
Indonesia	0·6	—	3·1	0·1	—	—	1·4	0·9
Iran	0·4	—	—	—	0·2	—	—	—
Korea (R)	0·9	—	—	—	0·4	0·1	—	—
Turkey	1·3	—	2·0	0·1	0·1	—	0·7	0·5
Others	5·4	0·1	0·4	—	1·5	0·3	—	—
TOTAL ASIA	65·8	0·8	6·7	0·3	36·1	7·3	2·4	1·7
Argentina	—	—	0·4	—	—	—	0·3	0·2
Brazil	4·0	0·1	6·0	0·3	2·5	0·5	5·6	3·9
Chile	2·4	—	2·1	0·1	—	—	0·1	0·1
Colombia	7·6	0·1	0·7	—	0·4	0·1	—	—
Mexico	5.4	0·1	—	—	0·9	0·2	—	—
Peru	1·0	—	—	—	0·1	—	—	—
Venezuela	1·6	—	—	—	1·0	0·2	—	—
Others	—	—	—	—	—	—	—	—
TOTAL LATIN AMERICA	22·3	0·3	9·2	0·4	4·9	1·0	6·0	4·2
Yugoslavia	0·1	—	10·8	0·4	—	—	8·4	5·9
TOTAL DEVELOPING COUNTRIES	203·3	2·6	27·0	1·1	48·2	9.8	17·0	11·8
WORLD TOTAL	7724·8	100	2400·4	100	492·5	100	143·9	100

Source; World Bank, *Coal Development Potential and Prospects in the Developing Countries*, October 1979.

world. Intensified exploration in developing countries is now identifying further deposits, and there is a cautious optimism that at least some of the world's very poor countries may possess useful amounts of coal.

Both tables show a great difference between the figures for resources and reserves. Present technically and economically recoverable reserves are just about 6 per cent of resources. It will be noticed that the proportion varies considerably between countries. In the USA the hard coal reserves are about 10 per cent of resources; in China they are only about 1 per cent. Price, quality of coal, availability of transport and capital equipment, and many other factors determine which coalfields can be mined economically at any particular time.

Although widespread in occurrence, the geographical concentration of coal is also extremely noticeable. The USSR possesses 52 per cent of the world's resources of hard coal and 36 per cent of those of brown coal. The USA has nearly 60 per cent of the world's brown coal resources and 15 per cent of the hard coal. The USSR, USA and China between them possess 85 per cent of the world's hard coal and 94 per cent of the world's brown coal. This is not to say that the reserves of other countries are negligible. Countries like Germany, the UK, Poland, Australia and South Africa (to take some of the present largest producers) have resources sufficient to last them hundreds of years at present rates of mining. Some of the developing countries, such as Colombia and India, are capable of meeting their own needs and becoming substantial exporters.

Production

The major European coal-producing nations have nearly all been running down their production in recent decades. In the UK, for example, production fell by more than half, from a post-war peak of 225 million tonnes in 1953 to 105 million tonnes in 1986 – the total number of miners fell from 715 000 to 119 000. In France production fell from 73 million tonnes in 1952 to 12 million tonnes in 1985. And in Holland, where production was over 12 million tonnes in 1950, coal-mining has now ceased completely. This kind of decline is difficult to arrest, let alone reverse.

Work-forces are hard to reassemble once the traditional mining communities have been dispersed. Mines once closed down suffer collapse and flooding and may be impossible to reopen.

Opening new pits and creating distribution and storage facilities in crowded, highly urbanized countries is almost prohibitively difficult. Coal-mining brings slag heaps, polluted waterways, dirt, heavy road and rail traffic and a big loss of otherwise usable land. There is also the problem of ground subsidence after the coal has been extracted. In some cases the ground may sink as much as a metre. This plays havoc with underground services such as sewers and water pipes. It also necessitates the replacement of damaged buildings. All these features are part of the way of life in a mining community; but it is very difficult to see them being easily accepted in areas which have not previously experienced them. The likelihood of any major restoration of the European coal-mining industry is therefore remote.

But far from being a dying industry as the European experience would indicate, coal-mining has been growing steadily in other parts of the world. Total production has quadrupled in the past forty years; the present annual growth in consumption is about 3 per cent per year. Table 8 shows the present distribution of coal production around the world. It is dominated by China, the USA and the USSR; together they account for about 60 per cent of the total.

At the present rate of consumption the world's geological resources of coal would last almost 3000 years. But, of course, production tends to rise with time, shortening the period over which a resource might be exploited. Theoretical studies of possible future patterns of production often use what is called a depletion curve. This assumes that production continues to grow until the rate of development of new mines becomes impossible to sustain. The growth in production then begins to slow down and eventually ceases; this is the peak in output. Thereafter production gradually declines.

In a study of world energy resources sponsored by the US National Academy of Sciences the geologist M. King Hubbert, using an extremely optimistic figure of 7.6×10^{12} tonnes of re-

Table 8. World coal production, 1985

Country	Hard coal (tonnes × 10⁶)	Brown coal (tonnes × 10⁶)	Total* (tce × 10⁶)
China	785	62	733
USA	743	60	705
USSR	566	160	519
Poland	191	58	199
India	150	8	146
South Africa	173	0	131
West Germany	94	121	118
Australia	125	36	117
East Germany	0	300	90
UK	94	0	82†
Czechoslovakia	26	103	71
Canada	51	10	57
Yugoslavia	0	67	29
Spain	16	24	26
Latin America	26	0	23
Romania	8	38	20
Others	123	22	177
World total	3171	1188	3243

* Converted to standard tonnes of coal equivalent (tce) on the basis of estimated calorific values applying in each case.
† Affected by the miners' strike: full year's production about 120 million tonnes.
Source: BP Statistical Review of World Energy, 1986.

coverable reserves, suggested the depletion curve for coal shown in Figure 3.[10] In this, world production grows for the next 175 years, peaks at about seven times the present consumption and thereafter declines, with final exhaustion occurring in about 800 years. Other depletion curves could, of course, be drawn: higher peaks mean shorter overall durations for the full production cycle; lower peaks allow it to be drawn out for a longer period. When a depletion curve is drawn, the area under the curve represents the total amount of the resource. In Figure 3 it is noticeable how small a proportion of total reserves have been consumed to date. Humanity has scarcely dented its coal resources.

The use of depletion curves is, however, of limited value when thinking about the future pattern of coal consumption. It helps to define the outer limits of what is possible. The main use of

Figure 3. Theoretical depletion curve for 7·6 × 10¹² billion tonnes recoverable reserves of coal

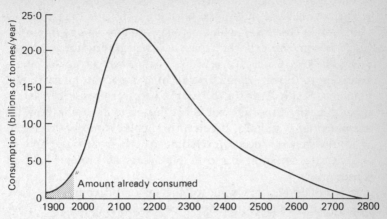

After M. K. Hubbert in *Resources and Man*, W. H. Freeman, San Francisco, 1969.

Figure 3 is that it shows that speculation about the ultimate exhaustion of coal resources is largely irrelevant, but it does not provide any guidance about what is likely to happen in practice.

The Outlook for Coal

The World Coal Study, which published its findings in 1980, envisaged world coal production at least doubled, and possibly trebled, by the year 2000. The time-scale for this has certainly slipped, and it is now highly unlikely that any such increase in production will take place before the turn of the century. It still remains at least a theoretical possibility for the early decades of the next century, but would require major changes in the coal markets of the world.

At present, most coal is consumed in the country in which it is produced. At the time of the World Coal Study, only 200 million tonnes of coal were traded internationally, of which 150 million tonnes were metallurgical coal, that special type of coal used to make coke for steel-making. If coal consumption were to increase on the scale envisaged, there would have to be a huge increase in the international coal trade. A major programme of investments in shipping, ports and railways would be required.

There would also have to be substantial shifts in the pattern of trade flows. The USA, which is today a major energy importer, would become an exporter, since it is well positioned to supply world markets. Canada, Australia, Poland and possibly China – exporting to Japan – could also become important international suppliers. South Africa also has the necessary resources and is already a coal exporter; but other factors will decide how far this potential is realized. It currently supplies almost 80 per cent of its own energy needs (excluding wood) from coal, and its reserves are sufficient for over 500 years at present rates of consumption.

It is noticeable that some of the major oil companies have already acquired large holdings of coal reserves both in the USA and abroad. Exxon, for example, has invested in Colombia; Shell has promoted developments in Botswana and Swaziland. Japan is another major investor with a programme of subsidized coal research-projects abroad and guaranteed loans for coal development-projects in foreign countries; these are all part of its long-term planning to secure its energy supplies.

Opposition to the use of coal on environmental grounds, however, is likely to become stronger, particularly in the USA, Western Europe and Japan, where lobbying groups are strong and well organized. The environmental record of coal has been a sorry one of smoke-blackened towns, devastated landscapes, polluted rivers and mine-workers with broken health. Coal was primarily responsible for one of the greatest environmental disasters when an estimated 4000 people who were old or suffering from respiratory troubles died in one of the great London fogs in 1952. The main reason was the amount of smoke and general pollution emitted by domestic coal fires.

In the general concern about nuclear power, it is sometimes forgotten what a potentially lethal cocktail of emissions there can be from a coal-fired power station. The particular combination varies depending on the coal being used and the degree of pollution control exercised, but it can include: sulphur oxides, heavy metals (lead, mercury, cadmium), radioactive elements such as uranium and radium, carcinogenic compounds such as polycyclic hydrocarbons, and, of course, plenty of carbon dioxide. All in all, coal-fired power stations are undoubtedly more polluting and in some cases may even be more radioactive than a smoothly running nuclear power station. This has been noted, with no little satisfaction, by the nuclear industry.

Awareness of the damage caused by the phenomenon of acid rain is also working its way into the broad public consciousness. For the Scandinavian countries and Germany, the evidence that something is going seriously wrong offered by dying forests and acidified lakes is overwhelming. There is little doubt in those countries that the sulphur-containing emissions from coal-fired power stations in the UK are at least partly to blame. The Canadians are similarly angry that the USA is exporting its acid pollution to them. Increasingly, people are wondering what the chemicals which devastate forests and destroy in a decade the stone façades of buildings which have stood for thousands of years also do to the tissues of human and animal respiratory systems.

There is enormous uncertainty about the exact numbers of people affected by the emissions from coal-fired power stations. The effects are statistically not very great and hence are difficult to measure. An international study entitled 'Environmental Implications of Expanded Coal Utilization', carried out at the Beijer Institute of the Royal Swedish Academy of Science in 1982,[11] quoted an estimate of American deaths from coal in 1975 which put the total in the range of between 1900 and 15 000 for the whole country; these are the sort of figures usually associated with estimates of the effects of a nuclear catastrophe, but are, in this case, referring to the normal operation of coal-fired power stations. An estimate from the USSR, quoted in the same study, put the figure at 299 deaths per year from each 1000-megawatt station.

Pollution-control devices can be used in coal-fired power stations. But the technical and economic difficulties are considerable. The sheer scale of a major power station and what is involved in 'scrubbing' out the sulphur dioxide from the emission gases are not generally appreciated. A 1000-megawatt power station uses about 2 million tonnes of coal per year. If this contains, say, 2·5 per cent sulphur, the total amount to be extracted is 50 000 tonnes. If the scrubber uses limestone to absorb the sulphur compounds, then hundreds of thousands of tonnes of a very noxious sludge are created which must be disposed of somehow. But the pressure to stop using high-sulphur coals and to install devices to 'scrub' sulphur compounds from power station flue gases is nevertheless becoming increasingly difficult for even the most obdurate of governments, such as that in the UK, to resist for much longer. The effect will be to reduce the economic competitiveness of coal.

Carbon dioxide is also emitted when coal is burned. Being mainly carbon, coal produces more carbon dioxide than oil or natural gas when it is burned. Per unit heat, the carbon dioxide production of coal is 25 per cent higher than oil and 75 per cent higher than that of natural gas. Much remains to be learned about the increasing level of atmospheric carbon dioxide and the dangers of a change in global temperatures. But in the light of the available evidence it is clear that a massive expansion in coal consumption could be a real threat to the global environment.

At present, coal supplies about 30 per cent of the world's energy. Its uses and importance are not as visible as those of oil. Electricity generation is, in fact, its principal use. But it would be completely impossible to dispense with it or to reduce consumption substantially without a major disruption of many of the world's industrial economies. It also offers some of the developing countries an indigenous fuel for electric power generation and industrial development. The short-term and medium-term prospect is that its use will continue to grow at something like the rate of the last few decades.

But the debate about its polluting effects has scarcely yet been joined. Almost certainly, it will develop in the coming decades. There is no question that the coal resources necessary to supply humanity with an abundance of energy for a long time to come exist. The unanswered question is whether the cost of using them will prove too high.

Peat

Peat is the first stage in the formation of coal from vegetable matter. Most of the world's present peat deposits have been formed within the last million years and are found at or very close to the surface, though some may be under water. The characteristics of peat vary greatly between deposits, but most contain a high proportion of sphagnum moss which gives the peat its cellular structure. The acidic environment of a peat bog can have a 'mummifying' effect, preserving animal or human remains for very long periods.

The methods of obtaining peat depend on local conditions. Usually trenches have to be dug to drain away the water in the deposit. The peat is then cut by hand or machine and left to dry in the sun and wind. When cut, peat may have a moisture content of up to 90 per cent. The peat is used as fuel at a moisture content of 30–60 per cent.

There are known peat deposits in about thirty countries. In general, they are found in the colder northern areas of the world. Canada, the USSR and the USA have very large resources. Indonesia is rather more surprising: the 1986 World Energy Conference lists it as having 200 billion tonnes of proved reserves. This is by a considerable margin the world's largest national reserves figure.

In Ireland, where it is called turf, hand-won peat has traditionally been very widely used as a domestic fuel; at present, it is mainly supplied in briquette form for household use. Sophisticated machinery has been developed by the National Peat Board for large-scale peat extraction and provides fuel for a number of the country's electricity generating stations. Production runs at about 7.5 million tonnes per year, but the quantity of recoverable resources is relatively small and is not likely to be able to sustain this level of production for more than about another two decades.

Finland produces about 2·7 million tonnes of peat per year, yet, like Ireland, its recoverable resources are relatively limited. The USSR, with a total production of about 17·5 million tonnes per year, is the world's largest producer, a rate of production which its resources would sustain for another thousand years. Apart from about 300 000 tonnes per year in Sweden, production elsewhere is negligible.

Peat is difficult and expensive to win and, unless it has been well dried, it is a difficult and smoky fuel to use. It is therefore difficult for it to compete economically with coal. There is, however, a large market for peat for horticultural uses, and it is probable that it has better prospects here than as a fuel for widespread use.

6

Petroleum

The word petroleum, meaning 'rock oil', is now used as a blanket term for a wide range of hydrocarbons – from the simple gas methane, or natural gas, through liquids of increasing viscosity to the solid paraffin waxes. Petroleum has been used as a fuel, lubricant, medicament and even building material for thousands of years. The biblical 'burning fiery furnace' was probably a lighted natural-gas escape, as were the eternal flames at various oracular shrines. In the Middle East bitumen has traditionally been used as a mortar, flooring and waterproofing material – it was reputedly used in the construction of the ill-fated Tower of Babel. It was also used in the preservation of mummies. Oil has also been used, more or less harmfully, as a salve or internal medicament for all kinds of ailments. It is now one of the basic raw materials of the pharmaceutical industry.

The origin of petroleum and natural gas have long been a subject of speculation. Under high temperatures carbon enters into combination with various metals to form carbides which are decomposed by water to give hydrocarbons such as acetylene (C_2H_2): it therefore seemed reasonable to suppose that petroleum products were formed in this way in the earth's crust. The great Russian chemist Dmitri Mendeleyev, who drew up the Periodic Table of elements in 1869, believed so and wrote a treatise explaining their origin. The majority opinion among chemists and geologists has, however, been resolutely against this and it is almost universally accepted that the great majority of the earth's petroleum is derived from marine organic material, laid down as part of the accumulation process by which the world's sedimentary rock basins were formed. Decisive proof of the biological derivation of the majority of the world's oil appears to be provided by the fact that petroleum contains complex molecules which have clearly come from organic material. The earliest oils, found in the lower Palaeozoic beds or even in some of the Precambrian formations, predate the formation of coal by hundreds of millions of years and were laid down long before the appearance of land vegetation.

The non-biological theory of the origin of oil has nevertheless continued to retain its adherents. There are unexplained anomalies in the occurrence of oilfields which fit better with the notion that the oil was carried upwards in association with methane rather than formed from marine deposits. The occurrence of organic molecules could be accounted for by the mixing of the petroleum with organically derived materials in sedimentary rock deposits. The theory is being now put to a practical test. In June 1986 work was started on drilling a deep borehole in the Siljan meteor crater in central Sweden. This is an area of granite rock rather than a sedimentary basin. Traces of hydrocarbons have been found in the area; if the borehole finds significant quantities of petroleum, then a major revision of the present theories of oil formation is likely to be required.[12]

Whatever the final story of its origins, a great deal is now known about where oil is most commonly found. It is, for example, never associated with coal; the two materials are always stratigraphically separated. The temperature rise associated with depth also appears to be a critical factor; many petroleum products break down at about 150°C. To date, very little liquid petroleum has been found at depths below 7600 metres.

Whereas coal is found in the geological stratum in which it was formed, petroleum usually migrates from the place of its origin. Under pressure from the overburden, liquid and gaseous hydrocarbons are displaced from the rocks in which they were formed and diffuse through the surrounding permeable strata until they are trapped, still under pressure, by an impermeable barrier. If no trap is encountered, the petroleum escapes to the surface where it is eventually broken down. The development of an oilfield thus has to be distinguished from the formation of the petroleum itself. The liquids and gases found in an oilfield do not necessarily have a common origin: the methane may, for instance, have come from the formation of coal. What they have in common is that their migratory progress through various permeable rock formations has ended in the same place.

The formation of an oilfield in any area therefore depends on the existence of suitable geological traps to which the petroleum can migrate and in which it can accumulate. But later faulting, folding or igneous intrusions can destroy or dissipate these accumulations. Such is the rarity of the coincidence of all the necessary conditions that only about one in twenty of the structures identified from geological evidence as being suitable as an oil reservoir actually yields petroleum in recoverable amounts.

Oil

The main blame for one of the commonest misconceptions about oilfields can possibly be laid on Jules Verne's *Journey to the Centre of the Earth*. The great underground caverns he so vividly describes seem ideal for the accumulation of lakes of oil. In fact, oil accumulates within the pore spaces of a variety of sedimentary rocks, such as the sandstones, or carbonates like limestones or dolomite. The volume of pore space available to be filled varies from about 35 per cent down to as little as 5 per cent of the total rock volume. Extracting oil is more like squeezing treacle out of a brick than lifting bucketsful of water from a well.

Within a reservoir, the oil, gas and water tend to separate into layers with gas at the top, oil next, and then water. The extent of this separation depends on the porosity of the rock, the viscosity of the liquid petroleum and the relative proportions of the liquids and gases. When the cap over the reservoir is punctured by a drill, the pressure is released and the liquids and gases shoot to the surface. In early years of oil exploration this frequently produced a 'gusher' which was completely uncontrollable until the pressure dropped. In these cases, most of the natural pressure of the well was lost and the amount of oil obtained was much less than it might have been. Obtaining the maximum yield from any oilfield requires careful management of the pressure by the spacing of wells and the control of rates of extraction. It is possible to mismanage the process so badly that the reservoir pressure is dissipated in driving up briny water, leaving the greater part of the oil deposit irrevocably trapped.

The extraction of oil using only the natural reservoir pressure has the technical name of 'primary recovery'. Wells used to be abandoned when the natural flow ceased, but it was discovered that injecting gas or water under pressure could restore the flow and this came to be called 'secondary recovery'. Efficient modern practice does not, however, allow pressures to decline to zero before commencing 'secondary' methods; the objective is to maintain the pressure at an optimum level for as long as possible. Often natural gas is reinjected into the reservoir from which it has been obtained in order to maintain the pressure for oil extraction. Gas injection was first used in the USA as early as 1891, but has come into widespread use only since the end of the Second World War. Secondary recovery by water flooding is also used, but it is more difficult to engineer and is not possible in many areas because of the amount of water required.

More elaborate 'tertiary' recovery methods use steam, solvents or underground combustion, fed with air or oxygen from the surface, to reduce the viscosity of the oil in the reservoir and allow it to flow more freely. The use of heat from underground nuclear explosions has also been suggested, but no way of preventing the oil from becoming radioactive, and hence unusable, has yet been convincingly demonstrated.

Viscous oils in rocks of low porosity have very low recovery factors, as little as 5 per cent. Even under ideal conditions recovery factors are rarely more than about 70 per cent. The average recovery factor in the USA is about 33 per cent; in the North Sea about 45 per cent; world wide it is estimated to be about 40 per cent.

Discussions about the exhaustion of the world's oil can cause considerable confusion. Some of it would be avoided if it were always clear what people were talking about. Here is one quotation:

If these rates continue to grow exponentially, as they have done since 1960, then natural gas will be exhausted within fourteen years and petroleum within twenty years.

And a contrasting view that

. . . the oil resource base in relation to reasonable expectations of demand gives very little apparent cause for concern, not only for the remainder of this century but also thereafter well into the twenty-first century at rates of consumption which will then be five or more times their present level.

The first is from 'A Blueprint for Survival',[13] one of the studies of the early 1970s which foresaw an early end to industrial society as a result of resource depletion and pollution. The second is from a paper by Professor Peter Odell,[14] who was unusually optimistic about oil resources during the 'crises' and excitement of the 1970s, and has so far proven himself to be more correct in his analysis than most of his critics. But quite apart from these differences in approach, the two quotations are actually about very different things. Professor Odell was talking about the 'resource base'; the 'Blueprint for Survival' was using figures for what are called 'proved reserves'.

The 'resource base' is defined as all the petroleum within the earth's crust in a particular area. It is sometimes called the 'oil in place'. Since recovery rates vary from 5 per cent up to 70 per cent of the oil in a reservoir, 'resource base' figures must always be qualified by reference to an expected rate of recovery.

On the other hand, 'proved resources' or, as they are sometimes called, 'published proved reserves' are defined by the oil industry as 'the volume of crude oil which geological and engineering information indicate beyond all reasonable doubt to be recoverable from an oil reservoir under existing operating conditions'. This is a very restricted definition. Its main purpose is to prevent fraudulent raising of money by oil companies publishing over-optimistic figures for their assets in the ground. There is nothing hypothetical about the proved reserves figure. It is, in effect, the verified inventory of an oil company's stock in hand.

The proved-reserves figure understates the true recoverable reserves in a number of ways. It is confined to oil which has been identified as recoverable in an oilfield: it does not include oil which may lie in extensions of the field yet to be explored, nor does it include oil which may be recoverable using secondary and tertiary methods until these are actually in operation. The figure for proved reserves is therefore one of limited applicability. At the beginning of the exploration of an oilfield it will necessarily understate the amount of recoverable oil. As exploration continues, an increasing proportion of the recoverable reserves will be identified until, finally, the estimate for remaining proved reserves will coincide with the figure for ultimately recoverable oil. A study published by the Alberta Energy Resources Conservation Board has shown, from the analysis of the production records of 128 oilfields in the province, that the quantity of oil finally recovered from each field was, on average, about nine times the published reserves declared at the end of the first year of exploration. The Alberta data can hardly be applied directly to other areas, but the general principle of the appreciation of the initially published reserves figure is certainly valid.

Table 9 shows the present distribution of the world's proved reserves. As in the case of coal, the unevenness of their distribution is very marked. The Middle East has 56 per cent of the total, with Saudi Arabia having almost half of this, or nearly a quarter of the world's reserves. The USSR, which is the world's largest producer, has 8·6 per cent; the USA, which is the next largest producer, has only 4 per cent. The North Sea accounts for 3·3 per cent of the total.

In 1970 the total proved reserves were $84 \cdot 1 \times 10^9$ tonnes. The 1985 figure is $95 \cdot 8 \times 10^9$, an increase of 14 per cent. Far from running out of oil, the world now has a considerably higher inventory of reserves than it had fifteen years ago. In other words, the pace of discovery is still more than keeping up with that of consumption.

Much work has been carried out on the estimation of the total ultimately recoverable reserves. Most of this is based on a careful analysis of the oil-bearing areas of the world. The main sedimentary basins have all been identified by now and most have been subjected to at least some exploratory drilling. Experience of oilfields which have been thoroughly explored can be used as a guide to what is likely to be found in the remainder. Some will be more prolific than expected, as was the case with the North Sea; others will be less so, as appears to be the case in Alaska. Normally such errors would tend to balance out. With time, as drilling reduces the uncertainties, the estimates will increasingly converge on the truth.

Table 9. Proved oil reserves at end of 1985

	Thousand million tonnes	% share of total		Thousand million tonnes	% share of total
NORTH AMERICA			AFRICA		
USA	4·6	5·0	Algeria*	1·1	1·3
Canada	1·0	1·0	Angola	0·3	0·3
Total North America	5·6	6·0	Egypt	0·5	0·6
			Libya*	2·8	3·0
LATIN AMERICA			Nigeria*	2·3	2·3
Argentina	0·3	0·3	Tunisia	0·2	0·3
Brazil	0·3	0·3	Others	0·2	0·3
Ecuador*	0·2	0·2	Total Africa	7·4	8·1
Mexico	6·9	7·0			
Venezuela*	3·7	3·6	ASIA & AUSTRALASIA		
Others	0·5	0·5	Brunei	0·2	0·2
Total Latin America	11·9	11·9	Indonesia	1·2	1·2
			Malaysia	0·4	0·4
WESTERN EUROPE			India	0·5	0·5
Norway	1·4	1·5	Australia	0·2	0·2
United Kingdom	1·7	1·8	Total Asia & Australasia	2·5	2·5
Others	0·3	0·4	TOTAL	84·8	88·5
Total Western Europe	3·4	3·7			
			CENTRALLY-PLANNED ECONOMIES (CPEs)		
MIDDLE EAST			China	2·4	2·6
Abu Dhabi*	4·1	4·4	USSR	8·3	8·6
Dubai*	0·2	0·2	Others	0·3	0·3
Iran*	6·5	6·8	Total CPEs	11·0	11·5
Iraq*	5·9	6·2	TOTAL WORLD	95·8	100·0
Kuwait*	12·4	12·7	Of which OPEC	64·6	67·1
Neutral Zone	0·8	0·8			
Oman	0·5	0·6			
Qatar	0·4	0·5			
Saudi Arabia	23·0	23·8			
Syria	0·2	0·2			
Total Middle East	54·0	56·2			

* OPEC member.
Source: BP Review of World Energy, 1986.

Table 10 shows various estimates of ultimately recoverable oil reserves for the world which have been made since the 1940s. The spread of these is large, with a factor of four between the highest and the lowest. But an important point should be noted: the unique magnitude of the Middle East fields was not fully appreciated until the mid-1950s. Until then, most of the detailed information on oil-bearing rock formations had come from borehole records available in the USA. They were used to make estimates of the likely productivity of oil-bearing sedimentary basins in other parts of the world. Oil geologists failed to see how radically the Middle East was going to break the established rules.

There is considerable ambiguity about these figures. Sometimes it is not clear whether the estimate includes the oil already consumed – about 60 billion tonnes. Looking at the list, however,

Table 10. Estimates of world ultimately recoverable crude-oil reserves

Date	Source	Estimate barrels × 10⁹
1946	Duce	400
1946	Pogue	555
1948	Weeks	610
1949	Levorsen	1500
1949	Weeks	1010
1953	MacNaughton	1000
1956	Hubbert	1250
1958	Weeks	1500
1959	Weeks	2000
1965	Hendricks	2480
1967	Ryman	2090
1968	Weeks	2200
1969	Hubbert	1350–2100
1970	Moody	1800
1971	Warman	1200–2000
1971	Weeks	2290
1972	Warman	1900
1972	Bauquis, Brasseur and Masseron	1950
1975	Moody and Geiger	2000
1978	Nehring	2025
1982	Coletti (AGIP)	2080
1982	Petroleum Economist	2190
1983	IEA	1500–2240

it can be seen that there is a marked clustering around the figure of 2000×10^9 barrels, or 274×10^9 tonnes. The International Energy Agency figure of 1500–2000×10^9 barrels represented the 'best estimate' of the total based on all the studies carried out up to that time. The figure of 274×10^9 tonnes remaining recoverable reserves is commonly accepted as a reasonable basis for discussion purposes.

The uncertainty in any such figure for ultimate reserves is, of course, still extremely high. It is worth remembering that about two thirds of this oil remains to be proved; this is about 100 times the published reserves figure for the North Sea. Some oil geologists, looking at their maps of the world's sedimentary basins, are unable to imagine where all the extra oil is supposed to come from.

Knowledge of geology and of how to extract oil is, however, improving all the time. An improvement in the average recovery ratio from 40 per cent to 50 per cent, for example, would represent an increase in reserves of 25 per cent. It is still possible that there will be a major upward revision of the estimated total reserves in the future. Professor Odell certainly supports this view and has suggested that the estimate could justifiably be trebled.

Figure 4 shows a theoretical depletion curve for oil typical of those which were being proposed in the late 1960s and early 1970s. It shows oil production continuing to increase at its historic growth rate of 7·5 per cent per year for a few more years. The growth rate then begins to slacken as discoveries are unable to keep pace with consumption. The peak is reached about the year 2000 and the production thereafter gradually declines. In fact, as can be seen in the figure, actual production grew much more slowly during the 1970s, and since 1978 has declined by about 7 per cent.

This levelling out of world oil consumption interrupts a pattern of growth which has lasted over a century. As Table 11 shows, from the 1890s onwards world consumption has doubled every decade apart from the period 1930–50, during which the Second World War destroyed Europe; even then, consumption trebled in twenty years. From the 1940s to the end of the 1960s the annual growth rate was about 7·5 per cent. For many planners it had almost become a law of nature that it would continue to do so.

80   *Resources*

Figure 4. Theoretical depletion curve for world oil reserves based on continued historic growth

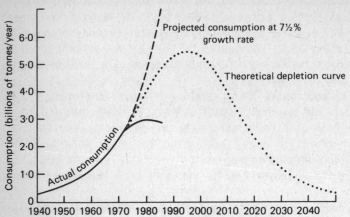

Note: Based on total reserves of 274 billion tonnes.
Source: H. R. Warman, The Future of Oil, *Geographical Journal* Vol. 138, 1972.

One reason for this unquestioning trust was that the question of security of supply had not yet arisen. In the 1950s and 1960s the international oil industry was almost totally controlled by just seven companies, the 'international majors', or 'Seven Sisters' as

Table 11. World oil production since 1890

	USSR, East Europe	North America	Latin America	Middle East	Africa	Asia	World total
1890	3·5	3·5	—	—	—	—	9·9
1900	9·6	10·1	—	—	—	0·1	19·8
1910	12·1	29·2	0·2	—	—	2·8	44·5
1920	6·1	82·2	1·0	1·7	0·1	4·1	95·2
1930	23·6	128·6	26·0	6·4	0·3	7·8	192·9
1940	36·9	192·6	36·8	14·1	0·9	11·2	293·9
1950	42·1	284·3	88·2	87·8	2·3	13·6	519·3
1960	163·0	392·3	173·5	263·5	14·4	31·1	1051·2
1970	372·3	563·3	237·0	706·0	302·5	89·6	2286·5
1975	514·8	557·4	227·5	975·1	248·5	109·1	2733·6
1980	626·0	565·8	298·5	927·4	301·7	135·3	3081·9
1985	617·1	578·4	334·0	532·5	252.6	158·5	2789·5

Source: E. N. Tiratsoo, *Oilfields of the World*, Scientific Press, 1973. *BP Statistical Review of World Energy*, 1986

they were called: Standard Oil of New Jersey (now Exxon), Standard Oil of New York (Socony Mobil), Standard Oil of California (Chevron), Gulf Oil, Texaco, Royal Dutch Shell and British Petroleum. Although they went through many of the rituals of competition and could at times behave ruthlessly towards each other and newly emerging competitors, they collaborated very effectively in the regulation of production and the distribution of petroleum supplies to the industrial world.

The 1970s put an end to the hegemony of the oil companies. Control of the industry is now much more fragmented. The producer countries have control over their own resources, but little over world markets. Oil supplies are no longer guaranteed to the industrial world by oil companies based in Europe and the USA; they depend on decisions made by governments in Riyadh, Teheran and Tripoli. There is a great deal more distrust between suppliers and consumers and doubts about security of supplies. For some countries, France notably, reduction in dependence on foreign oil suppliers was made an issue of the highest national priority after the oil embargo of 1973.

The Production Outlook

There is no question that oil remains a crucial fuel; the industrial world could not function without it. But there is a great deal more flexibility in the world energy system than there was fifteen years ago. Above all, there is a wariness in most oil-importing countries about increasing their dependence on oil if there are what appear to be more secure alternatives available.

On the other hand, oil has become an extremely cheap fuel once more. The international price at the end of 1986 was $15 per barrel. In real terms that was roughly what it was at the beginning of the 1970s. Nor is OPEC the threat it was in the 1970s. The immediate prospect is therefore that there will be a moderate increase in oil consumption over the decade or so. The level of prices will depend on how successful producers are in regulating production and preventing a glut in the market. Towards the end of the 1990s, as the North Sea and other non-OPEC production declines, producers will be in a stronger position and it is probable that prices will begin to rise significantly again.

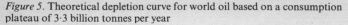

Figure 5. Theoretical depletion curve for world oil based on a consumption plateau of 3·3 billion tonnes per year

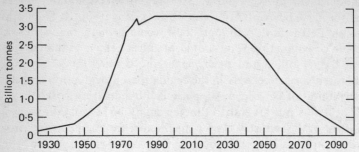

Note: Based on total recoverable reserves of 324 billion tonnes.
Source: World Energy Outlook, International Energy Agency, 1983.

Figure 5 shows a possible depletion curve, drawn up by the International Energy Agency in 1983. It is based on a hypothetical total remaining reserves figure of 324×10^9 tonnes, and shows consumption reaching a plateau of $3·3 \times 10^9$ tonnes per year in the 1990s, continuing at that level until 2020, thereafter declining to exhaustion in the year 2100. The IEA is at pains to point out that this does not represent its forecast of how oil production will actually turn out. It nevertheless represents a plausible future based upon the present state of knowledge. It also shows clearly that oil supplies can be maintained at near-present levels until around the middle of the next century. If the more optimistic views about ultimate resource levels turn out to be correct, or the shift away from oil continues, then the supply outlook is brighter. The days of unimpeded growth in consumption are almost certainly gone for ever. But there is still a great deal of oil left.

Natural Gas

Crude oil in a reservoir is always accompanied by a mixture of gases which, for convenience, is termed 'natural gas'. Its composition varies, but the principal component is methane (CH_4), which usually forms between 85 and 95 per cent of the total. The remainder is mainly composed of higher hydrocarbons such as

Table 12. Constituents and calorific values of natural gas

	% of total volume		
HYDROCARBONS	'wet'	←*(range)*→	'dry'
methane	84·6		96·0
ethane	6·4		2·0
propane	5·3		0·6
iso-butane	1·2		0·18
N-butane	1·4		0·12
iso-pentane	0·4		0·14
N-pentane	0·2		0·06
hexanes	0·4		0·10
heptanes	0·1		0·80
NON-HYDROCARBONS			
carbon dioxide		0–5	
helium		0–0·5	
hydrogen sulphide		0–5	
nitrogen		0–10	
argon		less than 0·1% of helium content	
radon, krypton, xenon		traces	
Calorific values: 9·31–11·38 kWh/m³ (900–1100 Btu/ft³)			

Source: E. N. Tiratsoo, *Oilfields of the World*, Scientific Press, 1973.

ethane, propane and butane. Helium, nitrogen and some of the rare gases like argon are also found. One of the most important non-hydrocarbons is hydrogen sulphide (H_2S). A natural gas contaminated with this will cause pollution problems and is termed a 'sour' gas; a 'sweet' gas has less than one part in a million of hydrogen sulphide. Table 12 shows a range of typical constituents and calorific values of natural gas.

Natural gas can occur almost entirely on its own; dissolved under pressure in oil; or in a layer above the oil in a reservoir – a so-called 'gas-cap'. Natural gas is also found associated with coal, when it is a major hazard because it forms an explosive mixture with air. Under some conditions, however, it can be extracted from coal seams in useful amounts. Natural gas from coalmines is sometimes called colliery methane.

In the technical language of the oil industry, gas which occurs on its own is called 'non-associated', that occurring together with oil is called 'associated'. It has been estimated that about 72 per cent of the world's proved gas reserves are non-associated, 17 per cent are dissolved, and 11 per cent are found in gas-caps.

There is also a group of compounds which occurs at the lighter end of the petroleum oils. These are known as 'natural gas liquids' or sometimes as 'natural gasoline' or 'condensate'. They are frequently found in conjunction with natural gas deposits. They may occur as liquids or they may condense from the gas when it is released from the high pressure of the reservoir. The term 'wet' is applied to a gas in which the extractable liquid hydrocarbon content is more than 1 litre per 25 cubic metres of gas (0·3 gallons per 1000 cubic feet).

Each mode of gas occurrence requires its own recovery technique. That for non-associated gas is relatively simple. If the gas is dry and sweet, it can be piped almost directly from the well to the consumer with little more than pressure regulation controls. Wet or sour gas, however, must be processed to remove the liquids or contaminants. Non-associated gas is obviously not extracted unless or until there is some use for it.

The problems with associated gas are greater. Because a well producing such gas is usually operated for optimum oil recovery, the gas is obtained, essentially, as an unavoidable by-product. In the early days of the oil industry associated gas was regarded as a complete nuisance and was either flared off or allowed to blow away. And it still causes difficulties. If no means of storing it or distributing it exists, it is usually flared. It can, however, under suitable conditions, be reinjected into the oil well to maintain the pressure for oil extraction. In that case it remains, at least theoretically, available for future recovery.

Dissolved gas bubbles out of the oil when it reaches the surface and is released from the reservoir pressure. The amount of gas held in solution in an oil is called the 'gas-oil ratio' and varies from less than a hundred to several thousand cubic feet of gas per barrel of oil. The gas must be removed before the oil can be safely sent in a pipeline or loaded into a tanker. The decision whether or not to flare the gas depends on the quantity of gas and the economics of distributing or reinjecting it.

The use of gas requires a distribution system or a conveniently situated petro-chemical works which can use it as a feedstock. In the USA these requirements are relatively easy to meet and there are legal penalties for wasting gas. But over the rest of the world the waste of gas up to quite recently was appalling. In 1978 the total amount of gas flared was estimated to be about 154 billion cubic metres, equivalent to about 130 million tonnes of oil. The Middle East flares and the Great Wall of China were the first distinguishable man-made objects sighted by one of the returning moon missions. In recent years, however, the position has greatly improved and the total amount of waste is very much less.

Table 13 gives the distribution of the world's present proved natural gas reserves. The most thorough exploration has been carried out in the USA, which is by far the largest producer and consumer of natural gas. In the oil-producing countries of the developing world there is usually no readily accessible market for gas, so it has not been a major concern of the oil companies to prospect for and prove gas reserves. Discoveries have therefore tended to be made fortuitously in the search for oil.

The total reserves figure of 98×10^{12} cubic metres is equivalent to about 90 billion tonnes of oil. Proved reserves are thus about the same as those of oil. The pre-eminence of the Middle East in oil reserves is not reflected in the picture for gas. The USSR has by far the largest amount, about 43 per cent of the total: a result of the extraordinary richness of Western Siberia. Iran has the next largest reserves with 13·5 per cent of the total, well over twice those of the USA. In 1970 the proved reserves of the world were about 38 000 billion cubic metres; they have thus more than doubled over the past decade.

Estimation of the world's ultimately recoverable gas reserves is subject to even greater uncertainty than that of oil. Some geologists suspect there are truly vast resources buried deeper than exploration has yet reached. The presence of methane in volcanic eruptions and its release in some earthquakes suggest it may be coming from greater depths and sources other than sedimentary basins. In principle, it is certainly possible that methane could be synthesized in large amounts from non-organically derived hydrogen and carbon.

There are also reserves at depths of 4000–5000 metres in what are called 'tight sands' and brine formations. These have generally been considered uneconomic or beyond the reach of currently available recovery methods. No reliable assessments have been

Table 13. Proved natural gas reserves at end of 1985

	Trillion cubic metres	% share of total		Trillion cubic metres	% share of total
NORTH AMERICA			AFRICA		
USA	5·6	5·7	Algeria*	3·0	3·1
Canada	2·8	2·9	Egypt	0·2	0·2
Total North America	8·4	8·6	Libya*	0·6	0·6
			Nigeria*	1·3	1·4
LATIN AMERICA			Others	0·4	0·4
Argentina	0·7	0·7	Total Africa	5·5	5·7
Ecuador*	0·1	0·1			
Mexico	2·2	2·2	ASIA AND AUSTRALASIA		
Trinidad	0·3	0·3	Brunei	0·2	0·2
Venezuela*	1·7	1·7	Indonesia*	1·0	1·0
Others	0·4	0·4	Malaysia	1·5	1·5
Total Latin America	5·4	5·4	Bangladesh	0·3	0·3
			India	0·5	0·5
WESTERN EUROPE			Pakistan	0·4	0·4
Netherlands	1·9	1·9	Australia	0·5	0·5
Norway	2·9	3·0	New Zealand	0·2	0·2
United Kingdom	0·6	0·9	Total Asia and Australasia	4·6	4·6
West Germany	0·2	0·2			
Others	0·5	0·5	TOTAL NCW	54·2	55·4
Total Western Europe	6·1	6·5			
			CENTRALLY-PLANNED ECONOMIES (CPEs)		
MIDDLE EAST			China	0·8	0·9
Abu Dhabi*	0·6	0·6	USSR	42·5	43·2
Bahrain	0·2	0·2	Others	0·5	0·5
Dubai*	0·1	0·1	Total CPEs	43·8	44·6
Iran*	13·3	13·5			
Iraq*	0·8	0·8	TOTAL WORLD	98·0	100·0
Kuwait*	0·9	0·9	Of which OPEC	31·4	32·2
Qatar*	4·2	4·3			
Saudi Arabia*	3·4	3·5			
Others	0·7	0·7			
Total Middle East	24·2	24·6			

* OPEC member.
Note: 1000 cubic metres natural gas = 0·9 tonnes oil.
Source: *BP Review of World Energy*, 1986.

made on the amounts of gas which might be recovered from such sources. Even assessments of conventional gas resources vary widely. All that can be said at the moment is that ultimate gas reserves appear to be roughly similar to those of oil; but if the deeper resources exist and prove exploitable, the total could be very much more.

Table 14 shows the world production and consumption of natural gas. This has been growing steadily at 3–3·5 per cent for about the last twenty years. It supplies approximately 20 per cent of the world's energy. The USSR is the largest producer and consumer, closely followed in both respects by the USA. Together, these two countries account for about two thirds of the world's total production and consumption.

Unlike oil, most of the world's natural gas is consumed in the countries in which it is produced. The reason for this is obvious. Natural gas is almost ideal as a fuel: it has a high calorific value, it is clean and efficient in use, and the only products of its combustion are carbon dioxide and water. But it is difficult to transport and distribute. For large-scale use it requires a network of underground pipes connected to every consumer. To establish such a system from scratch is a long and expensive undertaking. It can be justified only if a country has gas supplies under its own

Table 14. Natural gas production and consumption, 1985

Country	Production (million tonnes oil equivalent)	Consumption (million tonnes oil equivalent)
USSR	579	477
USA	422	444
Canada	67	50
Latin America	68	70
Netherlands	66	33
Middle East	46	40
UK	35	48
Algeria	32	—
Indonesia	29	—
Norway	24	—
West Germany	13	41
Italy	12	27
France	4	23
Total	1535	1492

Source: BP Statistical Review of the World Oil Industry.

control or is confident of the goodwill and political stability of potential suppliers and the countries through which supply pipelines must pass. It is a measure of how the political climate has changed since the 1950s that Europe is now firmly linked to the USSR by a natural gas pipeline that runs through Western Germany to the centre of France.

The alternative to pipelines for large-scale gas transport is the use of refrigerated tanker ships which transport liquefied natural gas (LNG). Some years ago there was considerable controversy about the dangers of these. There have, in fact, been a number of major disasters as a result of petroleum gas explosions. In 1944 an LNG tank ruptured in Cleveland, Ohio; the resulting cloud of gas exploded, killing 130 people. Spillages of propane or butane which liquefy under pressure at normal temperatures and are usually referred to as liquid petroleum gas (LPG) have also led to some horrific accidents. One was in Spain in 1978 when a road tanker started leaking close to a camp site; the resulting gas explosion engulfed the holiday-makers, killing more than 150 people. An even worse disaster was in Mexico City in 1984 when an explosion at an LPG distribution centre killed 500 people in the surrounding shanty town.

There does not appear to be any doubt that it is difficult to achieve the necessary atmospheric conditions under which an explosive cloud can form in the open air after a leak of LNG. But given that the energy content of a large LNG tanker is as great as that of a thermonuclear bomb, there is a strong case for siting loading and unloading docks for tankers well away from concentrations of people.

The future for natural gas is undoubtedly bright in the longer term. The USSR's gas reserves are sufficient to meet its own expanding needs and those of western Europe for at least a century. Countries with large resources such as China and the Middle East will increasingly turn to its use to meet their own energy needs. The use of gas in the oil-producing countries will also free a greater quantity of oil for world export markets.

7

Alternative Sources of Oil

Tar Sands and Heavy Oils

Sands or sandstones impregnated with heavy oils occur in a number of areas in the world. The largest deposit is near Fort McMurray on the Athabasca River in the Canadian province of Alberta. It covers an area of about 34 000 square kilometres, about the size of Belgium. In eastern Venezuela there is a 2300-square-kilometre deposit of somewhat lighter hydrocarbons in the Oficina–Temblador area. There is a further huge deposit at Olenek in the north of Siberia in the USSR. Although there are a score or more other large deposits around the world, none approaches these three in size.

Most of the development work so far has taken place on the Athabasca deposit, since economically and technically this is more promising than any other. The thickness of the tar sands there is between 40 and 80 metres, with an average of about 55 metres. In some places the tar sands are found at the surface, notably along the Athabasca River where there are cliffs of the material up to 45 metres high. More usually there is an overburden of glacial material of about 80 metres, though this increases to as much as 600 metres in some areas.

The precise origin of the Athabasca tar sands is still a puzzle to geologists. Some believe the bituminous material was formed where it now lies; others believe it migrated there from the underlying Devonian beds or downwards from the now mainly eroded Cretaceous deposits. The original petroleum may have resembled a conventional crude oil, but almost all the volatile components have been lost. The tar sand is a thick, heavy material with a sticky texture. In the ground it is interspersed with layers and lenses of sands, clays and shales. It is an awkward material to extract and process.

The presence of the tar sands in Athabasca has been known for a long time and many attempts have been made to extract the tar or to develop uses for the material. As early as 1915 a demonstration road surface, using the mined material as a kind of natural macadam, was laid and performed satisfactorily. But this and other ventures ended in commercial failure. The Athabasca region is very wild and desolate, with an appalling winter climate. The ground cover is mostly muskeg, a soft peaty substance which makes transport exceedingly difficult. S. C. Ells, one of the pioneers who spent his life exploring the area and trying to develop ways of using the tar sands, described the extreme discomfort caused by the myriads of flies with which the area is infested.[15]

It is not surprising that the development of the tar sands has been slow. As about 2 tonnes of mined material are required to produce a barrel of oil, the scale of operation necessary for an output of oil comparable with that from a conventional oilfield is gigantic. First, the overburden has to be stripped and dumped. Next, draglines or bucket-wheel excavators have to dig out the material which is then taken to the separation plant. An output of, say, 10 million tonnes of oil a year means digging out nearly 500 000 tonnes of material every day.

At the separation plant the raw sand is mixed with hot water and injected with steam to bring the mixture to a temperature of about 80°C. A series of filters and foam-raking processes then separates about 90 per cent of the bituminous material, which is taken for refining in an almost conventional way. One of the problems is that the bitumen has a high sulphur content and also contains metallic pollutants. The hot waste sand is dumped back into the excavated area of the mine and the processed water purified and recycled.

It was only during the late 1960s that the technical problems of separating the oil from the sand were solved on a commercial basis by a company called Great Canadian Oil Sands, which began work in 1967. The project ran at a heavy loss during the first five years but then showed sufficient promise to encourage further developments by other companies. Another plant operated by a company called Syncrude began production in 1978. Together, these two plants were producing 150 000 barrels per day, about 7·5 million tonnes of oil per year in 1983. The estimated production costs at that time were about $35 per barrel, which was roughly the market price of oil. A series of other projects were also considered. They had estimated production costs in the range of $40–80 per barrel. Luckily for their promoters, no decision was made to proceed with any of these developments at the time.

The only other significant tar-sand exploitation is at Yarega in the western USSR, where 600 000 tonnes of bitumen per year were being produced from an underground mine in 1985. The production system relied on steam injection into wells drilled from a tunnel-and-shaft system. A similar level of production was also being achieved from a variety of trial and pilot operations.

The world's tar sand resources are substantial. The world total of oil in place is estimated to be about 300 billion tonnes, more or less equally divided between the three major deposits. Only about 5–10 per cent of this is accessible from the surface and hence recoverable with presently available methods.

No way of recovering the remainder yet exists. Work is being done to devise ways of softening the deposits *in situ* by pumping steam down boreholes or by lighting fires and feeding them with oxygen from the surface. These processes, some of which are used in the tertiary recovery of crude oil, are aimed at reducing the viscosity of the tar so that it can be recovered by pumping it to the surface.

Given that oil prices are likely to remain relatively low over the next ten to fifteen years, it is unlikely that there will be any further major investments in tar-sands development projects in the immediate future. The oil recovered from them will never be cheap. It will never be available in the quantities to which the world has become accustomed. But it may well provide a welcome addition to world energy supplies when conventional oil supplies eventually begin their inevitable decline.

Oil Shales

Oil shale is a relatively common, finely textured sedimentary rock containing the solid organic material kerogen. The oil shales were formed in many different geological periods and hence vary considerably in composition and richness. They are found in many parts of the world. On heating to 300–400°C, in a retort or large distillation vessel, the kerogen breaks down into a number of gaseous and liquid hydrocarbons which can then be extracted. The liquids resemble a crude oil in some respects, but cannot be used directly in a conventional refinery: a preliminary upgrading process is required.

In the seventeenth century oil distilled from shale was used in the Modena district of Italy to provide street lighting. France had an oil shale industry as long ago as 1838. In Scotland shale oil was produced from 1848 until it became uneconomic to do so in 1962. Production was over 100 000 tonnes a year in the early 1950s. Pulverized oil shale is used as a direct fuel for electric power generation in Estonia, and in the manufacture of gas for Leningrad. Shale oil has also been produced in China since the 1920s.

The richest deposits of oil shale are found in the USA in the Green River area of Colorado, Utah and Wyoming. About 44 000 square kilometres here are underlain by oil-bearing shales. Within this area the richest deposits are concentrated in the Piceance Creek Basin (spelled 'Pissants' on the maps of a more robust age), which covers about 440 square kilometres and contains 80 per cent of the potentially recoverable oil in the area. The quantity of oil contained in these shales has given rise to some exaggerated optimism about their potential as a 'solution' to the world's energy problems.

This 'solution' remains to be found. The organic content of the Colorado oil shales varies from about 2 barrels per tonne down to near zero. The richest deposits are up to 100 metres thick, but these are generally deeply buried. Much of the oil is contained in thin layers interspersed with rocks of low or zero oil content. Although the oil shales outcrop along river valleys and some other areas, they cannot usually be mined by open-cast methods. In contrast with the tar sands the oil shales are hard rocks. Shale for retorting has to be quarried out of deep workings or mined in much the same way as coal. Only the richest deposits are worth working in this way. A tonne of coal is a tonne of coal. But a tonne of oil shale is a lot of rock and a little oil which has to be retorted and upgraded. Obtaining the same amount of energy from an oil shale which yields a barrel of oil per tonne requires five times as much mining as coal. Mining can, in fact, account for 60 per cent of the cost of oil from shale. It also causes big problems of environmental despoliation and waste disposal. For these reasons there is intense eagerness to develop a method of retorting the oil shales *in situ.*

Essentially this would have to duplicate the above-ground retorting process. The shale must be fractured, heated in a controlled manner, and the liquid and gas products drawn off. There are enough problems when these operations are conducted on a large scale above ground; when they are out of sight 100 metres below ground, the difficulties of control are quite daunting. For fracturing the rock, explosives, hydraulic pressure and high-voltage electricity have all been suggested. Combustion would be fed with air or oxygen from the surface. A method of keeping the temperature within the tolerances required by the retorting process is essential if the oil produced is not to vary unacceptably in quality and composition.

A wide variety of schemes for extracting shale oil were proposed in the USA during the 1970s and early 1980s. Some were developed to pilot plant stage, but all relied on government research and development funding provided through the Synthetic Fuels Corporation, which has since been abolished. The difficulties inherent in shale oil extraction are well illustrated by the extraction method by the Occidental Oil Company. Tunnels are driven horizontally inwards from a cliff face. A large chamber of fractured shale is then created with explosives. Natural gas is piped in to start a fire which is fed with oxygen. Oil which is dissociated from the shale by the heat flows to a sump from which it can be drawn off. None of these experimental shale oil extraction processes now shows any prospect of becoming economic over the next fifteen to twenty years.

In the USSR a number of oil shale retorts with a total output of about 500 000 tonnes per year are in operation. A very large retort, with an annual output of 1·2 million tonnes of oil per year, was under construction in 1986. Production of shale oil in China in 1985 was reported to be about 80 000 tonnes per year.

Inevitably, the use of nuclear explosions has been suggested to fracture the shale and provide sufficient heat to retort it. There are, however, difficulties in predicting the effects of underground nuclear explosions in detail. It also seems impossible to prevent the oil from becoming radioactive, which would make it unusable. As in the case of tertiary recovery from oil wells, the main supporters of this seem to be people with interests in the manufacture of nuclear bombs – for which, admittedly, it is difficult to find other productive uses.

Not surprisingly, there is confusion about the size of shale oil resources. Measured as 'oil in position', they are immense. A calculation of the total contained in all the world's deposits containing 5 gallons of oil per ton and over is quoted by Hubbert.[10] It is 2×10^{15} barrels, a thousand times greater than the world's recoverable conventional crude oil. But again the crucial question is how much of this is recoverable.

Table 15 shows the distribution of the world's shale oil deposits together with estimates of their oil content. The figures are indicative only; little work has been done to identify or evaluate shale oil resources throughout the world because on the whole they have not been economically attractive except in limited areas. It is now felt that only those shales with an oil content above 25 gallons per tonne will ever be economic. This reduces the size of the potential reserves by a factor of a thousand. At the 1978 World Energy Conference it was estimated that the recoverable oil from these resources was about 1500 billion barrels – about 90 per cent of it in the USA. The total is thus somewhat less than conventional crude oil. And of that only 5–10 per cent can 'be considered for immediate exploitation'.

In fact, to many people shale oil does not look at all promising as a major energy resource. The environmental problems are being viewed with increasing pessimism. The lack of water in the arid areas of the USA in which the richest deposits are located could well be the greatest constraint of all. Some oil industry experts believe this could limit the production of oil from the Colorado shale to a maximum of 50–100 million tonnes a year.

Table 15. Estimated shale oil resources of the world

	Total resources in position (barrels $\times$ 10^9)		
Oil content, gallons/ton	5–10	10–25	25–100
Africa	450 000	80 000	4 000
Asia	590 000	110 000	5 500
Australia and New Zealand	100 000	20 000	1 000
Europe	140 000	26 000	1 400
North America	260 000	50 000	3 000
South America	210 000	40 000	2 000
TOTAL	1 175 000	325 000	17 000

Source: Duncan & Swanson, 1965; quoted by M. K. Hubbert in *Resources and Man*, W. H. Freeman, 1969.

Hubbert is even more pessimistic. His comment is that '. . . the organic contents of the carbonaceous shales appear to be more promising as a resource of raw materials for the chemical industry than as a major source of industrial energy'.[10]

One of the most telling factors against shale oil is the sheer magnitude of the mining and quarrying operations necessary to produce yields comparable with those from coal or oil. If half the present US oil consumption were to be supplied from shales yielding a net quantity of 30 gallons per tonne, then the total amount of shale mined would amount to 4·25 billion tonnes per year. This is considerably greater than the output of the whole world's coal-mining industry. It is difficult to see how this could actually fit into the Piceance Creek area, quite apart from any question of whether it would be socially or environmentally acceptable there.

8

Nuclear Energy

Nuclear power is by far the most controversial of the world's energy sources. Seen by many as the only possible long-term source of energy for humanity, it evokes such fear and loathing in others that they are prepared to risk gaol, injury and even death in protests against it. It is also an energy source about which there is a great deal of ignorance. Nuclear physics, what goes on inside a reactor, and the measurement of radiation and its hazards are far removed from most people's knowledge and experience.

Fission Power

The energy released in a nuclear power station comes from the breakdown or disintegration of the atoms of the elements uranium and plutonium. If the products of this disintegration are added together, they do not quite make up the mass of the original atoms. The mass which has been lost has been transformed into energy. The amount can be calculated from Einstein's formula $E = mc^2$. The amount produced per kilogram of fuel 'burned' is prodigious in comparison with a coal-fired or oil-fired station; so also are the technical complexities involved.

An atom can be visualized as a miniature solar system in which electrons orbit around a compact core called the nucleus. The nucleus consists of particles called protons and neutrons. These have a mass about 1 800 times greater than that of the electron. The proton has a positive charge, the electron a negative charge and, as its name suggests, the neutron has no charge. An atom has no net electric charge because the number of electrons is equal to that of protons.

The mass of an atom, misleadingly called its 'atomic weight', is the total mass of the protons, electrons and neutrons of which it is made. If the small mass of the electron is ignored, the atomic weight can be expressed as a whole number representing the total number of protons and neutrons in its nucleus. The atomic weight of hydrogen, which has a single proton in its nucleus, is therefore 1; that of helium, the next heaviest, is 4 because it has two protons and two neutrons. But the picture rapidly begins to become more complicated.

In 1913 Soddy discovered that some atoms which behave chemically as though they were identical have different atomic weights. He named them 'isotopes', which literally means 'the same place', because they occupy the same place in the Periodic Table of the elements. The difference in mass occurs because they have a different number of neutrons in their nucleus.

Hydrogen has two naturally occurring isotopes: 'normal' hydrogen and deuterium. Normal hydrogen has a single proton in its nucleus; deuterium has a proton and a neutron. Chemically they are identical, but the mass of deuterium is twice that of hydrogen. Uranium has three naturally occurring isotopes: uranium-238, which has 92 protons and 146 neutrons; uranium-235, with 92 protons and 143 neutrons; and uranium-234, with 92 protons and 142 neutrons. Most elements occur in a number of isotopic forms.

Some isotopes are radioactive. The balance of neutrons and protons in the nucleus is unstable. These isotopes move towards a stable state by emitting energy or some of the sub-atomic particles of which they are composed. Radioactive decay is a complex phenomenon. The simple model of the atom composed of hard indestructible particles, protons, electrons and neutrons, does not fully explain what happens. In the radioactive decay of the atom some of the particles of which it is composed can themselves break down; the neutron may emit an electron and turn into a proton.

The early researchers, without clearly understanding what was happening, identified three kinds of 'emanations' or 'rays' emitted by radioactive substances. These they christened alpha, beta and gamma rays. Subsequent investigations showed these to be fundamentally different and scarcely deserving the common designation of 'ray'. Nevertheless, the names have stuck and are commonly used in discussions of radioactivity. Alpha rays are streams of heavy composite particles consisting of two protons and two neutrons. These particles are identical with the nucleus of the helium atom. Beta rays are streams of electrons. Gamma rays are true electromagnetic radiation. They have shorter wavelengths than X-rays and are extremely penetrating.

As a result of losing neutrons, protons or both, or in the transformation of a neutron into a proton, an atom changes its identity. It can become a different isotope of the same material or it can become a different material altogether. In radioactive decay a genuine transmutation of elements can and does take place. The process of reaching a state of stability through radioactive decay may be a long one. An atom decays and becomes something else which may itself be unstable; another decay takes place, and so on until stability is achieved. In the decay of the naturally occurring radioactive element uranium-238 there are nineteen separate decay stages (in one of which radium is formed) before the final formation of a stable isotope of lead.

Although it is impossible to predict the moment when any individual atom will decay, the overall rate of decay of a large number of atoms is totally predictable. For every radioactive material the time in which half its atoms will decay is an unvarying amount. It is called the 'half-life' of the material. If the half-life of a radioactive substance is a hundred years, then half the atoms in any quantity of it will decay in a hundred years, half the remainder in the next hundred years and so on. The half-lives of different radioactive substances vary from billionths of a second to billions of years. All radioactive substances are energy sources. In most cases, however, the rate of energy emission is far too slow for any practical use – though miniature devices are sometimes powered by radium.

Uranium-235 is the key element as far as nuclear power is concerned. It is a naturally occurring radioactive isotope with a long half-life of $7 \cdot 1 \times 10^8$ years. In nature it occurs in the proportion of 1 part in 140 with uranium-238, which is also radioactive but with a much longer half-life of $4 \cdot 5$ billion years. (The third natural uranium isotope, uranium-234, occurs in negligible amounts.) Uranium-235 normally decays by emitting an alpha particle. The unique property of uranium-235, among naturally occurring materials, is that its atoms occasionally split spontaneously into two approximately equal portions and emit two or three neutrons, as well as releasing a considerable amount of energy. This is nuclear fission, or 'splitting the atom'. Under normal circumstances, however, it happens so slowly that the amounts of energy released are too small to be of practical interest.

The nuclear industry is possible because uranium-235 can be split by hitting its nucleus with a slowly moving neutron. This means that if the neutrons which are emitted when an atom splits spontaneously can be controlled in speed and directed into another uranium-235 nucleus, this will split, releasing further neutrons to keep the process going. This is the 'chain reaction' on which nuclear power and nuclear weapons depend. When it is taking place, a considerable quantity of energy is released.

Another important process takes place as a result of the fission of the uranium-235 atoms. Some of the surrounding 238 atoms absorb a neutron and are transformed into plutonium 239. This is similar to uranium-235 in that it splits and releases neutrons if its nucleus is hit by a neutron; it has the advantage that it is split by fast-moving as well as by slowly moving neutrons.

Thorium has similar characteristics to uranium-238. It is a naturally occurring radioactive element with a very long half-life of 14 billion years. If it is exposed to neutron bombardment, it changes into uranium-233. This is an element which does not occur naturally, but behaves in the same way as uranium-235. Uranium-238 and thorium-232, while they are not themselves fissionable, are thus capable of being transformed into fissionable materials: they are termed 'fertile'. Both are 'second generation' nuclear fuels.

Although both nuclear reactors and atomic bombs rely on a chain reaction, the fundamental distinction between the operation of the two must be recognized. The aim in making a bomb is to produce a reaction which accelerates as rapidly as possible, so that all the fission energy of the uranium, or plutonium, is released in a concentrated burst lasting a minute fraction of a second, thus causing the maximum destruction. For this to happen, as many as possible of the neutrons must be available to cause further uranium-235 fissions. They must not be absorbed by other substances; neither must they escape from the mass of uranium. To meet these requirements, almost pure uranium-235 or plutonium must be used; otherwise the absorption of neutrons by the uranium-238 will prevent the rapid build-up of the reaction.

The production of the pure uranium-235 is carried out by a process called 'enrichment'. It is difficult to achieve because there is no chemical difference between the different isotopes of uranium; instead it is necessary to rely on the small differences in atomic weights. One enrichment process is called 'gaseous diffusion'. Uranium is converted to uranium hexafluoride gas and the enrichment relies on the fact that the molecules containing uranium-235 diffuse slightly more rapidly through a porous membrane than those containing uranium-238. Another technique which is gradually supplanting gaseous diffusion because it is simpler and cheaper relies on the use of gas centrifuges to separate the molecules of different weights. In both processes the concentration of uranium-235 is built up gradually through a large number of stages.

In a bomb it is also necessary that there is a certain minimum quantity of uranium-235 or plutonium-239 present. This is called the 'critical mass'. With a smaller quantity the ratio of surface area to volume is too large, and so many neutrons escape without hitting another uranium-235 nucleus that no chain reaction takes place. When an atomic bomb is being transported, the uranium or plutonium is divided into two separate sub-critical masses. The explosion is produced by firing the two together to create a critical mass.

Nuclear Reactors

The requirements of a reactor are entirely different from those of a bomb. It must be completely incapable of forming a critical mass. Nuclear reactors never use pure uranium-235. They rely either on natural uranium or on uranium in which the concentration of uranium-235 has been slightly increased by enrichment. The purpose of a reactor is to provide a steady chain reaction, the heat of which is drawn off to make steam which in turn drives electricity-generating plant. In a nuclear power station the reactor

Figure 6. Operation of conventional and nuclear power stations – schematic

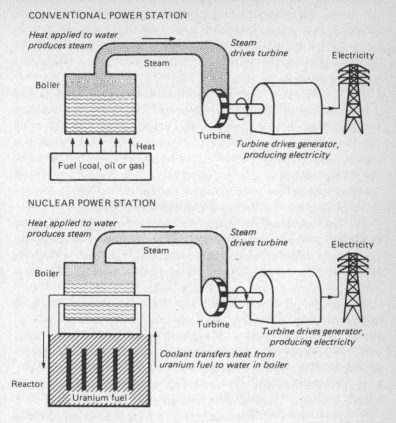

CONVENTIONAL POWER STATION

Heat applied to water
produces steam

Steam

Steam
drives turbine

Electricity

Boiler

Heat

Turbine

Fuel (coal, oil or gas)

Turbine drives generator,
producing electricity

NUCLEAR POWER STATION

Heat applied to water
produces steam

Steam

Steam
drives turbine

Electricity

Boiler

Turbine

Turbine drives generator,
producing electricity

Coolant transfers heat from
uranium fuel to water in boiler

Reactor

Uranium fuel

plays the part of the coal- or oil-fired boiler in a conventional
power station (see Figure 6).

When each fission produces, on average, one neutron which
causes another atom to split, the rate at which the chain reaction
is occurring is neither increasing nor decreasing. This is the normal
operating mode of a nuclear reactor.

One of the essential components of the reactor is the moderator. This is a substance which has the property of slowing neutrons down without absorbing them. Its role is to slow the faster
neutrons emitted by the uranium-235 fission down to a speed of
travel which will enable them to cause a further fission. Water is
a reasonably good moderator; so is carbon, which is usually used

in the form of graphite. One of the best moderators is heavy water. This is distinguished from ordinary or 'light' water because its hydrogen is in the form of the heavy isotope deuterium. Heavy water, or deuterium oxide, occurs naturally in ordinary water in the ratio of about one part in 6500; its separation is a costly and elaborate process.

Fine regulation, as well as start-up and shut-down of a nuclear reactor, is achieved by the use of control rods. These are made of a material which is a good neutron absorber such as boron or cadmium. When they are inserted into a reactor, they absorb a certain proportion of the neutrons being released, bringing the rate of fission below that required to sustain a steady reaction; they are used in this way to bring a reactor off power. To start it up again, the control rods are gradually withdrawn.

The heat produced by a nuclear reactor is transferred to the boiler in the power station by the 'coolant'. This is a gas or liquid which is circulated through the reactor, where it absorbs the heat being produced. This is then transferred by means of a heat exchange system to the water in the boiler in order to turn it into steam. A coolant should have a high heat-absorbing capacity; it should not, on the other hand, absorb too many neutrons. It should be non-corrosive and it should be stable within the operating temperature range of the reactor, with an adequate margin of safety. Gas-cooled reactors use carbon dioxide or helium. Liquid-cooled reactors use water, heavy water, liquid sodium or a molten alloy of sodium and potassium.

In some reactor designs the coolant is circulated directly through the electricity-generating turbines. In most cases, however, an indirect system is used and the coolant passes through a heat exchanger where it gives up its heat to produce the steam which drives the turbines, as shown in Figure 6. A wide variety of reactor types have been designed using different combinations of coolant, moderator and fuel type. They are usually referred to by sets of initials or technical nicknames.

There is some competition for the title of being the first country to harness nuclear power for public use on a commercial basis. The first supply of nuclear-generated electricity for public use was in June 1954, when a small power station of just 5 megawatts at Obninsk in the USSR was connected to the Moscow grid.

Two years later, in September 1956, a French reactor at Marcoule was connected to the public grid and brought up to a power of 5 megawatts. In October 1956 a 55-megawatt station at Calder Hall in Cumberland was connected to the UK national grid. Although the electricity from these stations was sold commercially, they were in no sense commercial ventures. Each of these reactors had been built to produce plutonium for their country's nuclear arms programme.

The UK, however, led the way in the large-scale application of nuclear power for civilian use. Calder Hall was the first in a planned series of stations; the intention was that nuclear power would be supplying half the country's electricity by 1975. The UK, in fact, led the world in the amount of installed nuclear power capacity and the quantity of electricity generated until the early 1970s.

Its first eleven stations were of the Magnox type, so called because of the special magnesium alloy which was used to cover the uranium fuel rods in the reactor. They had graphite moderators, carbon dioxide as a coolant, and used unenriched uranium. The reactors of the early stations were enclosed in a welded steel pressure vessel; in the later ones this was of prestressed concrete. Strenuous efforts were made to sell the Magnox design abroad, but only two stations were built outside Britain: one in Italy and one in Japan.

As the programme proceeded, British nuclear technologists decided that the engineering and economic limitations of the Magnox system were so great that a new reactor design was required. No further Magnox stations were ordered. Although there have been some problems with corrosion of reactor parts which led to a reduction in operating temperatures, the Magnox reactors have performed well. The early stations have now reached the end of their design life and are being assessed to see if they can continue operation or should be closed down.

In the early stages of its nuclear programme France also relied on carbon-dioxide-cooled reactors using graphite as a moderator. In all, seven of these were built. One was also exported to Spain in 1967, but interest in this type of reactor ended in 1970.

The early British lead in nuclear power stations was, in fact, deceptive. The main direction for nuclear power in the western world was set by the opening of a completely different type of nuclear reactor in Shippingport, near Pennsylvania, in 1957. This was called a light water reactor and it used ordinary water as a coolant and a moderator. It had been developed and used in the US nuclear submarine programme. Two varieties of this type of reactor have emerged: the pressurized water reactor (PWR) and the boiling water reactor (BWR).

The PWR was developed by the Westinghouse Company. It operates at the very high pressure of about 150 atmospheres (nearly 2000 pounds per square inch). This prevents water boiling at the operating temperature of around 300°C. The reactor is housed inside a welded steel pressure vessel. The high operating pressure places heavy demands on the quality of fabrication of the pressure vessel. From the beginning it has been a source of worry to critics of nuclear power and was apparently one of the major reasons why the British government rejected this kind of reactor for the next phase of the UK nuclear programme in the early 1970s. The accumulation of operating experience without any major pressure vessel problems has, however, reduced the level of concern about this aspect of the PWR. In the report of the inquiry into the Sizewell nuclear station, published in early 1987, it was not judged to be a reason for rejecting a PWR.

The BWR was developed by the General Electric Company. Conceptually, it is the simplest reactor of all, though like all nuclear power plant it is extremely complicated to build. It operates at a pressure of about 70 atmospheres and a temperature of about 300°C. Under these conditions the water turns into steam. It was originally thought that water boiling within the reactor core would make control impossible, but experiments showed that this was not the case. The first BWR was opened near Chicago in 1959.

Over the next two decades these two proprietary reactor types rose to complete dominance not just of the US nuclear industry but of that of the whole industrial world outside the communist countries. One of the milestones along this path was the decision in 1963 by the Jersey Central Power and Light Company to build a PWR on the purely commercial grounds that it would produce electricity more cheaply than coal or oil. Another key decision was that of the French nuclear authorities in 1969 to abandon the gas-cooled reactor and opt for the PWR. This took place after a long and bitter struggle between conflicting government agencies and industrial companies. Decisions to build either PWR or BWR plants were also made in Germany, Belgium and Italy in the late 1960s.

It was almost universally believed that a true commercial breakthrough had been made and that nuclear power was genuinely competitive with coal and oil. In reality there was very little real knowledge of construction costs; experience was later to demonstrate that nuclear power plants were considerably more expensive than had been thought. But enthusiasm among energy planners for nuclear power and light-water reactors in particular was unquenchable. The oil 'crisis' of 1973 dispelled almost all the remaining doubts about the economic attractiveness of nuclear power. In 1974 the French government decided to shift from oil to nuclear power as the basis for its electricity production.

A few pockets of resistance to the march of light-water technology remained. In the UK the advanced gas-cooled reactor (AGR) was developed as a successor to the Magnox stations. As in the Magnox stations, the coolant is carbon dioxide and the moderator is graphite, but they operate at the much higher temperature of 650°C. The fuel is slightly enriched uranium clad in stainless steel. These stations appeared to have considerable advantages over the Magnox design and there was hope that they would provide a competitive alternative to the light-water designs in export markets.

But, in the event, the AGR building programme which was announced in 1964 turned out to be a disaster for the British nuclear industry. Design changes and construction problems led to the bankruptcy of contractors. By 1980 only two of the stations ordered had been completed – one of which, Hunterston B, promptly disabled one of its reactors by sucking sea water into the reactor pressure vessel. Dungeness B, a large station on the Kent coast, turned out to be a construction nightmare: scheduled for completion in 1970, it was in the final stages of commissioning in mid-1987. The AGR stations have, nevertheless, a number of attractive technical features. The use of a massive pre-stressed concrete pressure vessel removes the safety worries associated with light-water reactor pressure vessels. This reactor type retains a certain amount of support in Britain and has not been entirely ruled out of a place in future programmes.

A further development of the gas-cooled reactor is the high-temperature gas-cooled reactor (HTGR). This operates at a temperature of at least 1000°C. The fuel is a mixture of highly enriched uranium and thorium in the form of small pellets which are baked into a shell of ceramic material. Helium is used as the coolant and graphite as the moderator. A small HTGR, called Dragon, was built and operated at Winfrith in the UK from 1966 until it closed in 1975 as a joint international experiment under the auspices of the OECD. Another small reactor was opened at Julich in West Germany in 1968; this was followed by a 300-megawatt unit which came on stream in 1985. A 330-megawatt commercial unit was built at Port St Vrain in Colorado and started operation in 1976.

The HTGR is inherently safer than most other reactor types and has a number of other technical advantages. It can also provide heat for industrial processes and high-temperature steam. It is tipped by some to make an eventual breakthrough as an alternative to light-water technology.

A Canadian reactor type called CANDU (Canadian deuterium uranium) uses heavy water as a moderator and coolant. Instead of the whole reactor being enclosed in a pressure vessel, this system uses a series of pressure tubes which contain the fuel and through which the coolant flows. The pressure inside the tubes is about 90 atmospheres. The tubes run through a large tank filled with heavy water, which acts as a moderator. The first CANDU station came on stream in Pickering in Ontario in 1971. This type of reactor is still the basis of Canada's nuclear programme. CANDU stations have been exported to the Argentine, India, Pakistan and Romania. The Indian nuclear bomb explosion in May 1974, however, caused Canada to review its export of nuclear technology to developing countries. The CANDU reactor has good safety characteristics and has proved reliable in operation, but it has not been able to compete commercially with light-water reactors in world markets.

The USSR has developed two kinds of reactors. The most commonly used is similar to the PWR. The other is called the

RBMK and is described as a light-water graphite-moderated reactor (LWGR). The first Soviet power station at Obninsk was of the RBMK type, as was that at Chernobyl. The RBMK is fuelled with slightly enriched uranium and is cooled by light water which is allowed to boil. The moderator is graphite. The reactor is similar to the CANDU in that the fuel is contained in individual pressure tubes through which the cooling water flows.

Numerous other reactor designs have been attempted. Early efforts in Switzerland and Sweden to develop indigenous designs came to nothing. A UK design called the steam-generating heavy-water reactor (SGHWR) was based on the same principles as the CANDU but used light water as a coolant. This was allowed to boil and was used to drive the turbines directly. The SGHWR was briefly considered as a candidate for the UK nuclear pro-gramme in the mid-1970s, but has now been abandoned.

Yet despite the success of light-water reactors and their almost universal acceptance, some nuclear engineers are beginning to have an uneasy suspicion that they are leading to a dead end. The growing demands of safety regulations have made them in-creasingly complex and difficult to construct and run. Thought is therefore being given to ways in which a radical simplification of reactor design might be achieved. One such design has been proposed by ASEA-ATOM, the Swedish nuclear company. It goes under the rather strained acronym of PIUS (process in-herent ultimately safe). The core of the reactor and heat exchanger are enclosed in a prestressed concrete vessel filled with water to which boron, which is a good neutron absorber, has been added. The reactor coolant circuit and the borated water are hy-draulically connected, but under normal conditions the pressure produced by the coolant pumps is just enough to prevent the borated water from entering the reactor core. Any disturbance in the core cooling system would, however, upset this delicate bal-ance and the reactor would be shut down as it was flooded by the borated water. No operator or mechanical device would be required to make this happen.

Table 16 shows the distribution of the different types of reactors throughout the world. In all, there were 374 nuclear reactors with a total generating capacity of about 250 megawatts connected to the grid at the end of 1985. Of these, 189 were PWRs and 79

Table 16. Type and net electrical power of reactors connected to the grid, 31 December 1985

	PWR		BWR		GCR		AGR		PHWR		LWGR		HTGR		FBR		Other		Total	
	No.	MWe	No.	MWe	No.	MWe	No.	MWe	No.	MWe	No.	MWe	No.	MWe	No.	MWe	No.	MWe	No.	MWe
Argentina									2	935									2	935
Belgium	8	5 486																	8	5 486
Brazil	1	626																	1	626
Bulgaria	4	1 632																	4	1 632
Canada									16	9 776									16	9 776
Czechoslovakia	5	1 980																	5	1 980
Finland	2	890	2	1 420															4	2 310
France	38	35 470			4	1 830									1	233			43	37 533
Germany, DR	5	1 694																	5	1 694
Germany, FR	9	9 194	7	6 893									2	309	1	17			19	16 413
Hungary	2	825																	2	825
India			2	296					4	844									6	1 140
Italy	1	260	1	860	1	153													3	1 273
Japan	15	10 856	16	12 502	1	159											1	148	33	23 665
Korea Rep	3	2 091							1	629									4	2 720
Netherlands	1	452	1	56															2	508
Pakistan									1	125									1	125
S Africa	2	1 840																	2	1 840
Spain	5	3 727	2	1 370	1	480													8	5 577
Sweden	3	2 630	9	6 825															12	9 455
Switzerland	3	1 620	2	1 262															5	2 882
Taiwan	2	1 814	4	3 104															6	4 918
UK					26	4 100	10	5 686							1	242	1	92	38	10 120
USA	60	51 654	32	25 820									1	330					93	77 804
USSR	19	11 394	1	50							28	15 616			3	696			51	27 756
Yugoslavia	1	632																	1	632
Total	189	146 767	79	60 458	33	6 722	10	5 686	24	12 309	28	15 616	3	639	6	1 188	2	240	374	249 625

Note: PWR – pressurized water reactor; BWR : boiling water reactor; GCR – gas-cooled reactor; AGR : advanced gas-cooled reactor; PHWR – pressurized heavy-water reactor (CANDU); LWGR – light-water graphite-moderated reactor (RBMK); HTGR – high-temperature gas-cooled reactor (HTR); FBR fast breeder reactor.

Source: *Atom*, December 1986.

were BWRs. The dominance of the light-water reactors is even more striking in terms of power: they account for 83 per cent of the world's total installed nuclear capacity. The USA leads with nearly 78 000 megawatts; France is next with 37 000 megawatts; the USSR is third with 28 000 megawatts closely followed by Japan. Sweden has over 9000 megawatts, giving it the world's highest nuclear power capacity per head of population.

Breeder Reactors

Plutonium is produced in all nuclear reactors which use uranium. Some of this plutonium contributes to the chain reaction taking place in the reactor; the CANDU reactor, for example, obtains up to half its energy from the fission of plutonium created within the reactor. The breeder reactor carries this logic further: it produces more fuel in the form of plutonium than it consumes in the form of uranium-235. There is nothing magical about this, nor is it violating any of the laws of physics or thermodynamics. It is simply that neutrons which would otherwise have gone to waste are used to transform the uranium-238 present in the reactor into plutonium.

In the breeder reactor there is a major effort to avoid neutron waste. Heavily enriched fuel, up to 75 per cent uranium-235, is used in a very compact core without any moderator. Around the core is placed a 'blanket' of uranium-238 which absorbs neutrons and 'breeds' new plutonium. The compactness of the core and the intensity of the fission activity there cause major cooling problems. A high heat-capacity material, moving very quickly, must be employed. This is why liquid metals, pure sodium or a sodium-potassium alloy, have been used as coolants in the breeder reactors built to date.

The term 'fast' is sometimes used when referring to breeder reactors. This has nothing to do with the speed at which plutonium is produced. This is, in fact, rather slow. Even under optimum conditions breeders built to present designs produce only about 10 per cent more plutonium than they consume each year. The term 'fast' refers to the use which is made of fast neutrons.

Breeder reactors are not new. The world's first nuclear-generated electricity, albeit a tiny amount, came from a US breeder reactor, the experimental breeder reactor-1 (EBR1), in Idaho in 1951; four years later, however, its core melted. The first true power-producing breeder reactors were the British Dounreay fast reactor (DFR) in the north of Scotland, which came on stream in 1959; and the EBR2 and the Edison Fermi reactor near Detroit, both of which began producing power in 1963. The DFR performed satisfactorily until it was closed down in 1977; the Edison Fermi had an adventurous history including a partial melt-down of the core in 1966, during which it is reported the evacuation of Detroit was seriously considered.

In France there has also been a long-standing interest in breeder reactors. Construction of a small research reactor called Rhapsodie began in 1961; this reactor was finally closed in 1983. The Phénix reactor of 250 megawatts came on stream in 1974. Although there have been some problems with the sodium circuits, once causing an eighteen-month shut-down of the plant, it has operated extremely successfully for a prototype up to the present. Construction of the much larger Superphénix, which has a capacity of 1200 megawatts, began in 1977 and this was expected to be commissioned in 1986. A collaborative agreement on future research and development on breeder reactor technology was signed between the governments of France, the UK, West Germany, Italy and Belgium in early 1984. Design studies for a 1500-megawatt Superphénix 2 are now under way.

In the USSR the 350-megawatt Shevchenko plant came into operation in 1973. Instead of being used entirely for electricity generation, this has the option of using about two thirds of its heat to produce distilled water from the Caspian Sea at a rate of 12 000 tonnes per day. A 600-megawatt plant also came into operation at Sverdlovsk in the Urals in 1980.

In the UK the Dounreay prototype fast reactor of 250-megawatts came on stream in 1974. Although it seems to have worked reasonably well on the nuclear side, it has been plagued with problems in the heat transfer circuit. In West Germany there have been long delays and considerable public protest against the 300-megawatt SNR-300 plant. In Japan the 100-megawatt Joyo reactor came on stream in 1977 and the 280-megawatt MONJU station is due for completion in 1991.

The USA is a notable omission from this list. Its prototype fast reactor project at Clinch River was subject to an endless series of design changes, delays and bitter disputes about the shares which should be borne by government and private industry. Finally, in 1984, the project was cancelled despite the very large expenditures which had been already made.

The attraction of the breeder reactor is that it makes use of the uranium-238 which for the most part remains unused in other reactors. Since uranium-238 constitutes by far the greater proportion of the world's uranium, the increase in effective energy resources is very large. In theory, breeder reactors improve the utilization of uranium resources by a factor of well over 100. If they were used entirely in breeder reactors, the world's uranium resources would provide a virtually inexhaustible supply of energy.

The plutonium has, of course, to be separated from the spent fuel in the reactor. This is done at a separation plant. The difficulties in doing this are considerable, as it is necessary to handle a complex mixture of highly radioactive materials. The breeder reactor may well be able to produce enough fuel to keep itself going, but the costs of doing so are extremely high. No commercial organization would dream of tackling it at present energy prices.

Breeder reactors are also considerably more expensive than conventional reactors. They operate at very much higher energy densities in their core, increasing the difficulty of guaranteeing their safe shut-down in an emergency. The engineering problems of controlling a mass of molten sodium as it hurtles round the cooling and heat transfer systems are formidable; sodium explodes on contact with water or steam. There are, on the face of it, grounds for apprehension about breeder reactors, which have not yet undergone the intense public scrutiny to which conventional reactor types have been subjected.

A decade ago the breeder reactor was being advocated with an urgency which implied that the future of industrial society hung upon its immediate introduction. Now that it is accepted there is no shortage of uranium in prospect for a long time to come, the ability to breed additional fuel is not particularly relevant. This is now reflected in the long-range planning of the nuclear industry. Except perhaps in France and the USSR, there is little serious pressure to build new breeder reactors to come on stream before the end of the century.

Nuclear Power in the World Energy Context

Since the heyday of its early commercial development in the 1960s, when it was confidently expected to resolve all the world's energy problems, forecasts of the future contribution of nuclear power to world energy needs have been constantly revised downwards. Figure 7 shows how OECD forecasts of what the installed capacity of nuclear power would be in 1985 fell during the 1970s. Only in 1978, when all the plants capable of being operational by 1985 had already been built or were under construction did the forecasters get the figure right. Up to then an invincible optimism – or wishful thinking – had prevented the nuclear interests and governments of the OECD countries from making a realistic assessment of the industry's near-term prospects.

In a study in 1974 the OECD estimated that the total installed nuclear generating capacity for the non-communist world in the year 2000 would be 2800 gigawatts (2.8×10^6 megawatts) and seriously suggested that an accelerated programme could result in 4100 gigawatts. It is now clear that OECD capacity by the end of the century will not greatly exceed 450 gigawatts. If it were going to be significantly more, a much larger number of stations would have to be built or under construction by now.

This does not, however, mean that the nuclear industry is dead or dying. The contribution made by nuclear power to world energy consumption is equivalent to using nearly 340 million tonnes of oil for electricity generation. It approaches the total conventional energy consumption of Latin America and is one and three quarter times the total for the whole of Africa. Between 1975 and 1985 it quadrupled its contribution; and it is still growing. At the end of 1985 a total of 157 reactors were being built. These had a total capacity of 142 000 megawatts. Unless construction of these stations is actually abandoned or they are built and not connected to the grid, nuclear generating capacity will continue to increase up to about 50 per cent higher than today's level – even if no further orders are placed.

Figure 7. Past projections of OECD nuclear generating capacity in 1985

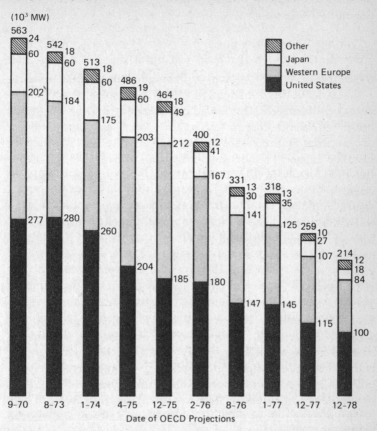

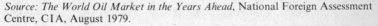
Date of OECD Projections

Source: The World Oil Market in the Years Ahead, National Foreign Assessment Centre, CIA, August 1979.

France has been the showpiece of nuclear energy. By April 1985 there were thirty-two PWRs in operation and a further twenty-one under construction, and nuclear power was supplying 65 per cent of the country's total electricity. The main problem facing the French nuclear programme is over-supply: electricity demand growth has been far below that forecast and the country is facing a huge surplus of generating capacity. There have been vigorous campaigns to promote the use of electricity. Electricity is also being exported to Germany, Switzerland, Italy, Spain and the Netherlands; a 2000-megawatt connection to the UK national grid has also been constructed beneath the Channel.

During 1984 nuclear power supplied 51 per cent of the electricity produced in Belgium; in Finland it supplied 41 per cent, and in Sweden 36 per cent. In Taiwan the figure was 52 per cent. The UK proportion was 17 per cent and in Japan it was 23 per cent. In all, nuclear power supplied about 15 per cent of the world's electricity.

The USA has by far the largest number of nuclear power stations. It accounts for about one third of the world's total capacity. The share of nuclear power in the national consumption of electricity is only about 13 per cent, but this does not reveal the full picture. The contribution in some states and areas is extremely high. The country's nuclear industry is by far the world's largest and it is still growing. Completion of the stations under construction will increase capacity by almost 40 per cent.

There is no doubt that the powerful environmental lobby in the USA has inflicted a number of severe defeats on the country's nuclear industry. But it would be wrong to attribute all the industry's present difficulties to these pressures. Many of its problems are rooted in the over-optimistic costings and exaggerated electricity demand forecasts of the late 1960s and early 1970s. These led to a stampede of orders for stations which were quickly found to be surplus to requirements as electricity demand failed to grow in accordance with the forecasts. Costs which had been pitched far too low in order to win orders also quickly rose as engineering reality asserted itself.

Utilities found themselves faced with the prospect of buying plant they did not need at twice the price they had originally assumed. Faced with public opposition to nuclear power, their simplest course of action was to cancel their orders. This they did on a huge scale. In some cases the utilities, who have a statutory duty to supply electricity and are at the same time restricted in their ability to increase tariffs, found their best course of action was to promote conservation so that they did not have to increase their generating capacity.

Uranium Resources

Uranium is a relatively common element. It is found in low concentrations in granite and sea water. In a more concentrated form it is found in the ore pitchblende, and as a constituent of many shales. The Colorado shale contains some and it is found in richer concentrations in the Chatanooga shale which underlies much of the states of Tennessee, Kentucky, Indiana and Illinois. It is also found in various conglomerate rocks in sedimentary deposits. According to the Canadian Department of Energy, Mines and Resources hundreds of thousands of square miles of the country are 'geologically favourable for uranium, and many are relatively unexplored'.[16]

Although it was discovered in 1789 and was mined first as a scientific curiosity and then as a source of radium, uranium has been regarded as an important mineral only in the past few decades. It has no long history of exploration as have coal, oil and the commercially valuable metals. Large-scale mining of uranium began, in Canada, only in 1942 in response to the military weapons programmes of the US and Britain. Once these requirements had been met, there was an almost total collapse in the market and uranium exploration was virtually dormant in Canada from 1956 to 1966. Another burst of activity occurred in 1966–9 but again declined.

In the 1970s exploration again picked up, but since 1979 there has again been a major fall-off. In the USA expenditure on exploration declined by 95 per cent, and in some other countries exploration has ceased. Table 17 shows the countries in the western world with significant known deposits which would be recoverable at prices of $80 and $130 per kilogram. The total is about 5 million tonnes. Data on the communist world are not available, but the evidence suggests that the level of resources is similar to that in the western countries.

The present rate of consumption of uranium in the western world is about 40 000 tonnes per year. At this rate of consumption the resources shown in Table 17 would last about 125 years. If consumption increases significantly, prices will rise, stimulating a resumption of exploration. Geologists are agreed that at prices of, say, $500 per kilogram the reserves of uranium would amount

Table 17. Uranium resources in the western world

Country	Reasonably assured resources up to $80/kg (t × 10³)	Reasonably assured additional resources up to $130/kg (t × 10³)	Additional estimated resources up to $130/kg (t × 10³)
South Africa	247	109	175
Australia	294	23	285
Brazil	119	—	81
Canada	230	28	760
EEC	62	53	88
USA	362	243	1097
Gabon	19	2	10
Namibia	119	16	53
Niger	160	16	53
Sweden	—	38	44
Others	135	34	74
Total	1747	546	2720
Grand total		5013	

Source: IAEA/OECD 1982, quoted in *Revue de l'Energie*, October 1982.

to hundreds of millions of tonnes. There is no fear of nuclear power being brought to a halt through lack of uranium resources for a very long time to come.

The Problem of Nuclear Wastes

Like all large industrial undertakings, nuclear power stations produce waste. Compared with paper pulp making or many of the metal industries, which produce large quantities of permanently toxic waste materials, nuclear power stations are extremely clean. But a proportion of the waste they produce has its own particular quality: it is radioactive.

Contrary to what might be expected, the fuel going into a nuclear power station is a minor hazard. Natural uranium fuel rods can be packed in cardboard boxes. But once it has been inside the reactor, the fuel becomes a very nasty and dangerous substance indeed. Used fuel contains the fission products created when the uranium-235 atom splits; these are usually highly radioactive. It also contains plutonium and other elements not found in nature. One of the reasons why fuel elements are clad in some strong material is to prevent these radioactive substances leaking into the coolant, which would carry them to the heat exchange system or the electricity generating plant. The fuel cladding material, because it is subject to the intense neutron flux in the reactor core, also becomes radioactive.

When the spent, or poisoned, fuel elements are removed from a reactor, they are dumped in a deep cooling pond until the shortest-lived isotopes have decayed sufficiently to allow the fuel to be transported to a reprocessing plant. It is taken there in heavy metal casks which have to be cooled in transit. In the reprocessing plant the uranium and plutonium are separated and, in principle, stored for reuse in reactors. There are regular but unconvincing denials by governments that the plutonium is used for military purposes.

The reprocessing of nuclear fuel is an extremely difficult and expensive process. In the UK it is carried out at a big plant on the coast of Cumbria. Formerly this was called Windscale, but after a variety of incidents in which radiation was unwittingly released the name was changed to Sellafield. However, the incidents continued and in 1986 Britain's nuclear safety inspectors threatened to halt nuclear fuel reprocessing if the plant were not brought up to a satisfactory standard of operation. Despite previous warnings, the cost and complexity of carrying out operations in a safe and reliable manner had proved to be beyond the capabilities of the plant management.

When the plutonium and uranium have been separated, the remaining waste materials must be isolated from the biosphere until their radioactivity has decayed to a sufficiently low level. Some authorities consider this would be after twenty half-lives. In the case of the common fission products, such as strontium-90 with a half-life of twenty-eight years, and caesium-137 with a half-life of thirty years, the isolation period is therefore 600 years. Some of these high-level wastes, as they are called, are highly corrosive and, being highly radioactive, they emit considerable amounts of heat. If they are to be stored safely, they must be sealed against leakage and their heat must be conducted away to prevent them melting or turning any water in their vicinity into steam.

A great deal of work has been carried out on the development of a method of solidifying high-level wastes by vitrification; that is, binding them into a glass-like solid. This would make the wastes much more manageable and greatly reduce their volume. Only about four cubic metres of treated and solidified high-level waste would be produced by a 1000-megawatt station every year. The plan is that the blocks of vitrified wastes would be stored for perhaps thirty years in underground caverns during the period of their most vigorous radioactivity and heat emission. After that, they would be buried deep in the earth – perhaps a kilometre down – and sealed off. A small-scale vitrification process has been in operation at Marcoule in France since 1978, and there are plans for the building of a major vitrification plant at the reprocessing plant at Cap de la Hague on the tip of the Normandy peninsula.

The difficulties and expense of fuel processing have led many experts to question whether it is even a worthwhile activity; it is simpler and cheaper to mine fresh uranium than it is to extract it from the used fuel. A number of countries, such as Sweden and the USA, are therefore seriously considering the permanent disposal of the spent fuel as a high-level waste. This would eliminate the expense and dangers of reprocessing. It would, of course, prevent the recovery of plutonium for nuclear weapons. In Canada it has never been intended that the fuel from CANDU reactors should be reprocessed.

There are other wastes from nuclear power stations and reprocessing plants. Anything which is used in a radioactive area becomes contaminated. Ancillary reactor parts, valves, pipes, switches and all the equipment which is replaced in routine maintenance, protective clothing, the whole of the industrial detritus resulting from running and maintaining the station, have to be carefully collected and buried at the site or put in casks and dumped elsewhere.

A certain amount of radioactivity is also released to the atmosphere or discharged at sea. High chimney stacks take radioactive gases like krypton-85, which has a half-life of 4·5 hours, up to levels which allow them to be widely dispersed before they reach the ground. Other soluble or dispersible radioactive material is taken several miles out to sea by pipeline and released.

The reactor itself becomes a waste product. Once it has been in operation, a nuclear reactor and all that surrounds it become highly radioactive. Work is being carried out on the use of remote-controlled equipment that will be able to demolish a nuclear reactor which has reached the end of its useful life. The expense will be extremely high. In many cases the most practical thing will be to leave it sealed with concrete for the next few thousand years.

Risk of Major Accidents

The need for caution when dealing with nuclear power is great. Nuclear engineering is at the edge of technical knowledge. The total accumulated experience is rapidly increasing, but it is still relatively small. Most of the world's largest nuclear stations have come on stream within the last ten years. The long-term effects of radiation and operational stresses on critical components remain to be discovered. Engineering has a long history of finding things out the hard way while at the same time making bland statements about how safe and well understood everything is.

The failure of steel bridges and welded tankers after the Second World War was because of the phenomenon, unknown up till then, of rapid crack propagation, which can occur in stressed steel when the temperature is low. The mysterious crashes of early Comet aircraft were a result of unforeseen metal-fatigue failures. The collapse of the Tacoma Narrows suspension bridge occurred because no one thought structural resonance could be induced by a wind of moderate speed. The rash of failures of welded box-girder bridges in the UK, Europe and Australia was because designers had not fully understood the behaviour of steel diaphragms under heavy buckling loads. The failure of the Challenger space shuttle was because those in charge would not believe that a failure of a sealing gasket in one of the fuel tanks was possible.

Nevertheless, there are some certainties. The fear that a nuclear power station could explode like a nuclear bomb is completely unjustified. Under no circumstances could this happen to a reactor containing natural or slightly enriched uranium fuel. In the case of the breeder reactor, however, this remote possibility cannot be totally excluded. If there were a catastrophic melting of the core, the highly enriched uranium could, theoretically, achieve the configuration necessary for an albeit very inefficient, but quite definite nuclear explosion.

The worst accident which designers consider, the maximum credible accident, is a complete failure of the coolant supply to the reactor. If this happens, the intense heat in the reactor core builds up and the whole assembly melts – this is called a 'melt-down'. This may result in the destruction of the pressure vessel and reactor building and a massive spewing of radioactivity into the environment. The possibility that the whole molten assembly will then burn downwards through the reactor floor carries the mordant title of the 'China Syndrome' in the USA because of the general direction of progress of the molten mass.

There are, of course, numerous mechanisms which shut down the reactor if anything starts to go wrong. Control rods, for example, may be automatically dropped into the reactor through the operation of 'fail-safe' systems which come into operation if any abnormality is detected in reactor functioning. But one of the big problems with nuclear power is that, even when it has been shut down, a reactor continues to generate a large quantity of heat because of the amount of radioactive material it contains.

To prevent a melt-down in the case of a serious accident, emergency core-cooling systems are installed. A difficulty is knowing whether these will work; the accident which triggers their operation may also prevent them behaving in the predicted way. Elaborate computer simulations have been made of reactors under various disaster conditions. While these have more or less satisfied the builders of nuclear power stations and the regulatory authorities, they tend to be rather divorced from the ingeni-ousness of human fallibility, which finds ways of making mistakes beyond the dreams of most safety engineers.

It is unlikely, for example, that any computer simulation en-visaged the possibility of a man with a candle setting fire to cables under the control room, thereby disabling the emergency core-cooling system in a nuclear power station. But this actually happened in March 1975 in the huge Brown's Ferry nuclear station in Alabama. An electrician and his mate were checking

airflows through wall openings for cables when a dra
out the candle and set some foam-plastic packing aligh
seven hours to put out the fire. During that time all five en
core-cooling systems on one reactor were knocked out of
luckily, they were not needed during that time.

The accident at the Three Mile Island nuclear plant in Pennsylvania has been used in both pro-nuclear and anti-nuclear arguments. The fact that nobody was killed and the release of radiation was small has been held to demonstrate that, in the last resort, safety systems do work. The fact that nobody quite knew what was happening and the station was on the brink of disaster nevertheless gave the majority of people a frightening intimation of what might have happened.

Two coolant pumps failed; a valve stuck open; the reactor overheated; and the fuel rods ruptured with a huge release of radioactivity. A large bubble of hydrogen formed above the reactor core. If it had exploded, there would almost certainly have been a major release of radioactive material. The true condition in the plant was not immediately revealed to the public for fear of adverse publicity. When it was, the State Governor recommended the evacuation of pregnant women and children from within five miles of the plant. The station staff managed to get the situation under control, though the reactor was destroyed and repairs to the station have not yet been completed.

The Chernobyl accident in April 1986 brought the previous nightmares of the industry into reality. It was the result of a bizarre sequence of events. The irony is that it resulted from an attempt to increase the safety of operation by investigating a possible response to a very unlikely event. Station engineers wanted to check the ability of one of the electricity-generating turbines to produce enough power to drive the cooling-water pumps while freewheeling to a standstill. If the station were accidentally disconnected from the grid, this would provide some additional power while other emergency systems were being mobilized.

They set the experiment in motion. As the generator slowed, so did the cooling-water pumps. This would normally have shut down the reactor automatically, but the operating staff had shut off that part of the safety system in order to carry out the test.

The reactor started to overheat; this caused extra steam to be formed in the cooling circuit, reducing its effectiveness and setting in motion a runaway process of overheating. The engineers tried to release the control rods to trip the reactor, but it was too late. The temperature soared upwards, fuel disintegrated, there was a massive explosion blowing the roof off the containment building, the graphite moderator went on fire, and several tonnes of radioactive material were released into the atmosphere. Thirty-one people were killed and many more were injured severely, some in truly heroic and self-sacrificing efforts to deal with the disaster. Hundreds of millions of people across the USSR and Europe were affected to some extent by radiation; many were badly worried.

Radiation Units

The radiation emitted by radioactive substances is sometimes referred to as ionizing radiation. When it hits an atom of a particular substance, it can cause it to lose or gain an electron, thus changing its electrical charge. The effects on living tissue vary according to the type of radiation. Alpha and beta rays are effective as ionizing agents; gamma rays and neutrons much less so. On the other hand, alpha rays are not very penetrating: they are stopped by a piece of paper or the skin. The greatest danger is when an alpha-emitting substance is inhaled or ingested with food into the body. Beta rays are more penetrating, and gamma rays need a very heavy shielding such as that provided by thick concrete or lead to stop them.

One of the difficulties facing anyone trying to understand the debate over the effects of radiation is the bewildering variety of radiation units. Part of the problem is that a distinction is made between the radiation emitted by a radioactive source and that absorbed by a person. The most commonly used measure of emitted radiation, or activity, up till recently was the curie (Ci): this expressed the radiation of a source in terms of the radiation of a gram of pure radium. The rate of radioactive decay of radium is $3 \cdot 7 \times 10^{10}$ disintegrations per second. A curie is the quantity of a radioactive substance which produces this number of disintegrations per second.

The use of the curie has now been superseded by the SI unit for emitted radiation which is called the becquerel (Bq). This is a rate of disintegration of one per second. A curie is equal to 3.7×10^{10} becquerels. Another unit of radioactive activity is the roentgen (r). This is defined as the amount of X-ray or gamma radiation which causes a specified amount of ionization in a kilogram of air.

Such measures of emitted radiation are of little value when studying the effects of radiation on human beings. For this it is necessary to know the amounts of radiation actually absorbed by the body. The most common unit for this is the rad, and this is defined as an amount of absorbed radiation which is equivalent to 100 ergs of energy per gram of irradiated material. It is a very tiny dose: it would raise the temperature of the tissue absorbing it by about two millionths of a degree. The SI unit of absorbed radiation is the gray (Gy), and is the energy in joules absorbed by 1 kilogram of irradiated material; 1 gray is equal to 100 rads.

The rad and the gray, however, are unsatisfactory in that they do not distinguish between the effects of different types of radiation on the body. Radiation studies therefore tend to use units in which an adjustment is made for the different biological effects of each type of radiation. The most commonly used 'dose equivalent' unit is the rem – which stands for roentgen equivalent man – and is the radiation dose which has the same effect as one roentgen of X-rays. The SI unit of dose equivalent is the sievert (Sv). One sievert is equal to 100 rem. Radiation doses are frequently measured in millisieverts.

Radiation and Health

There is no dispute about the effect of exposure to massive doses of radiation: they are quickly fatal. This was grimly demonstrated in the bombing of Hiroshima and Nagasaki, the accident at Chernobyl, and the fortunately rare instances in which workers in the nuclear industry have been caught in major radiation releases. A slower death from 'radiation sickness', which may develop into leukaemia, also takes place as a result of the destruction of white blood cells in heavily irradiated people, although a bone marrow transplant may be able to save such a victim.

There are huge disagreements about the effects of radiation releases. An example of this was the variation in the estimates of the long-term effects of the Chernobyl accident: these varied from a few hundred cancer deaths up to hundreds of thousands. The disagreement was not about the effects of radiation; it is fully agreed among experts both inside and outside the nuclear industry that low-level radiation can cause cancer and genetic damage. This happens as part of a two-stage process. First comes the cell damage caused by an ionizing ray or particle; for the most part, the body deals with this without any problem as cells are always being damaged and replaced. But sometimes a cell is damaged in such a way that its DNA is altered so as to make it potentially malignant. If this 'rogue' cell then eludes the body's defences, it may form the starting-point for a cancerous growth. The occurrence is relatively rare; not all cell damage produces malignancy, nor do all malignant cells result in cancers.

There is roughly the same problem in demonstrating the fatal effects of cigarette smoking. No one now seriously denies that smoking cigarettes causes lung cancer. All cigarette smoking is therefore dangerous; smoking one cigarette can be the cause of a fatal cancer. But many people survive smoking forty cigarettes a day until they die of something else. Similarly, all radiation is dangerous, but not everyone who has had a few dental or chest X-rays is doomed to die of a radiation-induced cancer.

Moreover, it is extremely difficult to identify those who actually die as a result of exposure to radioactivity. When a person develops a cancer, it is usually impossible to say exactly why this happened. It could be the result of exposure to radiation, but it could be something else entirely. The cancer might be a result of air pollution, special carcinogenic hazards at work, sunbathing, wearing a luminous watch, a virus or a 'spontaneous' breakdown in the body's normal functioning. Similarly, a deformed birth may be the result of any of a variety, or even a combination, of causes.

The evidence on which assessments of the number of cancers and the amount of genetic damage are based is statistical. Just as in the case of cigarette smoking, where studies have shown that the proportion of lung cancers increases with the number of cigarettes smoked, investigations of people exposed to substantial radiation doses such as uranium-miners, atom-bomb survivors, early workers with radioactivity and others have shown that the greater the radiation dose, the higher the number of cancers. On the assumption that the same proportional relationship holds for lower doses, an estimate can be made of the numbers of people likely to be affected by a given radiation dose.

The huge differences in the estimates of the ultimate number of cancers likely to occur because of the Chernobyl accident were a result of the different assumptions made at a time when there was very little quantitative evidence available. The calculation of the long-term effects depends on the amount of radiation emitted, its distribution in the atmosphere, how and where and when it returns to earth, the numbers of people it affects and the actual dose they receive. The opportunities for producing the answer one would prefer are limitless.

Radiation has not always been regarded as dangerous. In the early years of the present century, radium spread on copper sheets was fastened over warts, scars and patches of dermatitis as a means of treatment, with reasonable success. The alpha-emitting radioactive gas radon, which is one of the 'decay daughters' of uranium, came to be highly regarded as a treatment for rheumatism and gout. Various ingenious methods of treating patients were devised: one London doctor had an 'Inhalatorium', or small room in which radon was released; radioactive spas were popular in Europe in the 1920s; radioactive tonic water was on sale in London; and there were advertisements for ladies' corsets lined with radioactive material – or customers could have their own corsets lined.

Studies of uranium-miners and of workers in factories where uranium was used, however, gradually accumulated evidence of the long-term damaging effects of radiation. In 1928 the International Commission on Radiological Protection (ICRP) was established. By the 1930s the dangers were becoming more widely recognized. Intensive study has also been carried out on the 285 000 people who survived the nuclear bombs on Hiroshima and Nagasaki. The United Nations established a Scientific Committee on the Effects of Atomic Radiation (UNSCEAR) in 1955. It has regularly reviewed and assembled the state of knowledge on all aspects of radiation, producing regular authoritative summaries of the position.[17]

In fact, the human race and the whole biosphere have evolved within a radioactive environment. The principal source of radiation is the earth itself. Uranium and other radioactive materials are dispersed throughout the earth's crust, and their decay provides a ceaseless background of radiation from which there is no escape. The intensity of this varies considerably. Granite rocks tend to have a higher concentration than others, but meat, vegetables and water also contain a certain amount of natural radioactivity. The estimated 'normal' dose from background radiation from the earth is about 0·35 millisieverts per year; in some places, however, it can be five to ten times as much. The internal irradiation from ingested radioactive material is about the same. Still, no pattern of increased cancer incidence in more radioactive areas has been clearly identified.

Radiation is also received in the form of cosmic rays from space. People living at higher altitudes have less protection from the atmosphere and hence receive a greater dose than those at sea level. Travelling by high-flying aircraft also increases exposure to radioactivity. The exposure to radiation from cosmic rays increases by a factor of 20 in ascending from 4 to 12 kilometres. The dose at sea level is about 0·3 millisieverts per year.

Radon is produced in uranium-bearing rocks and percolates its way to the surface of the earth and mingles with the atmosphere. Radon concentrations can be particularly high in coal and uranium mines. It has received increasing attention in recent years because it has been found to become concentrated in buildings built in some of the more radioactive areas; there is no way of preventing it being absorbed in breathing. The irony is that draught-proofing as a means of energy conservation can increase the level of radon in a building substantially. The average radiation dose from radon is about 0·8 millisieverts per year, but in some dwellings it may be up to ten times as great.

Human activity has also introduced a wide variety of sources of radioactivity into daily existence. Coal contains trace levels of various radioactive substances. Burning coal in a power station distributes these to the atmosphere. Medical X-rays are a well-known hazard. A few decades ago they were over-used in routine diagnostic tests to an extent which makes scientists of today shudder. The use of medical X-rays is now heavily curtailed and the ordinary member of the general public is subject to few, but those working as radiologists receive an appreciable additional exposure to radiation.

Luminous watches, which used to use radium and now more commonly employ tritium, subject their wearers to a certain amount of radiation. The starters in fluorescent lights, anti-static equipment in factories, smoke detectors, exit signs in buildings and a variety of other devices may incorporate radioactive materials. In some cases the emission of radiation during normal operation is negligible, but a hazard may be caused if the device is broken.

There is also a substantial contribution from the fall-out from nuclear bomb tests. Vast quantities of radioactive material were hurled into the atmosphere in the 1950s and 1960s. Governments and scientists on both sides of the ideological divide seemed willing to collaborate tacitly in a quite remarkable act of scientific and governmental irresponsibility. It is estimated that about 3 tonnes of uranium-235 and 17 tonnes of uranium-238 as well as a vast array of other radioactive materials have been thrown into the atmosphere by the 420 or so atmospheric weapons tests to date. UNSCEAR calculations show that the total average exposure from nuclear weapons tests to the end of 1980 was about 3·8 millisieverts; but many of the military personnel involved were subjected to very much more. Much of the radioactive debris remains in the atmosphere and will continue to make its contribution to the radiation dose of the world's population for thousands of years to come.

Nuclear power adds to all this radioactivity in a variety of ways. Uranium-mining brings radioactive material to the surface of the earth. Huge piles of mildly radioactive waste, called tailings, are produced when the uranium ore is extracted and taken for processing. Wind and water distribute some of this material into the atmosphere and water courses. Processing uranium ore into fuel for reactors releases more radiation as does the operation of the power station itself. Waste disposal has its own pattern of radiation releases. Very roughly, the total radiation resulting from nuclear power activities is about one five-hundredth of the background radiation.

At each of these stages in the production of nuclear power, however, some individuals receive radiation doses which are considerably greater than the global average from the processes on which they are working. These vary, depending on the standards which have been set for exposure; on the degree to which working practices conform to these; and on whether there are accidents. Broadly speaking, the risks of working in a well-run nuclear installation are very small. The health of nuclear workers compares well with that in most other occupations. Uranium-mining is a different matter: it is a dangerous way of earning a living.

The discharge of nuclear wastes into the sea and air is also a cause for worry. The stable and radioactive isotopes of the same material are indistinguishable. Nature concentrates some elements within parts of the body – iodine in the thyroid, for example. It also successively concentrates substances along food chains. Even if a radioactive isotope of one of these elements is dispersed sufficiently widely to be biologically almost completely innocuous, natural processes can concentrate it dangerously.

Bass, for instance, produce a concentration of caesium in their flesh which is 1000 times greater than that in the surrounding water, while plankton have been recorded as concentrating strontium-90 up to 75 000 times the level of that of the water in which they live. An accident occurred at the reactor at Windscale in the UK in 1957 in which a considerable amount of radioactive material was released into the atmosphere. One of these substances was iodine-131, which emits beta rays. It was found that this became concentrated alarmingly in cow's milk. All deliveries of milk from the area had to be stopped until the radioactivity had decayed to a level which was considered acceptable.

Under normal operating conditions, nuclear power stations emit very little radiation. Neither those who work in them or live near them are subjected to any significant extra risk. But nuclear accidents do happen. Some 135 000 people in the vicinity of Chernobyl received radiation doses which have certainly increased their chances of getting cancer. It is the world's first major nuclear disaster in some 4000 years of reactor operating experience. Statistically, other accidents in which radiation is released are bound to happen.

A Question of Choice

The argument that no human activity should be permitted which increases the risk of death is clearly absurd. There is virtually nothing human beings like doing which does not carry some risk to themselves, the environment and society as a whole. Doing nothing to secure future energy supplies or adopting a non-nuclear strategy also carries a risk. The argument about nuclear power therefore cannot usefully start from the premise that it is acceptable only if there is no risk from it. The question is whether in the context, and considering the alternatives available, these risks are acceptable.

This question has scarcely been broached. A large measure of the blame for this must rest with the nuclear industry itself and with the governments supporting it. Far too often the industry has been arrogant and secretive. Its military antecedents and continued connections foster such attitudes. Many of its activities are shrouded in a veil of secrecy which may often conceal nothing, but can leave people extremely uneasy about what lies behind it.

Forecasts of the need for nuclear power have often been blatantly tendentious, if not completely absurd. It is difficult to believe that the U K Atomic Energy Authority, in its evidence to the 1976 Royal Commission on Nuclear Power and the Environment, seriously projected an installed nuclear capacity of 104 gigawatts by the year 2000 – that is about fifty large power stations – and no less than 426 gigawatts by the year 2030. The casualness of the attitude of the Authority and the Department of Energy towards what the Commission called 'long-term issues of unusual range and difficulty which are political and ethical as well as technical in character' thoroughly alarmed the Commission's members. The final report said:

We are perfectly clear that there has so far been very little official consideration of these matters. The view that was expressed by the Department of Energy in their evidence to us was that there were reasonable prospects that the safety and environmental prospects posed by nuclear power could be satisfactorily overcome and that, if this proved not to be so, other forms of energy would have to be used or consumption reduced somehow. We see this as a policy which could lead to recognition of the dangers when it would be too late to avoid them.

More is needed here than bland, unsubstantiated official assurance that the environmental impact of nuclear power has been fully taken into account.[18]

In France, Britain, the USA and other countries, governments have appeared to ally themselves almost uncritically with nuclear power. Indeed, among some there is a tendency to see support for the nuclear industry as a test of patriotism. It is not particularly conducive to rational discussion if criticizing the energy forecasts on which nuclear programmes are based is branded as somehow subversive of freedom and democracy. On the other hand, much of the opposition to nuclear power has been hysterical and uninformed. Tiny incidents which would pass completely unremarked in any other context have been blown out of all proportion. Double standards have often been used: if some of the arguments against nuclear power were applied universally, a great number of other industries and human activities would also have to be banned.

The case for nuclear power is a strong one. Oil resources are undoubtedly limited; the next generation, if not the present, is likely to see them becoming scarce. Coal poses not just local environmental problems, but threatens to affect the atmospheric temperature on a global scale. Nuclear power has shown that it has the potential to provide energy in the quantities that human society has grown to require.

Alvin Weinberg, one of the early leaders of the US nuclear programme, made the following remarkable and revealing statement in 1970:

We nuclear people have made a 'Faustian Contract' with society: we offer an almost unique possibility for a technologically abundant world for the oncoming billions, through our miraculous, inexhaustible energy source; but this energy source at the same time is tainted with potential side effects which, if uncontrolled, could spell disaster.[19]

If it is to win public assent, nuclear power will have to be discussed openly, freely and honestly. Newer and safer reactors can be developed. If reactor vessels were buried underground, for example, as are many hydro stations, the risks to the public from even the worst accidents would be minimal. Waste can be stored safely and securely if enough money were spent on building the necessary facilities deep under the sea. But these are costly measures and would make electricity dearer.

Hardly anywhere has there been a proper discussion of the real options available to society over the next few decades. For the most part, nuclear power has simply been imposed on an uninformed public, which has become increasingly disenchanted and suspicious. The feeling is clearly growing that if there is to be a Faustian bargain, it is only right that those on whose behalf it is being made should have a share in the discussions leading to it.

Fusion Power

Nuclear fusion is the source of the energy of the sun and the stars. In the extremely hot cores of these bodies atoms of the lightest elements coalesce to form heavier elements. Some mass is lost in the process and released as energy. If the same process were harnessed on earth in a fusion reactor, many people believe humanity's energy problems would be solved for ever.

Fusion reactors, however, do not exist. They are products of the technological imagination. The nearest man has come to harnessing fusion power is in the hydrogen bomb. It remains to be seen whether it will ever be possible to control a fusion reaction and make use of its energy. Professor Lidsky of the Massachusetts Institute of Technology, writing in 1972, summed up the attitude of probably the majority of scientists working on nuclear fusion:

The search for economically controlled fusion power is a scientific hunt for the Lost Dutchman Mine. Only a few believers are *absolutely* certain that the goal exists but the search takes place over interesting ground and the rewards for success are overwhelming.[20]

The position is little different at the end of 1986.

About thirty different energy-releasing fusion reactions are theoretically possible, but only those using the hydrogen isotopes deuterium and tritium* and the common metal lithium are of practical interest. If all the deuterium in 1·5 cubic kilometres of sea water were used in a fusion reactor, the energy released could be equal to that in the world's recoverable crude oil. Since there

* Tritium is hydrogen with two neutrons in its nucleus and hence has an atomic weight of 3.

are about one and a half billion cubic kilometres of sea water, the rewards for the successful development of fusion power are indeed overwhelming.

There is a simple and engaging logic about the processes which would occur in a fusion reactor. When two deuterium atoms combine, they either form a helium atom and release energy, or form one tritium atom and one ordinary hydrogen atom, also releasing energy. The tritium in turn combines with deuterium, again forming an isotope of helium and releasing energy. If lithium is introduced, it is broken down into helium and tritium (a process of nuclear fission) with a release of energy and the tritium fuses with deuterium. All the radioactive components are thus 'consumed' and the final products of the whole reaction are helium, hydrogen and energy. As, however, there is a neutron release during the reaction, the containment vessel and exposed equipment would become radioactive, though probably not to the same extent as in a fission reactor.

Its logical simplicity, however, does not mean the process is easy to achieve in practice. Fusion can occur only between the nuclei of atoms which are brought into contact with sufficient kinetic energy to overcome the extremely high forces with which they repel each other. Such conditions can be obtained at a temperature of about 100 million K. At this temperature substances are not only gaseous, but they exist in a state in which their atoms have been stripped of their electrons. This high-energy condition of dissociated nuclei and free electrons which is found in the sun is called a plasma.

Obviously such a plasma cannot be kept in a material container. It would instantly vaporize it. The only way yet envisaged of holding a fusion plasma is by the use of an immaterial container made up of very strong magnetic forces. The problems of holding the plasma stable at the correct temperature and extracting energy from it are well beyond the present powers of science. Theoretical and experimental work to date has, therefore, not even attempted to produce all the conditions necessary for an energy-producing reaction. Instead it has been concentrated on separate aspects of the problem.

Theoretical solutions are emerging, but the next stage is more difficult because experiments to confirm the theoretical results have yet to be devised and carried out. Many of these require hundreds of millions of dollars' expenditure and years of work with no guarantee of producing anything more constructive than the conclusion that a theoretically attractive approach does not work in practice. In the early 1960s there was much premature, and ill-informed, enthusiasm for a British device named ZETA which was supposed to have answered most of the questions. It had answered some but its use revealed a host of problems previously unsuspected.

Scientists in the USSR, however, made a significant breakthrough in 1969. They were using a toroidal, or ring-shaped, machine within which the plasma is confined by magnetic forces; it was called a Tokomak. Experiments revealed higher temperatures and greater plasma stability than had hitherto been achieved. The success spurred further efforts in the USSR and the Tokomak approach was soon adopted by other fusion researchers; it now represents the main line of fusion research. The Joint European Torus (JET) was opened at Culham in the UK in 1983, and a further large Tokomak (JT-60) has been built in Japan.

It is difficult to make an assessment of how close researchers are to constructing a working fusion reactor. One criterion of progress is known as the 'Lawson Product', or Lawson Criterion. This is the product of the density of the plasma in ions per cubic centimetre and the confinement time. When a plasma meeting the requirement of the minimum value of the Lawson Product is confined at a temperature of 100 million K, it becomes theoretically possible to extract more energy from it than is being put into heating and confining it. The minimum necessary Lawson Product is $1 \cdot 0 \times 10^{14}$ seconds per cubic centimetre. Experiments to date have given results with a Lawson Product value of $1 \cdot 0 \times 10^{13}$, which is about a tenth of that required.

It must be borne in mind that all this work is at a theoretical and experimental level. Even if a Tokomak can achieve a plasma state which satisfies the Lawson Criterion, no one expects to get any useful power from the machine; it will simply have confirmed that a fusion power station is practical in principle. In a power-generating fusion reactor it is envisaged that the neutrons emitted in the fusion reaction would be captured in a blanket surrounding the plasma. Heat from the blanket would be used to raise steam.

An alternative approach to nuclear fusion emerged in the USA during the 1970s. This relied on the focusing of laser beams on tiny pellets of deuterium and tritium in such a way that they are compressed and heated sufficiently for the fusion reaction to take place. A quotation from one of the leading scientific groups working on this method of laser 'implosion' speaks eloquently for itself:

In addition to a substantial advance in laser technology, a laser-fusion power plant will require the solution of many other technological problems. The high-efficiency detonation of fusion-fuel pellets for practical electricity generation will occur on a time scale of 10^{-11} seconds or less. Since the energy released will be at least 10^7 joules, the peak rate of fusion power production will be at least 10^{18} watts. This rate (which, to be sure, is intermittent) is a million times greater than the power of all man-made machinery put together and is about 10 times greater than the total radiant power of sunlight falling on the entire earth. The technological challenge of laser fusion is to wrap a power plant around fusion micro-explosions of these astronomically large peak powers that can endure their effects for dozens to hundreds of times every second for many years.[21]

At this stage of uncertainty there is no point in dwelling on the amount of fuel available for fusion reactors. For practical purposes it can be regarded as infinite: sieving the oceans of their deuterium could continue for millions of years. Lithium can also be recovered from sea water and could eventually provide a near-infinite source of supply of this element at essentially constant costs. An interesting discussion by Kulchinski,[22] however, suggests that the availability of materials for constructing fusion reactors could well be a limiting factor. Any potential fusion reactor would appear to need large quantities of comparatively rare materials such as vanadium, niobium and molybdenum.

It is also unreasonable to go too deeply into the question of the safety, or otherwise, of fusion power at this stage. The potential hazards seem to be fewer than those associated with fission-power stations. If it can be mastered, fusion is likely to provide electricity more cleanly than any other method.

In summary, then, fusion power is an attractive but still distant promise. Slow progress is being made in the major research centres, but the difficulties and the costs are immense. The Tokomak Fusion Test Reactor Project at Princeton University, for example, which was completed in 1982, cost $314 million. The US Congress passed a Magnetic Fusion Engineering Act in 1980 which proposed that a demonstration reactor should be built as soon as possible, perhaps by the year 2000, but this is now regarded as hopelessly over-optimistic. Even if the energy break-even point is reached in the present generation of experimental machines, it will be just the first step in the right direction. It will have to be followed by other more elaborate experimental machines, an operating prototype and a full-scale demonstration plant before fusion energy can make any contribution to world energy needs. None of these steps is without major problems. The world will surely have to wait at least fifty years for any help from fusion power.

9

Renewable Energy Sources

The sun, the rivers, the tides and waves of the sea, the wind, the earth's internal heat, and the natural growth of plant life can all be used as energy sources. They are often classed together and referred to as 'renewable' or 'non-depleting'. But this is not accurate. Only the sun, the wind and the waves remain unaffected by man's use and are truly non-depleting over centuries.

In the case of hydro or tidal power the installations used for channelling and damming the water become silted up and eventually unusable. The river or estuary may then have to be abandoned as a source of power. Geothermal energy is obtainable only at certain favourable sites, usually reservoirs of hot water or steam, and these are depleted when the heat is drawn from them faster than its natural rate of renewal. And timber, or any other plant life used as fuel, cannot be cropped without depleting the soil of the nutrients on which renewed growth depends.

Solar Energy

The most tantalizing feature of the sun's energy is its abundance. The solar flux at the outer edge of the atmosphere is 1·4 kilowatts per square metre. Although absorption and reflection reduce this, about 50 per cent of it reaches the earth's surface. The noon intensity of solar energy on a clear day in the tropics can exceed a kilowatt per square metre. This energy falling on an area about 8 kilometres square is equivalent to the output of the whole of the United Kingdom's electricity generating system.

The desert areas of the world extend over about 20 million square kilometres. On this area of land, which grows no food and supports no population, the total annual solar radiation is about four hundred times the world's present energy consumption of all kinds. This obvious superfluity of energy, with no known way of collecting more than a tiny fraction of it, makes solar-energy research both extraordinarily challenging and maddeningly frustrating.

The most commonly used collecting device is the flat-plate collector. In its simplest form it is no more than a flat black surface with water trickling across it. Evaporation losses can be cut down by running the water through pipes embedded in the absorbing surface or by using a device like a flat central-heating radiator. Insulation at the back and sides improves performance by cutting down heat losses to the surroundings. Convection and re-radiation losses from the absorber surface are reduced by covering it with one or two glass plates. Glass has the useful property of being almost transparent to most of the energy from the sun and almost completely opaque to the infra-red radiation emitted from an object which has been heated by the sun. The glass plate over the collector therefore absorbs heat emitted by the absorbing surface and radiates some of it back again.

A further refinement is the use of a selective absorber. This is usually a polished metal plate covered with a thin layer of a black material such as oxide or sulphide of nickel. At any particular temperature the rate of heat emission from a polished surface is less than that from a black one – a shiny teapot keeps the tea warm for longer than a similar one with a black surface. On the other hand, a black surface absorbs heat more effectively than a polished one. The selective absorber is one of those happy instances in which the best of two worlds is provided: it absorbs like a black body and emits like a polished one. The black layer, however, has to be applied under tightly controlled conditions, usually by electrolytic deposition; and it is delicate and easily worn away. Its performance is also seriously impaired by dust, which can be a big problem in desert conditions.

The main application of flat-plate solar collectors is in the provision of hot water for domestic or small-scale commercial and industrial uses in countries with plenty of sun. In such locations they are clearly an economic proposition under present economic conditions. Australia, Japan, Israel, Turkey and the southern United States are among the areas where they are commercially available. In Israel, for example, there were about 700 000 households using flat-plate collectors for their hot water in 1984; a similar number is reported for the USA; the figure in Japan was about 300 000.

In the temperate countries, with their much cloudier climates and lower intensities of insolation, flat-plate solar collectors are much harder to justify economically. They are able to provide very little hot water in the dark cold months of winter. Their main use is restricted to topping up hot water supplies in the summer. Given the expense of the collector and the plumbing required to integrate it into the hot water system, the savings are too low to pay back the cost of the installation at present energy prices.

Further research is unlikely to alter this basic picture. There is no scientific breakthrough in prospect; terrestrial engineers are unable to control the intensity with which the sun emits its radiation or the position of the earth in space. Very large sums of money were spent on research into exotic refinements of the flat-plate collector during the 1970s, some of it by companies mainly devoted to aerospace technology. While some improvements in efficiency and general thermal performance resulted from this research, most of it was far removed from the mundane requirements of domestic and small-scale industrial and commercial water heating. It is not an extra few per cent of thermodynamic efficiency which attracts potential customers; the real need is for cheap, durable and simple systems which can be installed and maintained easily.

Another application of solar energy is the distillation of water. Solar distillation was being successfully used in Chile in the last century and since then the basic method has not changed much. Salt water flows along trays with a black heat-absorbent floor. When the sun is shining, the heat absorbed causes the water to evaporate and it condenses on a sloping glass cover plate and runs off into a collecting channel. The output of a solar still is low: it produces about 3 litres per square metre per day. This is a major limitation on the widespread use of solar distillation. The capital costs of a plant with a large output would be so high that they are unlikely to be able to produce water for domestic or industrial use at an affordable price. There is hope, however, that simple designs using low-cost materials may be able to supply limited supplies of drinking water in parts of the developing world.

Much higher temperatures than those common in flat-plate collectors can be obtained by using focusing collectors. A 'magnifying' glass is one such device, and Lavoisier used a lens as big as a man for some of his experiments in 1774. The application has an even longer history if Archimedes really did use focusing mirrors to set the Roman fleet on fire in 212 B.C.

The modern focusing collector uses a mirror rather than a lens. The temperature at the focus is determined by the area of the collector and by the precision with which the energy is focused. Simple concave collectors about 1·2 metres in diameter can bring a litre of water to the boil in about fifteen minutes, but temperatures as high as 4000°C have been achieved in the Odeillo furnace in the French Pyrenees. Here, ranks of adjustable mirrors on a hillside reflect sunlight down on to a large concave mirror, which in turn focuses on to a furnace. The absolutely clean heat supplied and the high temperature are useful in many research programmes.

A number of electricity generating stations relying on the sun's heat, sometimes referred to as solar thermo-electric stations, were built during the 1970s and early 1980s. Two 500-kilowatt installations costing a total of $30 million were opened in Spain in 1980. One of these used an array of mirrors, or heliostats, to focus the heat on a central receiver from which the heat was conveyed to the steam boiler by a liquid sodium coolant. The other used a series of long parabolic solar collectors each of which had a heat-absorbing pipe at its focus on which the radiant energy was concentrated; the heat transfer medium in this case was oil. Other solar thermo-electric plants have been built in Italy, Japan and the USA. The Japanese efforts proved particularly disappointing and solar thermo-electric research was abandoned in 1984.

The future is not at all bright for solar thermo-electric generation. The capital costs of these plants are extremely high. They occupy large areas of land for very small power outputs. They can function only during the hours of bright sunlight. The costs of maintenance and keeping the mirrors clean are also high. There are few who now believe they have any practical role in supplying future energy needs.

Another application of focusing collectors for which there have also been many hopes is as domestic cookers in the developing world. But in spite of many efforts to promote their use little has happened. The reasons for this are not hard to find. Solar cookers cost money; most of the people at whom they were aimed in the developing countries are very poor; even when fuel is scarce, there is usually enough to be found in the form of wood or waste agricultural materials to meet cooking needs without having to spend any money. There are also social and technical reasons why solar cookers are unpopular. Many people cannot or do not want to eat at midday, when it is easiest to use the cooker. Using the cooker involves cooking in the intense heat of the midday sun. Furthermore, the cookers tend to be large, cumbersome and dangerous to use: it is easy to be burned or scalded when trying to lean across to position a pot at the focal point of a cooker. The continual adjustment necessary also means that the woman doing the cooking is unable to carry out the manifold other tasks with which she is usually burdened. In short, solar cookers are almost invariably far more trouble than they are worth.

A major disadvantage of focusing collectors of all types is that they depend on clear sunlight. The flat-plate collector is able to use indirect solar radiation which has been scattered by clouds and atmospheric constituents on its way to the earth's surface, but this is useless to the focusing collector. Even slightly hazy conditions put it out of action. In addition, the focusing collector needs continual adjustment when it is operating: the flat-plate collector will pick up heat if it is oriented in the general direction of the sun, but the focusing collector is useless unless it is pointed precisely at the sun.

There have also been attempts to develop solar-powered mechanical engines. The laws of thermodynamics dictate that those which rely on flat-plate collectors will inevitably be very inefficient. A solar-powered engine depending on heat delivered at, say, 65°C and working over a temperature drop of 40°C would have a theoretical operating efficiency of only 12 per cent. In practice, operating losses will bring this down to 2–3 per cent.

To obtain any useful amount of power, the area of collector has to be immense: at 2 per cent efficiency, 50 square metres are required to deliver a 1-kilowatt output. A number of experimental solar engines were installed in the West African Sahel during the 1970s, but they were extremely expensive. Typical costs (in 1979 figures) were around $50 000 per kilowatt, compared with around $150 per kilowatt for a diesel engine. Not surprisingly, the solar engines did not proceed beyond the experimental stage.

Higher mechanical efficiencies can be obtained by using focusing collectors to make steam which is then used to drive conventional reciprocating or turbine engines. Such engines have been made – one which ran a printing press was exhibited in Paris in 1878. The most successful seems to have been one built in Egypt in 1913 which developed up to 40 kilowatts and was used for pumping water from the Nile. The fact that these engines can work only when there is bright direct sunshine limits their use, though it is possible to imagine circumstances in which short bursts of operation, whenever conditions are favourable, could be turned to some useful purpose. In the early part of the present century J. A. Harrington, a solar enthusiast in New Mexico, used a solar-powered engine to pump water into a high-level storage tank from which it ran down to operate a water turbine and electricity generator. But the cost, operating limitations and general impracticality of these engines have rendered them little more than curiosities.

The solar technology which has evoked the greatest interest, and which probably has the greatest worldwide potential, is that of solar photovoltaics – the direct production of electricity from sunlight. This is possible because of what is called the photoelectric effect: when light falls on certain materials electrons are displaced; if enough can be made to do this and they can be collected and passed through an external circuit and returned to the parent material, a means of electricity generation is created. The photoelectric effect was first noted by Hertz in 1887; its explanation by Einstein in 1905 was one of the major steps on the way to the development of the quantum theory.

A photovoltaic cell is designed to exploit the photoelectric effect for practical purposes. It is in two layers with a barrier between: one layer contains electrons which can be displaced by light and is known as the negative layer, or N-layer; the other is called the positive layer, or P-layer. When a photon of light of the correct energy level is absorbed, it detaches an electron in the N-layer and creates a positive 'hole' in the P-layer. The electrons flow through a wire connecting the two layers and are neutralized by the 'holes'. A current is created in the wire, no material is consumed and the cell can continue operating indefinitely. A solar panel consists of an array of cells fitted into a rigid supporting framework.

The most common material used for making photovoltaic cells is silicon, which is one of the most abundant elements in the earth's crust. The silicon is purified so that the content of other materials is less than 1 part per million. A trace of arsenic or phosphorus is then deliberately added to the silicon used in making the N-layer; that used in the P-layer has a trace of boron added. This process, known as doping, is essential if each layer is to have the required electrical properties. Between the two doped layers there is a barrier layer of pure silicon.

The manufacture of solar cells is a high-precision process which is very expensive. A vast amount of effort has been devoted to developing ways of making it cheaper. One of the most promising approaches is the use of amorphous rather than crystalline silicon. Amorphous silicon absorbs more light and so can be used in much smaller quantities. Work has also been carried out on gallium arsenide cells. The original photoelectric light meter cell which was developed around the turn of the century used selinium, but its low efficiency makes it impractical for electricity generation.

Most practical solar photovoltaic cells have operating efficiencies in the range of 5–7 per cent, though laboratory cells have been made with efficiencies of 20 per cent and higher. It is possible that cells with efficiencies of 8–10 per cent will be commercially available within the next five years or so.

The cost of photovoltaic cells remains the biggest barrier to their use. They first found application on a significant scale in the space programmes, where they were used to provide power for satellites and spacecraft. The amounts of power required were tiny and there were virtually no economic restrictions on costs: prices of $50 000 per kilowatt of output were quoted in the late

1960s and early 1970s. Since then costs have fallen, though at nothing like the rate forecast by the solar industry. The costs of solar photovoltaic panels are now in the range of between $8000 and $10 000 per kilowatt of peak operating power. This leaves them still a long way from being economically competitive with alternative sources of electricity generation.

At present, solar photovoltaic panels are used to provide electric power for buoys, telecommunication relay stations and other applications where other power sources would be very expensive. Small-scale lighting kits, in which a solar panel charges a battery during the daytime, are also being used for holiday cabins or, in a few instances, for remote medical stations in the developing world. Photovoltaic-powered water pumps have also been installed by technical assistance agencies and charities in some parts of the developing world. There is a lively debate about their economics in comparison with other power sources; but for people with little or no money it is largely academic since they cannot afford the cost of between $10 000 and $15 000 required for a solar pumping installation.

The day when solar photovoltaic systems become a part of everyday life is thus a considerable way into the future. Nevertheless, slow progress is being made. This is a research area of intense interest and enormous potential.

One of the most curious methods of harnessing the sun is the 'solar pond' developed in Israel by Harry Tabor in 1958. The pond is about a metre deep with a black heat-absorbent bottom. The lower part is filled with a concentrated brine solution and over this is carefully poured a layer of ordinary water; the difference in density prevents the two from mixing. The brine is heated by its contact with the heat-absorbent bottom, but because of its high density remains trapped below the ordinary water, which acts as an insulation. Quite remarkably high temperatures, approaching 100°C, are attained in the brine. The heat is drawn off by an organic fluid with a low boiling point which evaporates and drives a special low-temperature electricity-generating turbine, also developed in Israel.

Work ceased between 1966 and 1974 because of low petroleum prices, but in 1975 development of the solar pond was declared a 'national project' with a budget of $20 million. In 1979 a prototype generating station with a peak output of 150 kilowatts was opened on the shores of the Dead Sea; it drew its power from a solar pond with an area of 7500 square metres. Following its success, construction of a 5-megawatt station was commenced in 1983.

Solar energy can also be used to cool buildings. The mechanical equipment for this is akin to that used in the domestic refrigerator, which uses the mechanical energy supplied by a compressor pump to take heat from the refrigerator cabinet and expel it to the outside air. In the solar cooling device an absorption-desorption circuit is used, employing principles which were demonstrated as long ago as 1824 by Faraday. The thermodynamics are complicated but, basically, cooling is achieved by evaporating ammonia and absorbing it in a 'carrier fluid' which is then regenerated by being passed through a solar collector. Here the ammonia is re-vaporized and then passed through a condenser where it loses its heat and is liquefied to begin the cycle again. There is an inherent logic in the use of solar energy for cooling. The greatest need for cooling occurs when the solar energy required to provide it is available. This is in contrast with solar heating applications, which are most needed when there is no solar energy whatsoever. The application of solar cooling for cold storage, commercial and domestic use thus has considerable potential. But the cooling systems so far developed are more elaborate, expensive and unreliable than those powered in more conventional ways.

In the last decade or so, the term 'passive solar design' has come into use to describe the design of buildings to increase their utilization of the solar energy falling upon them. All buildings are, of course, passive solar collectors. They are heated by the radiation falling on their roofs and walls and by that passing through their windows. Indeed, one of the problems with many modern buildings is that they can be so effective in collecting solar energy that they have to be air-conditioned in order to make them habitable during sunny weather.

Many traditional types of buildings deal with the problems of heating and cooling very well. A variety of techniques are used. Thick walls intercept the solar radiation during the day, preventing an excessive build-up of heat inside the building. But at night this heat is slowly released, providing warmth as the outside temperatures fall. Windows may be shuttered against the noonday sun and later opened to provide cooling draughts. Overhangs and courtyards are strategically positioned to provide shade and prevent an excessive build-up of heat.

Modern passive design of buildings seeks to incorporate and build upon these traditions. In the USA, France and Scandinavia a large number of so-called 'solar houses' have been built in which a variety of techniques are used to try to capture and utilize the incident solar radiation to the best effect. The 'Trombe wall' developed by Professor Felix Trombe in France is one such feature. It is illustrated in Figure 8. A glass sheet is fixed in front of a wall facing the sun. The wall absorbs heat and in turn heats the air in the gap between wall and glass, causing it to rise. To cool the building the bottom flap in the glass sheet is kept shut and the top one opened. The heated warm air flows upwards and draws cool air into the house from the shaded rear. To heat the building the top flap is closed and the bottom left open.

It is thus clear that solar energy can be harnessed and used in a variety of ways. At the same time, because of its very nature, it poses considerable technical problems. One of the biggest obstacles to its wider use is its variability. During the day its intensity varies from zero at sunrise and sunset to a peak at noon. The noon peak itself varies from a minimum at the winter solstice to a maximum at the summer solstice. On top of these inherent, and regular, variations must be superimposed the random fluctuations imposed by weather conditions. The regular processes of industrial society are ill suited to such a varying and unreliable energy source. Solar energy cannot be used as the primary supply in any application where regularity and reliability are important. This means that solar energy applications are restricted to topping up heating systems when the sun is shining, or supplying heat for swimming pools or other such purposes where interruption of supply does not particularly matter. Only in areas where there is reliable, year-round sunshine, which in fact tend to be deserts below latitudes of about 40°, can solar energy be relied upon as a primary energy source. Many of the present difficulties could, however, be overcome if a cheap way of storing solar energy could be devised, and this is the aim of much modern research.

Figure 8. 'Trombe' wall

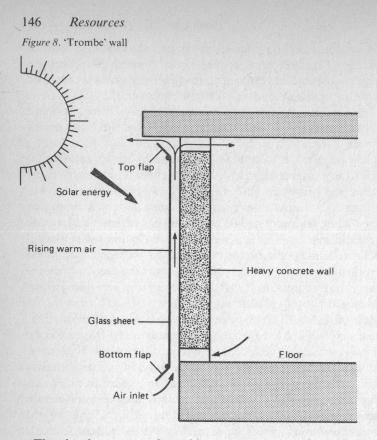

Solar energy

Top flap

Rising warm air

Heavy concrete wall

Glass sheet

Bottom flap

Floor

Air inlet

The simplest approach avoids any energy transformation and just relies on the capacity of materials to store heat. Thus the water heated by a flat-plate collector during the day can be stored in a well-insulated tank and drawn off in the evening. In a 'solar house' depending on solar collectors to provide some of its space heating, heat from the collector is passed, as hot water or air, to a water storage tank or a bed of concrete or rock fragments underneath the house; in the evening the heat is drawn off and circulated through radiators or a hot-air heating system. Depending on the size of the heat store and the collector, enough heat can be retained to bridge over cold periods lasting up to perhaps a week. But this system is obviously quite expensive and almost impossible to install in anything except a large new building. An ingenious variation of this method is the use of a pool of water on the roof of the house. In winter it absorbs heat during the day, and at night heavily insulated covers are drawn across and the stored heat is released downwards into the house. In summer the process is reversed: the pool is covered during the day and absorbs heat from the house, and this heat is released to the atmosphere at night when the covers are drawn back.

Such methods of solar heat storage introduce no novel principles. They are variations on the age-old principle of using massive wall construction to store heat during the day and release it at night. At most they can store about a week's supply of energy. They are mainly applicable in areas where there is regular year-round sunshine but a sharp drop in night-time temperatures which make it necessary for houses to be provided with some form of heating system. They are of little relevance in a climate such as that of the UK, where the mean daily sunshine in December and January is just about an hour and a half, and for six months of the year scarcely exceeds three and a half hours a day. Under these conditions the collector would not be able to charge the store sufficiently during the day to keep the house warm overnight, let alone carry it through a week of dark and frosty weather. To solve that problem and enable a house to obtain all its heat from the sun a method of storing heat in summer for use in winter is required.

Work has been carried out on methods of heat storage which rely on the heat absorption during a change of state from liquid to gas or from solid to liquid. When, for instance, ice melts, a large amount of heat is absorbed without any rise in temperature: it takes about eighty times as much heat to turn a quantity of ice into water as it does to raise its temperature the last degree from $-1°C$ to $0°C$. When the ice re-forms, this 'latent heat' is given off. For solar heat storage a substance is required which melts at the temperature reached by water from a flat-plate collector, and which can then be easily stored at that temperature.

The most promising substance investigated thus far is Glauber's salt ($Na_2SO_2.10H_2O$). It melts at about $32°C$, dissolving in its own water of crystallization, and absorbing 67 watt-hours per kilogram – so 1 kilowatt-hour of energy storage would require about 15 kilograms. When the liquid is cooled slightly it recrystallizes, giving off this heat. This is, obviously, an expensive method of energy storage and to date has not been made to work particularly effectively. Repeated cycles of heating and cooling cause variations in concentration to occur in the liquid and can prevent recrystallization occurring at all within the temperature range required. The search for a better medium goes on, but with few reports of promising discoveries.

During the 1970s there were numerous fanciful proposals for solving the world's energy problems. One of these was that huge satellites with arrays of silicon solar cells should be placed in geostationary orbit round the earth so that they could collect solar energy and beam it back to earth as microwave radiation. While this is certainly an attractive idea for the companies involved in aerospace research, as an energy proposition it is more dubious. A rather scathing comment on this by Professor H. C. Hottel, a leading solar energy scientist, was:

> The proposal that ... we put up giant satellites to intercept solar energy, convert it there to microwave radiation, beam it to earth in a dilute enough form not to make a death ray of it, reconvert it to electrical energy and then transmit it to our cities appears even less attractive in its long-range possibilities. It puts in series at least four steps each one of which is far beyond our present capability except at prohibitive cost.[23]

There is now little talk of such schemes. Most of the euphoria about solar energy which was such a feature of the 1970s and early 1980s has now vanished. Progress in harnessing solar energy remains disappointingly slow. There are good reasons for this. Although solar energy is abundant, it is diffuse and difficult to collect. The energy may be free, but its collection is expensive. Nor is there any prospect of this changing greatly. This is not because the secrets of solar energy have not been penetrated; the barriers to progress are the well-understood laws and principles of thermodynamics.

In 1971 Hottel summarized the existing position and immediate prospects for solar-energy use as follows:

> Domestic hot water from the sun is economically significant in many areas today, solar house heating in some, and its prospects are improving; solar distillation to produce fresh water from saline water is economic in areas of extremely high fossil-fuel cost (certainly not in the US main-

land); solar electric power from photovoltaic cells is significant in space research where the laws of terrestrial economics are inapplicable and it has some chance of becoming much cheaper. There are certainly enough of these areas to justify a vigorous research programme, but a major effect on the national energy picture is not to be expected.[23]

Sadly, the picture has scarcely changed today. Nor is there anything yet in sight which could alter it.

Hydro Power

The energy of fast-flowing or falling water was recognized at least as long ago as 85 BC. At about this time, a poem by the Greek poet Antipater celebrates the liberation of maidens from the task of grinding corn by hand: a waterwheel enables the water nymphs to do the work for them. Mithridates, whom Pompey defeated in 65 BC, was famous for his possession of a watermill. And Vitruvius, writing in about 20 BC, described in detail a watermill for grinding corn.

The Roman empire developed water power as a means of freeing for military use horses which were previously used to drive corn mills. It was not the first, or last, technological advance to be spurred by military objectives. Their development of water power, however, made the Romans vulnerable to interruptions in its supply. When the Goths cut the Trajan aqueduct in AD 536, an alternative source of power had to be found and Belisarius is said to have developed the floating watermill. This operated between two boats moored on the Tiber, being driven by the water flowing between them. Mills of this type were used for centuries afterwards and in medieval towns were frequently moored beneath the arches of the larger bridges. Although the output of power was small, the mill had the advantage of being able to work irrespective of the water level.

The Domesday Book records no less than 5624 watermills in Britain, indicating the heavy dependence of the medieval economy on water power. At the peak of their use in Britain there were as many as 20 000 mills in action. They were used not only for grinding corn but for operating bellows and hammers in forging iron, for sharpening tools and weapons, for textile manufacture, for tanning and even for pumping water from mines. By modern standards, however, the output of power from the watermill was small. The larger mills rarely delivered more than about ten kilowatts, while the smaller domestic ones produced little more than half or three quarters of a kilowatt.

There were numerous designs of watermill. Water was delivered through a 'flume', or channel, to the top of the 'overshot' wheel and at mid-height in the 'breast wheel' design. At their best, these were able to capture about 60 per cent of the energy in the flowing water. They also suffered from the limitation of being unable to make effective use of a head of water much greater than their own diameter. The 'undershot' wheel was the simplest type and basically just dipped into the flowing water; it had a maximum efficiency of only about 20 per cent.

John Smeaton, builder of the Eddystone Lighthouse, was one of the later designers who brought the waterwheel to its most refined form. A mill built by him at Merthyr Tydfil in 1800 was capable of producing about forty kilowatts. One of the largest mills ever built was in the Isle of Man and delivered 150 kilowatts from a wheel twenty-two metres in diameter.

The waterwheel, in any of its traditional forms, was, however, a technical dead-end. Further advances in harnessing water power did not come until the development of the turbine. Much of the pioneering work was done in France during the nineteenth century when Poncelet, Burdin and Clapeyron were the most prominent workers. Other notable work was done by J. B. Francis in America and James Thomson in England. Two main types of turbine were developed: the impulse and the reaction. The impulse turbine has a wheel with a set of buckets fixed around the rim. A high-speed jet of water shoots from a nozzle into the buckets, causing the wheel to spin rapidly. The most commonly used turbine of this kind is now the Pelton wheel, patented in 1880 by L. A. Pelton in California. These are usually used where there is a high head and a low volume of water flow, conditions typical of high mountainous country. Pelton wheels delivering 60 000 kilowatts have been built and, under ideal operating conditions, efficiencies of over 90 per cent are obtained.

Reaction turbines have vaned wheels inside a curved pressure casing through which the water flows. There are numerous designs which have been developed to suit different conditions. In tidal flows, or slowly moving rivers, efficiencies are low, but with a moderate or high head of water they can exceed 90 per cent. Reaction turbines with very high output capacities can be built. On the Yenisey River in Siberia there is a power station with twelve turbines each of 500 megawatts, and a further plant of twelve 550-megawatt turbines under construction. Churchill Falls in Canada has eleven 480-megawatt turbines. Units producing up to 1 500 megawatts are theoretically possible. One of the main reasons for not building such large units is the big change in load which occurs when they are switched in or out of service.

Hydro power installations are now invariably used to produce electricity. This makes good energetic sense. The use of water power to generate electricity is not subject to the thermo-dynamically inevitable 'heat-engine' energy losses which occur in a fossil-fuel-powered generating station. In a hydro power station up to 90 per cent of the potential energy is converted to electricity. Even for small-scale applications, therefore, it is, with rare exceptions, more efficient to produce electricity and use this to power any machinery than to use the mechanical power of the turbine directly. The old picturesque watermill transmitting the energy it took from the water through a series of creaking gears and belts was extremely inefficient.

There is plenty of energy to be obtained from the world's rivers. The theoretical amount obtainable from any river system is given by the volume of water multiplied by the drop through which it falls, but, of course, much of this cannot be recovered in practice. Dams cannot be built everywhere there is a harnessable fall in a river. Confinement in reservoirs increases the evaporation losses, hence reducing the river flow. Seasonal peaks or floods tend to exceed the generating capacity of the plant installed and have to be run to waste once the storage reservoir has been filled; during the dry season the flow may be too small for use. The potential output of a river system is usually calculated for 'average flow conditions'. It can be quite a small fraction of the figure obtained from a purely theoretical calculation of the total energy available.

The yield of every hydro-electric installation is progressively reduced by silting of its reservoirs. This is an inevitable process. All rivers carry some silt which is deposited in the still waters of the reservoir, thus decreasing its storage capacity. In some locations provision can be made for flushing out part of the reservoir but this is often impossible. The wide expanses of water behind most hydro-electric dams are thus destined to become the swamps and mudflats of a later age. Conditions vary so much between river systems that no general figures can be given, but the life of many reservoirs is probably not much more than a century. While a river is non-depleting, each hydro-electric station has a finite life determined by the rate at which its reservoir is filled with silt. Some rivers are so silt-laden that it would be pointless even to try to harness them.

But, even with these reservations, the hydro-electric potential of the world is very large. Some individual rivers are particularly notable. The potential of the Yenisey–Angara in the USSR is estimated at 64 000 megawatts, about the same as the whole electricity generating capacity of all kinds in the UK; that of the Inga River in the Congo at 25 000 megawatts; and that of the Bramaputra in India at 20 000 megawatts.

Table 18 shows the distribution of the world's potential hydro-electric resources. It lists the possible generating capacity which each country might install, and it gives an estimate of the output which might be obtained from this. Note how much the output per megawatt of installed capacity varies. This is because of the different flow characteristics of each river system. It is obvious from the table that some countries get very much better value than others for each unit of installed capacity. It is also noticeable that South America, Africa and South East Asia, regions poor in coal and oil have major water-power resources, only about 20 per cent of which are yet developed. In Europe some 80 per cent of the total potential is already exploited; in America about 60 per cent.

The present installed hydro-electric capacity in the world is about 490 000 megawatts, about 22 per cent of its potential. These installations contribute the amount of electricity which would be obtained from burning about 500 million tonnes of oil. This is 6·7 per cent of the world's present primary energy consumption. The output of hydro-electricity has been growing at about 3·5 per cent per year over the past decade.

If the whole of the world's hydro-electric potential were har-

Table 18. World hydro-electric potential: 'average flow conditions'

	Theoretical capacity (usable MW)	Theoretical annual output (GWh)
China	330 000	1 320 000
USSR	269 000	1 095 000
USA	186 700	701 500
Zaire	132 000	660 000
Canada	94 500	535 200
Brazil	90 200	519 300
Malagasy	64 000	320 000
Colombia	50 000	300 000
India	70 000	280 000
Burma	75 000	225 000
N. Vietnam and Laos	48 000	192 000
Argentina	48 100	191 000
Indonesia	30 000	150 000
Japan	49 600	130 000
Ecuador	21 000	126 000
Papua-New Guinea	17 800	121 700
Norway	29 600	121 000
Cameroon	23 000	114 800
Peru	12 500	109 200
Pakistan	20 000	105 000
Sweden	20 100	100 300
Mexico	20 300	99 400
Venezuela	11 600	98 000
Chile	15 800	88 600
Gabon	17 500	87 600
All other nations	514 800	2 011 800
WORLD TOTAL	2 261 100	9 802 400

Source: World Energy Conference, *Survey of Energy Resources*, 1974.

nessed, the contribution to world energy consumption would be equivalent to using 2·45 billion tonnes of oil to generate electricity, about 33 per cent of the present world total energy consumption. But a full development of the world's hydro resources would come into conflict with some of the other vital needs of human society. Water is required for many other purposes besides electricity generation. Irrigation is one of the most important in many of the developing countries. The use of rivers for navigation and fisheries may also be difficult to reconcile with their harnessing for electricity generation. The creation of large lakes can also cause immense social and ecological damage; the opposition campaigns which are mounted against many large hydro-electric schemes are growing steadily more sophisticated and effective.

Hydro-electric schemes flood large areas of land. The Cabora Bassa Scheme in Mozambique has a lake 250 kilometres long, covering an area of 2700 square kilometres, with an output capacity of just 2000 megawatts – though there are plans to double this. As long as the land is in barren mountainous regions its loss may be acceptable, but many countries would not find it easy to flood their fertile lowland valleys, no matter how great their need for electricity.

Finance is also a problem: hydro-electric schemes require heavy capital investments, and the long construction times involved usually mean that benefits are delayed for at least a decade. Many of the developing countries with exploitable hydro-electric potential find they have more immediately pressing demands on their available capital. International lending agencies such as the World Bank and the major industrial nations have been willing to provide funds for projects such as Aswan, Kariba, and Cabora Bassa in the past. But the emphasis in international technical assistance has switched away from such projects over the past ten to fifteen years, and it is now very difficult for a developing country to find the funds for a large hydro-electric project.

One of the reasons for this is that electricity is irrelevant to the problems afflicting the majority of people in most of the poorer developing countries. A high level of electricity consumption presupposes a level of wealth sufficient to enable people to purchase electrical appliances. When this is so, domestic energy consumption can be extremely high. In the UK, for example, 37 per cent of the total output of electricity is used by domestic consumers; home use is actually greater than the total used by industry. The poor farmers and shanty-town dwellers of the developing world have no way of consuming electricity on a scale remotely approaching this.

There is a danger that hydro-electric schemes in such countries, unless carefully integrated with the development of productive uses for electricity, will exacerbate rather than ease the problems of poverty, malnutrition and scarcity of capital from which they chronically suffer. The only beneficiaries of indiscriminate hydro-electric development can, too easily, turn out to be those who live in the wealthy areas of the big cities and those involved in big industrial enterprises such as aluminium smelters, which are usually outposts of the industry of the developed countries.

Hydro power nevertheless continues to make progress around the world. Power stations in mountainous areas are increasingly being built as underground constructions for economic and technical reasons. It is also being found that some natural lakes can be utilized as reservoirs without building dams, but simply by piercing the lake from below. Small-scale and mini-scale hydro power stations are also being used to meet the needs of isolated communities in many countries.

The development of hydro power is thus likely to carry on. It can be a very important resource in a country which has steeply falling rivers and the capital and technical resources to exploit them. Norway, for instance, obtains all its electricity from hydro power. The greater proportion of the resources so far untapped, however, are in the developing world. It will be a long time before they are harnessed to meet the energy needs of the countries in which they are found.

Tides, Waves and Thermal Gradients

Watching the waves breaking on the shore, or the daily rise and fall of the tides, gives the feeling that there should be a simple way of harnessing this obvious source of energy. The frustrations of practical research in solar energy and in tidal or wave power have many similarities. The energy is there, and in quantity, but extremely difficult to tap.

Historically, the development of the tidal mill parallels that of the river mill, but the obvious geographical limitations and the inherent difficulties in use prevented it from becoming a comparably important source of energy. One of the earliest British wheels was in operation in Wapping in 1233; it was owned by the Priory of the Holy Trinity at Aldgate. Many of these wheels operated successfully for centuries: one of the last to cease working was that of Pomphlett in Devon, which went out of action only in 1956.

The typical tidal mill was situated some distance inland on a tidal creek. The incoming tide flowed into a millpond, the gates of which were closed at high water. After the tide had ebbèd, the gates were opened and the outflowing water was used to drive the mill.

The disadvantages are obvious. No two consecutive milling days could be the same because of the timing of the tide. And because of the variation in flow between spring and neap tides, a different amount of water was stored each day, thus altering the output of the mill. Also, since the output of any mill depends on the head of water driving it, the power output of a tidal mill varied throughout each period of operation, being greatest when the pond was full and declining as it emptied. Much ingenuity went into coping with these problems. Many mills used two or more ponds to store water for use during low tides or to boost output as the water level dropped in the main pond. A variable mode of operation was also developed, with sluices being used to make the wheel operate as overshot, breast or undershot, depending on the water level.

Much the same limitations apply to modern tidal power installations. The station is available only about a quarter of the time, and its peaks of power output vary not in accordance with loads on the electricity supply system, but in accordance with the times of the tides. These disadvantages can be overcome only by the use of elaborate secondary or even tertiary storage basins. As with other renewable energy sources, the costs of recovering the 'free' energy are prohibitive in all but the most favourable circumstances.

The total estimated potential electricity supply from tidal power is about 200 000 gigawatt-hours. If it were produced, the saving would be about 250 million tonnes of oil, or about 3 per cent of the world's total primary energy consumption. This is the outer limit and only a very small fraction of this is ever likely to be developed. In fact, only four areas have any real possibility of development within the next few decades. These are the Bay of Fundy, which lies between Nova Scotia and mainland Canada, the Severn Estuary in the UK, the Sea of Okhotsk on the eastern coast of the USSR, and La Rance on the north-west coast of France. In each of these areas the average tidal range is considerably higher than normal: ten metres in the Bay of Fundy, six metres in the Severn, seven in the Sea of Okhotsk, and eight metres at La Rance.

At present, only one large tidal power station is in operation. This is at La Rance and was opened in 1966; it has a maximum output of 240 megawatts. It has operated satisfactorily but has led to little significant follow-up in other countries. Both the USSR and China have built small experimental stations of about 500 kilowatts and an 18-megawatt station was opened at Annapolis in the Bay of Fundy in 1984. There have also been numerous studies: the Severn, which has been investigated on and off for many decades, was restudied in the early 1980s and the report is being considered by the government. The French government also examined the possibility of building further tidal stations between 1980 and 1984, but finally rejected the idea.

Even though they are in themselves almost completely non-polluting, one of the major obstacles to tidal power stations is environmental. They introduce major ecological changes and can destroy the habitats and nesting places of water birds, as well as interfering with fisheries. A tidal station at the mouth of a river can also block the flow of polluted water into the sea, thereby creating health and pollution hazards in the estuary.

The outlook for tidal power is thus not particularly promising. But the efforts of inventors to harness the energy of the waves has been even less rewarding. The list of dotty technical ideas which has been proposed is a long one. A surprising addition was provided by no less august a body than the UK government's Central Policy Review Staff, its 'think-tank', in 1974. The suggestion was that a system of 'wave-generators' [sic] over a length of 900 miles of coastline would be able to produce about 30 000 megawatts, or sufficient to meet half the country's electricity requirements. The proposal deserves quoting if only for its optimism and technical naivety:

The technology required for wave-generation is not expected to be particularly sophisticated. It could, for example, take the form of a system of floating tanks located about a mile offshore, tethered to each other and to concrete blocks on the seabed. The 'up and down' motion caused by the waves would be used to drive a high-pressure water pump with the resultant high-pressure water being used to drive a turbine generator located on the shore. A 60-megawatt installation would extend to a length of about 1·7 miles and the tanks would have a height above water of about 4 feet . . . Wave-generators could not be installed immediately and some development work would have to be undertaken, but lead times would be comparatively short. Wave-generators would certainly have objections on aesthetic grounds and could cause some hindrance to coastal shipping. There would, in addition, be the danger that floats might break loose.[24]

Not surprisingly, nothing came of this suggestion. But the attention of the press and public was caught by the proposal of Dr Stephen Salter of the University of Edinburgh. In order to get away from the idea of an object bobbing up and down, he envisaged using the motion of the waves to drive a series of rocking vanes; they acquired the nickname of Salter's nodding· ducks. The original proposal was nothing if not ambitious. Huge assemblies of these devices were to be set floating in the stormy reaches of the Atlantic out beyond the Hebrides; there they would generate electricity which would be used to produce hydrogen by the electrolysis of water. He said:

> The installations could be self-propelled. They could move line-ahead, a low drag condition, out into the Atlantic, turn abreast to the waves and be driven slowly back by wind and wave thrust, storing hydrogen on the way. Most of the hydrogen would be discharged at a shore terminal leaving enough to get to sea again.[25]

At a more practical level, a considerable programme of theoretical and practical research into large-scale wave power was carried out in the U K during the 1970s and early 1980s. The various devices investigated included a version of the Salter ducks, rafts hinged at the middle with pistons and pumps at either side of the hinge, columns of water oscillating up and down inside tubes, a 'sea clam' which harvests energy when waves force air out of a bag, and pressure-sensitive devices sitting on the sea bed. There is no question that the energy in the waves is extremely large, and that, in principle, devices such as these can tap it, but the practical problems are immense. Any sailor, harbour engineer or offshore oilrig constructor knows the awesome power of winter storms at sea. Producing a device which can survive these conditions and generate useful amounts of electricity has proved itself a daunting task. In 1985 the U K government more or less abandoned its research into large-scale harnessing of wave power.

Work in Norway on land-based wave power stations has, however, been successful. A 500-kilowatt prototype has been built on the coast at Tostestallen, north of Bergen. The design is referred to as an oscillating water column. Waves enter at the bottom of a 20-metre-high cylinder; the oscillation of the column of water drives air through a special turbine at the top. These turbines, which were developed by Professor Alan Wells in Queen's University, Belfast, go round in the same direction regardless of the direction of the air flow. This station has been delivering electricity to the Norwegian national grid since 1985.

Development work is continuing and there are plans for a 10-megawatt station made up of a series of elements using the oscillating water column principle. Time and further experience are required to iron out some of the operating difficulties found in the prototype and to establish the real operating costs; but the outlook is promising. Even if very large stations are not found feasible, there would appear to be a considerable number of island or isolated coastal communities where such electricity generating stations might be able to provide electricity more economically than the diesel engine generators used today.

An interesting idea for harnessing the energy of waves breaking on a coral reef has been worked out in some detail by Noel Bott, former general manager of the Central Electricity Board of Mauritius. An impounding lagoon is built behind the coral reef. The high waves coming in from the Indian Ocean break on a slipway and run up into the lagoon which fills to a level of 1·5–2 metres above sea level. The water in the lagoon is then used to drive a series of pumps which lift water to the top of a nearby hill, whence it can run down to generate electricity.

A completely different approach to taking energy from the oceans is to exploit the thermal gradient which exists in the tropical deep oceans. In some areas the temperature difference between the surface and depths of about 1000 metres is as much as 25°C. In theory this difference could be used to drive a heat engine. The possibility was suggested by the French physicist Jacques d'Arsonval as long ago as 1881, and a 22-kilowatt trial plant was constructed in Cuba in 1930 and operated satisfactorily until it was destroyed in a hurricane.

This method of energy extraction is referred to as ocean thermal energy conversion (OTEC). Two types of energy converter can be used. In one, called the open cycle, the warm water is flash-evaporated to steam at low pressure, used to drive a turbine and then condensed by the cold water. In the other, called the closed cycle, a working fluid with a low boiling point such as ammonia is vaporized in a heat exchanger and recondensed in a cold water heat exchanger. The operating efficiency is very low because of the small temperature difference: a figure of 2·5 per cent overall is probably the best that can be achieved. As a result, installations have to be very large if they are to have a substantial output.

During the 1970s a number of 'conceptual designs' were proposed by companies in the USA such as the Lockheed Corporation, Westinghouse and others with experience in the outer reaches of military and space technology. These clearly showed the extent to which the sheer size of OTECs is a major obstacle to their development. For example, a 200-megawatt floating station would require a 30-metres diameter pipe stretching 1 kilometre deep into the ocean and drawing up some 1500 cubic metres of water per second. This is the equivalent of the normal flow of a major river such as the Missouri. The weight of the machine would be around 200 000 tonnes. Much of the metal work would need to be in titanium or stainless steel to resist corrosion.

Smaller land-based machines would avoid some of the problems inherent in such floating monsters, but they are still on a remarkably large scale considering their output. A 10-megawatt project proposed for the Nauru Island in the Pacific was to have four 2·3-metre-diameter pipes running 750 metres along the steeply sloping ocean bed to a depth of 500 metres. Laying such pipes is a major engineering feat more usually associated with the development of large petroleum resources rather than a minor power station.

The theoretical size of the potential OTEC resource is, in principle, more or less infinite. But it is obvious that only a very small proportion of this can ever be tapped economically. The only likely applications for OTECs are remote tropical islands with the appropriate ocean conditions immediately offshore. Another necessity is oil prices considerably higher than their present level.

Geothermal Power

The precise origin of the earth's internal heat is still debated. It is now estimated that about 40 per cent is generated by the radioactive decay of uranium, thorium and their derivatives, with the remaining 60 per cent being residual heat from the original formation of the earth. The rate of heat flow is tiny: about 0·0015 kilowatt-hours per square metre a day. The problem with geothermal power is the familiar one of concentrating a highly diffused energy flow into usable amounts. The fact that the temperature rises at an average rate of about 10°C for every kilometre of depth into the earth is apt to delude people into thinking that all that needs to be done is to drill a hole deep enough to reach the boiling temperature of water, pour water down it and use the resulting steam to drive turbines. It is not as simple as this. While the temperature rises with depth, the flow of heat remains almost the same: there is no more energy flowing through a square centimetre 10 kilometres down than there is at the surface. Water poured down a 10-kilometre-deep hole would therefore rapidly cool the surrounding rock by withdrawing from it its stored heat. After a first flush of energy recovery the maximum rate of heat extraction would drop down to the slow rate of natural heat flow through the rock. If geothermal energy is to be usable, this natural heat flow must be increased and concentrated.

The solid rocks of the earth's crust are usually about 30 to 40 kilometres thick in the land areas. At the base of the crust is the Mohorovicic discontinuity; below this is the mantle in which the rock is in a molten or semi-molten state. In some areas the mantle pushes upwards into the crust, increasing the local rate of heat flow. Sometimes the mantle breaks through to the surface in areas of volcanic activity; at other times it merely creates a local 'hot spot' detectable only with sensitive thermometers or aerial infra-red surveying.

If this increased rate of heat flow is to create a usable energy resource, it must occur in an area in which the geological conditions are favourable to the formation of a geothermal reservoir. This is similar to the rock trap within which oil or natural gas accumulates: a permeable reservoir rock capped by an impermeable stratum. Ground water which has been heated by contact with hot rocks percolates into the reservoir, where it becomes trapped beneath the cap-rock. If there are fissures in the cap-rock, some of the hot water, steam, or both, may escape to the surface, forming hot springs or geysers. In such cases the underground system is replenished by further infiltrations of ground water. In nature the rate of energy loss is usually closely matched by the rate of energy gain and the system can remain active for a long time, though activity gradually diminishes. Geyser basins have a life of up to ten thousand years; lower-temperature hot springs last considerably longer.

The use of natural hot springs goes back a long way. The Romans made systematic use of them for medicinal and recrea-

Table 19. World installed geothermal electricity generating capacity

	Installed capacity (megawatts)
USA	2002
Philippines	894
Mexico	645
Italy	479
Japan	215
New Zealand	167
El Salvador	95
Kenya	45
Iceland	39
Nicaragua	35
Indonesia	32
Turkey	21 *
China	11
USSR	11
Guadeloupe	4
Azores	3
Total	4719

* Presently inactive.
Source: World Energy Conference Survey of Energy Resources, 1986.

tional purposes as well as for domestic heating. Appropriately, the Italians were the pioneers of the use of geothermal energy for electricity generation. The first such plant was opened in Lardarello in northern Italy in 1913. By the end of 1985 the total installed capacity in the world was over 4700 megawatts. Table 19 shows how it is distributed between countries.

Heat from geothermal sources is, of course, still widely used in spas and hot baths – balneology, to give its formal title. Japan accounts for about two thirds of the total worldwide consumption for these purposes. Geothermal hot water is also used for domestic, industrial and horticultural heating. Excluding the amount used for balneology, the total geothermal heat utilized throughout the world is equivalent to about 2 million tonnes of oil per year. Iceland, where it is widely used for domestic and commercial heating, is the largest user, closely followed by the USSR. The next highest consumers are France, where it is used for domestic heating in the Paris region, and Hungary, which uses it mainly for horticulture.

Because steam temperatures tend to be low by modern power station standards, the use of geothermal energy for electricity generation tends to be very inefficient, often down to around 10 per cent. This means that 90 per cent of the energy is completely wasted. Where the heat can be used directly in buildings or greenhouses, the generating loss is avoided and a much more efficient use is made of the energy.

Harnessing geothermal energy is not without its problems. When used for electricity generation, the mineral properties of hot springs which give them their curative reputations are a real nuisance. The waters are rich in minerals because hot water under pressure is a powerful solvent; when the pressure is reduced, the water flashes into steam and a proportion of the mineral content is deposited. One result of this is that boreholes which supply power stations gradually have their diameter reduced and have to be redrilled every seven to ten years, which is both difficult and expensive. Serious pollution problems are also caused when these mineral-rich waters are run to waste from power stations: they can have very damaging effects on natural watercourses. One way of avoiding this is by reinjecting the water into the zone from which it has been extracted, but this adds considerably to the operating expenses.

Being accumulations of hot water, geothermal reservoirs deplete when they are tapped by boreholes. The life of any particular reservoir will obviously depend upon the rate at which energy is being used. As a rough generalization, the life of a large geothermal field at its maximum rate of exploitation should be in the range of between 50 and 100 years.

It is also possible in principle to obtain heat from deep-lying 'hot-dry' accumulations of heat. This involves drilling a borehole several kilometres deep and then fracturing the rock at the bottom by high-pressure water or the use of explosives. Heat can be recovered by pumping water down the borehole, through the fractured rock and up a second recovery borehole. But the techniques for achieving this are still at an experimental stage.

Work has been carried out in the USA and at the Camborne School of Mines in Cornwall in the UK in which experiments at a depth of about two kilometres in granite have given encouraging results. There are still difficult problems to be overcome. Even when the rock has been fractured, it is still difficult to drive the water through it. There are also major water losses through leakage into fissures which do not lead to the recovery borehole. It is thus not yet clear whether this technique is likely to be technically practical. Certainly, the energy produced by it would not be economically competitive at present energy prices. At best, it is a long-term possibility.

The amount of energy stored in the top five kilometres of the earth's crust is estimated to be about 40 million times that of world petroleum reserves, but because it is so diffused and at such a low temperature, only an infinitesimal proportion of this is recoverable. The exploitable resources tend to be in geologically active areas which may also show signs of volcanic activity along the western side of the Americas from Alaska to Chile; in Kenya, Uganda, Zaire, Tanzania and Ethiopia; in the Philippines, Indonesia, Burma and India; and in the countries around the Mediterranean, especially Turkey.

The annual growth in the output of electricity from geothermal power has been remarkably rapid over the past decade and a half: since 1970 it has averaged 14·5 per cent per year, doubling every five years. The technology is improving and economic drilling depths are increasing. While the high growth rates of the recent past are unlikely to be sustained for very much longer, the prospects for a steady increase in the use of geothermal energy for both heat and electricity generation are good. But until the far-distant possibilities of tapping into the very deep high-temperature rocks of the earth's crust are realized, geothermal energy will remain a minor energy source in the global context.

Wind Power

Old-fashioned sail windmills are perhaps the most aesthetically pleasing of all devices for harnessing energy. The earliest wind-mills, however, were of the vertical axis type and are reputed to have been in use in China more than 2000 years ago. In the west, windmills are mentioned in Arab writings of the ninth century. The first recorded northern European mills were in France in 1180 and in England in 1191.

Early windmill technology was often derived from that of the waterwheel, but in time a distinctive response to the very different problem of extracting energy from the wind was evolved. Air has a density nearly eight hundred times less than that of water. Therefore, to capture the same amount of energy from the same speed of flow, the windmill needs eight hundred times the blade area of the watermill. The windmill's requirements of size, light-ness, robustness and adaptability to varying speeds and directions of wind made heavy demands on the ingenuity and skill of its designers.

Windmill technology developed steadily over the centuries. Means of braking and feathering the sails and of remote control, and improvements in gearing and power transmission, combined to give it a role in the medieval economy comparable with that of the watermill. A particularly ingenious innovation was the fantail. Before its invention the difficult and dangerous job of keeping the sails facing into the wind had to be done by hand. The fantail was a small vaned wheel, another windmill in fact, mounted at right angles to the main sails, behind the cap of the windmill. When the wind veered out of alignment to the main sails, it began to turn the fantail. This operated a gearing arrangement which slewed the main sails back into the wind. This early example of a negative feedback device made a great difference to the safety and efficiency of windmills. It was patented in England in 1754 by Edmund Lee.

Large windmills could develop up to 30 kilowatts, which was enough for the milling needs of a small community. Holland, the country most famous for its windmills, had 8000 of them in the middle of the eighteenth century. But Germany had 18 000 in operation in the nineteenth century; Britain had 10 000, mainly in the windy south-eastern counties; and Portugal had 1000 operational as late as 1965. Small windmills, or 'windchargers', were a familiar sight in rural areas a couple of decades ago. These generated a small amount of electricity which was stored in batteries and used to operate domestic lighting circuits and radios. Many small wind machines are still in use in different parts of the world today, principally for pumping water for irrigation.

The sail windmill in its developed form was a beautiful solution to a very difficult set of problems. It is an immense tribute to its designers that it could in many cases compete with the watermill. Both, however, were the end of a line of technical development. The waterwheel was completely superseded by the much more efficient water turbine. The analogous development in wind power is the propeller mill. Most modern windmills are of this type, which rotates more quickly and is a generally more efficient energy collector than the sail mill. Unfortunately, no progress in the general development of wind power comparable with that which has occurred in the case of water power has taken place. Since the winds cannot be manipulated, dammed or pumped, like water, wind power has been relegated to a very minor role in the important business of generating electricity.

Most of the early work on generating electricity from wind was carried out in Denmark, starting at the end of the last century and continuing into the 1940s. Machines capable of generating up to 70 kilowatts were built. During the 1930s the Lucas 'Freelite' machine was on the commercial market in the UK; this could power four or five light bulbs of about 40 watts each. Similar machines were on sale in the USA. A 30-metre-diameter machine delivering 100 kilowatts was built in Russia in the 1930s.

The largest of all these machines was built during the 1940s in the USA at Grandpa's Knob in Vermont. This had a two-blade propeller 52·5 metres in diameter and delivered a maximum of 1250 kilowatts. Wartime difficulties with spare parts and finally an accident in which one of its blades broke off during a storm ended the life of this machine. Just after the war there was a surge of interest in the UK: a 100-kilowatt machine was built at St Albans and another in the Orkneys. Enthusiasm for these experiments was not sustained as electricity generation using coal or oil was then so cheap. The 1970s saw a renaissance of interest in wind power. Amateur enthusiasts and large engineering and aerospace companies alike became involved in reviving old designs or trying to produce new approaches to the harnessing of wind power.

The majority of windmills, or wind turbines as they are now generally described, are still of the horizontal axis type. In addition to an unknown number of older machines which are mainly used for water pumping, around 8000 wind turbines have been installed in the USA for electricity generation in the past decade or so. They range in size from 10 metres up to 45 metres in diameter, with outputs from 50 to 200 kilowatts. Most of the recently installed machines are in California; large numbers have been built in 'wind farms' in windy mountain passes. Over 2000 machines with a total generating capacity of 142 megawatts are found in the Altamont Pass near San Francisco. State legislation which provides substantial financial incentives to windmill builders and also compels electricity generating utilities to buy the electricity made wind energy a profitable investment in the late 1970s and early 1980s.

Research into large wind machines has also been carried out in Germany, Sweden, the UK and the USA. The world's largest wind turbine is in northern Germany; it has blades 100 metres in diameter and has an output of 3 megawatts. An even more powerful wind turbine, with an output of 4 megawatts, has been built in Wyoming in the USA; its rotor diameter is 78 metres. The higher power is a result of design differences and a more favourable wind regime. A 3-megawatt machine with a rotor diameter of 60 metres has also been built on Orkney Island to the north of Scotland and is due to be commissioned in late 1987.

There has also been a renewed interest in the vertical axis windmill. The main advantage of this is that it can be driven by wind blowing on it from any direction, and this obviates the expense and complexity of a device for keeping it oriented into the wind. The French engineer George Darrieus was granted the first patent for a vertical axis machine in 1920. Most vertical axis designs use a curved airfoil section in the form of a hoop – sometimes referred to as a 'tropeskein' shape – which eliminates the problem of bending, since the ring is primarily subjected to tension forces as it is spinning. Experiments are also being conducted in Canada and the UK into an H-shaped version with straight vertical airfoil sections at the ends of a horizontal axis. Machines of the vertical axis type look quite improbable as sources of power and will not start by themselves, but once under way they function perfectly adequately. Vibration as a result of the varying angle of attack as the blades rotate can, however, cause problems.

Wind energy is widely available, but it is also highly variable. Speed is a very important criterion: the power available in the wind varies as the cube of its velocity. When the wind speed falls by half, this means that it has only one eighth of the power. The ideal locations for wind turbines are where there are strong steady winds. Most commonly these are on high ground, or on wide flat plains where there are no obstructions to the flow of the wind.

Because of the low energy density of the wind, machines have to be extremely large if their output is to be substantial. For a peak generating power of a few megawatts, the rotor diameter needs to be in the range of 50 to 100 metres, set on a large steel lattice tower like a high-voltage transmission pylon. Such a machine is extremely noisy and highly dangerous if there is a blade failure in strong wind. It may also interfere badly with television reception. The modern wind turbine is thus far removed from the gentle and romantic image of the traditional windmill. Any attempt to replace a large conventional power station with, say, 500 giant wind turbines is likely to raise considerable public opposition on environmental and safety grounds.

Siting wind turbines in shallow offshore waters would obviate many of the problems associated with land-based machines. The wind regimes would also tend to be more favourable. But the construction and maintenance costs would be considerably increased. Studies in the UK, however, indicate that in the longer term such schemes might become technically and economically viable.

The outlook for wind power over the coming decades is not particularly encouraging. The progress made in the USA is unlikely to be sustained if, as seems likely, the financial incentives are withdrawn and wind power has to survive in commercial competition with other power sources. Nor are the large wind machines likely to find favour anywhere except in the most sparsely populated areas. Nevertheless, a solid technical foundation has been created. It is possible that a reasonable number of small or moderate-sized machines may find applications in isolated areas and island communities for electricity generation and pumping water.

10

Energy Conversion, Distribution and Storage

Electricity Distribution and Use

Electricity came into commercial use towards the end of the nineteenth century. Coal had been the foundation of the Industrial Revolution, making energy available in quantities for which there was no historical precedent. But it was an awkward fuel, dirty, unwieldy, difficult to transport and inefficient in use.

Electricity overcame most of these difficulties. It was clean. It could be transmitted instantly. It was versatile in its uses. It was economical in labour and space. Electricity also permitted the abundant energy of rivers and waterfalls to be harnessed and transmitted to distant consumers.

The first electric power station began operation in London on 12 January 1882; the next began in New York in September of the same year. Problems with payment of electricity bills must have been immediate. People who do not pay their bills in Britain today are disconnected under the provisions of the Electric Lighting Act of 1882. These early supply systems were small and primitive, using direct current transmitted at a low voltage. Service areas were limited by the length over which current could be transmitted economically, which was only a few kilometres. Transmission losses were so high that inter-city services were quite prohibitively expensive.

But technical advances and the use of higher voltages soon opened the way to transmission over longer distances. The loss when electricity is transmitted through a conductor is inversely proportional to the square of the voltage. Doubling the voltage therefore reduces the losses by a factor of four. The first long-distance transmission of electricity took place in Italy in 1886 – over a distance of twenty-seven kilometres. Technical progress was rapid, and direct current gave way to alternating current. One of the main advantages of this was that it made it practical to step up the voltage for transmission and step it down again for safety at the point of use. In 1896 an 11 000-volt line began to bring power from the generating station at Niagara Falls to nearby Buffalo, and by the turn of the century electricity was being transmitted at 40 000 volts over a distance of 110 kilometres in California.

Thereafter there was a continued increase in transmission distances and voltages. In 1936 the Los Angeles Department of Water and Power brought electricity from the Hoover dam over a distance of 430 kilometres at a voltage of 287 000 volts. Swedish engineers raised the voltage to 380 000 volts for the transmission line from the Harspranget power station, just north of the Arctic Circle, to southern Sweden, a distance of almost 1000 kilometres. In the 1960s and 1970s transmission lines at 765 000 volts were built in Canada and the USSR.

Table 20. Growth of world electricity production – 1929–82

Year	Production (TWh)
1929	(287)*
1935	(333)
1940	(482)
1945	(572)
1950	(858)
	957
1955	1535
1960	2301
1965	3377
1970	4923
1975	6530
1980	8237
1982	8459

* Figures in parentheses exclude USSR and China.
Source: UN, *Statistical Yearbooks*.

Electricity proved itself an almost ideal form of energy for domestic, commercial and industrial consumers. Many new uses were devised for it. Electric light superseded all other forms of illumination. Electric motors could be made tiny enough for the most delicate tasks or robust enough for heavy industrial use. Safe, clean, urban transport systems could be powered by electricity; domestic drudgery could be reduced by using cookers, refrigerators, vacuum cleaners and washing machines for clothes and dishes. Table 20 shows how its use has grown since 1929, roughly doubling every ten years.

More detailed figures of how electricity production is shared between the different regions of the world are given in Table 21. Of the total 1982 consumption, 33 per cent was produced in the USA, 26 per cent in Europe and 16 per cent in the USSR. The rest of the world shared the remaining 24 per cent. The picture for Africa is particularly abysmal: of its meagre share of the 1982 total, just over half is produced in South Africa.

Table 21. World electricity production by regions in 1970 and 1982

	1970 production (TWh)	1970 (% of total)	1982 production (TWh)	1982 (% of total)
Africa	87	1·8	206	2·4
North America	1898	38·6	2818	33·3
South America	108	2·2	295	3·5
Europe	1407	28·7	2180	26·2
Asia	612	12·4	1423	16·8
USSR	741	15·0	1345	15·9
Oceania	70	1·4	131	1·5
Total	4923	100·0	8459	100·0

Source: UN, *Statistical Yearbook*, 1985.

Of the world total production in 1982, the nuclear share was about 11·5 per cent, and that of hydro was about 24 per cent. The remainder was generated using coal, oil or gas, and required an input of about 1·4 billion tonnes of oil equivalent, about 18 per cent of the world's total energy consumption for all purposes. The table also shows figures for 1970. Although there was an increase of over 70 per cent in the world's total production of electricity in the period 1970–82, it can be seen that there was very little change in the proportional shares used in the world's different regions.

The use of electricity is now so all-pervasive that modern life is virtually inconceivable without it. The increased efficiency of transmission has allowed national and even international grids to be created. These link the generating systems in an area into a common system. A central computer monitors the changing load conditions in different parts of the grid and switches stations in and out as required. Areas of high load can be supplied from those where there is a surplus of generating capacity. The stations are arranged in what is often referred to as a 'merit order', so that the modern efficient ones are used as much as possible with those of low efficiency only being brought in to supply short-term peaks.

The larger the total grid capacity, the greater its ability to deal with breakdowns. In a large grid such as that of the UK, even if a large station breaks down suddenly, its load is taken up within fractions of a second by the remaining stations without consumers noticing anything. A disadvantage is that the effects of a major breakdown or loss of central control can result in the failure of the total system.

More Efficient Electricity Production and Distribution

The search for more efficient methods of electricity production and distribution continues. Higher transmission voltages are possible and research work is continuing, but reservations are being expressed about the practical advantages of further increases. Noise levels from present high-voltage lines are high, especially in humid weather and rain. There are also worries about the health effects of the electrostatic field created around the transmission line. As a result, it is only possible to run such high-voltage lines through areas in which a wide uninhabited corridor of land is available.

There has also been a major revival of interest in the use of direct current for very high-voltage transmission. Sweden was the modern pioneer in this technology: the underwater line connecting Gotland to the mainland at over a distance of 100 kilometres at 100 000 volts was opened in the late 1950s. The Pacific

Intertie, between the northern and southern portions of the US West coast, came into service in 1970: it is 1354 kilometres long and operates at 800 000 volts; the Volgograd–Donbass link in the USSR is somewhat shorter, but also operates at 800 000 volts. In recent years there has been an increasing number of such schemes throughout the world, with high-voltage direct current (HVDC) being constructed in Brazil, Zaire, Australia and the USA. The 2000-megawatt underwater connection between France and the UK opened in 1986 also uses direct current.

One of the transmission possibilities for the future is the use of superconductors. These can cut transmission losses dramatically. When the temperature of a conductor is near absolute zero, transmission losses almost completely disappear. The resistance of copper, for example, is reduced to one five-hundredth of its normal value at a temperature of 20°K.

Although superconductivity was discovered in 1911, it has had very limited practical application because of the cost of achieving and maintaining such a low temperature. But the early months of 1987 have seen astonishingly rapid progress in superconductor technology. Following a report in 1986 that researchers in the IBM laboratory in Zurich had found evidence of superconductivity in a mixture of lanthanum, barium, copper and oxygen at a temperature of 35°K, there was a flurry of scientific activity in physics laboratories across the world. A joint team from the universities of Houston and Alabama announced in January 1987 that they had achieved superconductivity at 93°K in a ceramic mixture of yttrium, barium, copper and oxygen. A fortnight later scientists in Beijing announced that they had also achieved superconductivity with a similar mixture. An announcement on the same lines came two weeks later from Tokyo University. Since then, numerous other research groups have also reported achieving superconductivity at temperatures of around 100°K with yttrium mixtures. In April researchers at the Argonne National laboratory in Illinois reported that they had managed to form a wire, albeit weak and brittle, from material which was superconducting at a temperature of about 85°K.

It is, of course, impossible to tell how long this rate of progress will be sustained or where it will lead. But already the breakthrough is extremely significant. Reaching a temperature of 20°K is an expensive process, requiring the use of liquid helium; but temperatures of around 100°K can be achieved relatively easily using liquid nitrogen. This reduces the cost by a factor of about fifty.

These new superconductors are likely to find a variety of laboratory and scientific applications in the near future. It is quite possible that they will also move into the electric power industry and specialist industrial uses within the next ten to fifteen years. In the longer term, if the breakthrough to room-temperature superconductivity is achieved as many scientists now believe is possible, they hold out the promise of dramatically increasing the efficiency of electrical transmission and utilization, as well as greatly reducing the amounts of material used for conductors.

Much work has also been done to increase the efficiency of electricity generation. Since the beginning of the century, the efficiency has risen by a factor of four, from around 10 per cent to the 40 per cent obtained in a large power station. Partly this has been achieved by increasing the size and output of units; the higher efficiency is obtained because the heat and friction losses are proportionally less in large units. Steam turbine generating sets now frequently have an output of 600 megawatts or more. One of the problems with these is the big change in the generating capacity of the system when one of these is brought in and out of service. The system needs to be large enough to damp this effect to an acceptable level. The other major reason for improved generating efficiency is the increase which has taken place in the operating temperature of the steam turbines. This is now around 600°C, which is close to the working limit of reasonably available materials. Further increases in efficiency will thus be hard to win.

There are, however, several possible methods of generating electricity which completely eliminate the turbine and offer greatly increased efficiencies in the use of fuel. One of these is called magneto-hydrodynamic generation (MHD). If an ionized very high-temperature stream of gas is passed at high speed through a strong magnetic field, an electric current is generated and can be extracted by placing electrodes in the stream of gas. Another method of electricity generation with a high theoretical efficiency is the fuel cell. Again, the principle is old – the first fuel cell was made by Grove in 1839 – but development has been slow. Various types of cell are possible. The most common is the hydrogen-oxygen cell with a sulphuric acid electrolyte. The cell is divided into three compartments. The two outer ones are the electrodes, which are porous; one is fed with hydrogen and the other with oxygen. The gases penetrate into the electrolyte where, in the presence of a catalyst such as platinum, they combine to form water, and also produce a flow of electrons – an electric current – through an external circuit connecting the two electrodes.

A great deal of research into fuel cell technology has been carried out in the past two decades. They have proved their worth in space, but have so far been too highly priced for terrestrial use. But cheaper fuel cells are emerging. The most promising use phosphoric acid as an electrolyte, natural gas as a fuel, and platinum as a catalyst; they operate at a temperature of about 200°C. A 4·5-megawatt test plant was opened in Tokyo in 1983 and operated successfully for two years before being dismantled for tests. It is therefore probable that fuel cells will gradually begin to find commercial applications over the next decade or so. They are likely to remain expensive and will consequently be used in specialist applications. One possible use, if they can be made cheaply enough and safety fears can be allayed, is in electric-powered vehicles. Few people, however, envisage them being used in large power stations or making a significant contribution to electricity generation at a national or global level this century.

Electricity Storage

A major difficulty with electricity is that it must be used immediately it is produced. It cannot be stored directly. This is particularly irksome when there is little or no control over the energy source used for generation. Wind, solar and tidal power must be used when they are available or not at all. Nuclear power stations have great difficulties in following the rise and fall of electricity consumption throughout the day and night. Most of these difficulties would be eliminated if a cheap and effective means of transforming electricity into a stored energy form, from which it could be recovered at will, could be developed. This has been the objective of a great deal of research.

Transformation into chemical energy is the most common approach. Despite immense efforts, the lead-acid battery, or accumulator, as used in cars, remains the most practical device.

It was invented in 1858. Most of the remainder are alkaline electrolyte batteries, either nickel-cadmium or nickel-iron, both of which were invented around 1900. Apart from a few small expensive types for special applications, no new batteries have become commercially viable since then.

Every battery has a number of essential components. The first is an electrolyte, which is a solution which conducts ions. An ion is an atom or group of atoms which has become electrically charged by the gain or loss of an electron. Positively charged ions, called cations, have fewer electrons than required to be electrically neutral; negatively charged ions, called anions, have more. The electrolyte, in addition to conducting ions, must also be an insulator against the conduction of electrons.

The battery must also have two electrodes: an anode and a cathode. The anode is usually a metal such as lead, zinc, cadmium, sodium or lithium. The cathode is usually a metal oxide, sulphur, chlorine or bromine. The two electrodes are connected by an external circuit. In some battery types the electrolyte is absorbed in a porous material which serves to keep the two electrodes apart.

When the battery is discharging, electrons are liberated at the anode and pass through the external circuit to the cathode, thus providing the electric current. The electrolyte carries ions from the cathode to the anode. In, for example, a lead-acid battery, both the electrodes are made of lead but the cathode is covered with lead oxide when the battery is charged. As the battery discharges, both electrodes and the electrolyte change their chemical composition; provided the process is not carried too far, the battery can be recharged by sending a current through it in the reverse direction.

For large-scale use, a battery needs to be cheap, robust and capable of being charged and recharged a large number of times. So far, the lead-acid battery meets these criteria best; in particular, it can be charged and recharged a large number of times without undue deterioration. Its main disadvantage is that it is cumbersome and heavy: a battery to store 1 kilowatt-hour weighs about 45 kg. Even though scientists feel that substantial improvements can still be made, so that it can be used, for example, in high-performance electric vehicles, it is quite impractical for large-scale energy storage.

Promising results have been obtained with a zinc-air battery in recent years. The plates are made of zinc and the oxygen is obtained from the air. The electrolyte is potassium hydroxide and the zinc is converted to zinc oxide in the discharge cycle. It can store about five times the energy per unit weight of the lead-acid battery. Higher energy-storage densities can also be obtained with sodium-sulphur and lithium-chlorine batteries operating at temperatures in the range of 300 to 600°C, but these are far from ready for the commercial market.

Another approach to large-scale energy storage is to use surplus electricity to pump water into a high-level reservoir from which it can be withdrawn at periods of peak electrical load. Some large-scale pumped-storage schemes, as they are called, have been built, and many more are being discussed in various countries. They can play a valuable part in balancing loads and stabilizing the output of a country's electricity system. But they are very expensive and as the reservoir needs special topography the number of suitable sites is limited.

To extend the possibilities of this principle, underground pumped hydro-electric storage systems are being considered. The lower reservoir would be constructed as an underground cavern in hard rock. As the drop between upper and lower reservoir can be much greater – several thousand feet – much smaller reservoirs are required for the same output.

Underground storage of compressed air could be even more advantageous. No surface-level reservoir is necessary and the underground caverns could in some cases be leached out of salt formations. A large compressed-air storage system on these lines was built in the late 1970s near Bremen in West Germany; it can produce 290 megawatts for about two hours. Surplus generating capacity is used to compress air to about 1000 pounds per square inch. At times of peak demand the air is expanded into a turbine. At the moment, the air has to be cooled after compression and reheated on expansion using an energy input, but a method of storing the heat of compression would obviate this.

Some investigations have been carried out into the use of flywheels to store energy. Huge flywheels weighing between 100 and 200 tonnes and spinning at 3500 revolutions per minute could store between 10 000 and 20 000 kilowatt-hours.[26] Flywheels have the advantage of absorbing and releasing energy rapidly. But they are expensive. They are also extremely dangerous if an accident happens, as can be appreciated from the above figures, and for safety reasons would probably have to be housed underground.

Off-peak electricity could also be used to electrolyse water. When an electric current is passed through it, water breaks down into hydrogen and oxygen, a familiar experiment in junior science classes. The hydrogen thus produced can be stored and used as fuel for combustion or for electricity generation in a fuel cell.

Hydrogen has a great deal to recommend it as a fuel. It can be piped, stored in gasholders or liquefied and stored under pressure. It can be burned in cookers, furnaces, motor cars and aeroplanes. It is clean – the only by-product of its combustion is water. Its only obvious disadvantage is its comparatively low calorific value, which is about a third that of natural gas. But it can be combined with carbon, obtained from the almost limitless supplies of limestone, to form methanol, a liquid fuel with most of the desirable attributes of petrol.

Hydrogen, however, is not an energy source. It is a manufactured fuel, like electricity; and like electricity its manufacture consumes more energy than can be obtained from the resulting hydrogen. In electrolysis about half the energy of the electricity used can be recovered from the hydrogen produced. Using coal to produce electricity which in turn produces hydrogen therefore results in a conversion efficiency of 15 to 20 per cent even under the best conditions. It can be justified only under exceptional circumstances, for instance, to produce hydrogen for use in chemical processes. In fact, hydrogen is more usually produced for this purpose by breaking down natural gas.

There has been some speculation about a possible future 'hydrogen economy'. This is an industrial society in which hydrogen or synthetic fuels derived from it are used instead of the present petroleum fuels. Essentially, it relies on the postulate that there are vast surpluses of electricity available, either from nuclear or fusion power. These would be used to produce hydrogen by the electrolysis of water. It is an unlikely eventuality for a very long time to come.

This is not to say that using electricity to produce hydrogen has no future whatsoever. If a cheap and simple electrolysis 'kit' could be produced, the intermittent and unpredictable output of a wind-powered generator could be stored and the surplus energy of a solar-powered generator could be slowly accumulated during the summer and used in winter. On a larger scale, electrolysis could be used to serve the same purpose as today's pumped-storage systems and store some of the energy which would otherwise be wasted at nuclear, hydro or tidal power stations and use it to help meet peak loads. But the evolution of these uses into a full-scale hydrogen economy is a matter for the distant future, if at all.

Another long-term possibility is to use the heat from nuclear reactors to produce hydrogen directly from water, without an intermediate conversion to electricity. This could have a great deal to recommend it in terms of efficiency, at least in theory – it should be possible to devise a process with an efficiency of considerably more than the 15 to 20 per cent obtained by first using the heat to produce electricity and then using the electricity to produce hydrogen. But there are still large difficulties to be overcome before this can happen, as can be seen from the following quotation:

> The scheme to which most attention has been given is based on reactions between $CaBr_2$, $HgBr_2$ and water. While many of the basic chemical parameters have been studied, a very large chemical engineering development programme would be needed . . . criticisms which have been levelled at this scheme relate to the environmental implications of handling mercury on such a scale, the mercury investment required and the corrosion problems inherent in such corrosive materials.[27]

Gas from Coal

Another way in which coal can be made more convenient to use is to turn it into gas. This has a long history. In Europe, coal gas was used for illumination in the late eighteenth century. The London and Westminster Gas Light and Coke Company was granted a charter in 1812 and the first US company was chartered in 1816 in Baltimore.

The basic process was very simple. Coal was heated in airtight retorts to drive off its volatile constituents. About 70 per cent of the coal was left behind as a coke of almost pure carbon, which was used for metal smelting and as an industrial and domestic fuel. The gas produced was a mixture which depended for its exact characteristics on the coal from which it was formed. With time, the manufacturing process became more sophisticated; passing a certain amount of steam through the retort enabled engineers to control both the quality of the gas and the quantity of coke. Later, the addition of a certain proportion of oil allowed further control of the quality of the final gas.

In Table 22 a typical range of constituents in gas made from the Durham coalfield in the UK is shown. Over half the gas is hydrogen, with a fifth to a third being methane. The carbon monoxide is also extremely important: it is the lethal constituent. When inhaled it reacts with the haemoglobin in the blood, preventing it from carrying oxygen from the lungs. The introduction of non-toxic natural gas was welcomed, amongst other reasons, for discouraging 'easy' suicides.

Another coal gas with a long history of manufacture is 'producer gas'. In this, the whole of the coal is converted into gas. In

Table 22. Constituents and calorific values of town and producer gas

CONSTITUENTS, percentage	Town gas*	Producer gas†
Carbon dioxide	1·6–5·2	5–10
Oxygen	0·3–0·5	—
Unsaturated hydrocarbons (ethylene, propylene, butylene)	2·0–4·0	—
Carbon monoxide	6·2–16·4	25–30
Hydrogen	52·9–55·3	10–18
Saturated hydrocarbons (methane, ethane)	19·2 30·2	0 5–3 0
Nitrogen	5·1–7·4	50–60
CALORIFIC VALUE	5·17 kWh/m³ (500 Btu/ft³)	1·34–1·55 kWh/m³ (130–150 Btu/ft³)
YIELD OF COKE PER TONNE	0·655–0·755 tonnes	—

* Constituents of town gas are those obtained from a Durham coal processed in a variety of ways.
† Constituents of producer gas are those obtained from processing a range of fuels from coke to anthracite.
Source: E. C. Pope, ed. *Coal: Production, Distribution, Utilisation* (Institute of Fuel and Coal Industry Society), Industrial Newspapers, 1949.

the gas-manufacturing process, steam and air are passed over an incandescent bed of coal. The steam and oxygen from the air react with the carbon in the coal to produce a mixture of gases which includes as its main combustible components carbon monoxide, hydrogen and a small proportion of methane. Table 22 shows the composition of a typical producer gas. The calorific value is low, less than a sixth that of natural gas, because the main component is the inert gas nitrogen, which comes from the air used in making it. Producer gas was used exclusively in manufacturing processes; the point of it was that it provided a method of utilizing the energy of coal in a much more controlled and versatile manner.

More elaborate gas production processes in which oxygen rather than air was used were developed in the early decades of the present century. Most of this work was done in Germany. One of the best-known methods was the high-pressure Lurgi process for the production of medium calorific value gas. Plants using this method were built in many countries before the Second World War.

Most gasworks producing town gas have now closed, and the use of producer gas in industry has largely disappeared. The superior calorific value of natural gas, twice that of town gas, its non-toxic and non-pollutive characteristics, its cheapness and availability in huge quantities, led to its complete dominance of the US gas market after the Second World War. In the UK the discovery of the southern North Sea gas fields led to a similar elimination of town gas within about a decade. In a remarkably quick and smooth operation, the British gas authorities managed to modify or replace every gas-using appliance in the country, illustrating what can be done given a significant improvement in energy-using technology and a strong political commitment to its widespread dissemination.

Interest in coal gasification revived, however, during the 1970s when there was concern about depleting gas reserves in the USA and worries about security of supply in Europe. There was considerable work on developing and improving established methods of manufacturing medium calorific value gas such as the Lurgi process. Some of the major oil companies, Shell and Texaco in particular, invested considerable amounts of money in the development of new gas-manufacturing methods. The aim was to achieve economical high-volume methods of producing a gas which could be used directly as a fuel by industry, or as a feedstock for further processes which would upgrade it to a liquid fuel or synthetic natural gas (SNG).

Despite the large sums of money spent on SNG research in the 1970s, and despite its undoubted technical feasibility, only one commercial-size plant was built. This was in North Dakota and came on stream in 1984. It produces 4 million cubic metres of gas per day which is distributed in an existing natural gas pipeline. The plant was given loan and price guarantees by the US government's Synthetic Fuels Corporation, without which it would not have been able to survive commercially.

Research activity has now declined greatly and it is unlikely that SNG manufacture will take place on a significant scale before the turn of the century. The exception is South Africa. There, a combination of political isolation and plentiful coal, which can be mined cheaply, have encouraged the development of coal gasification on a substantial scale. The technologies in use are based on those used in Germany during the Second World War. Although they have a proven technical record, it is only the special circumstances of South Africa which make them economically feasible.

The underground gasification of coal, which would eliminate the problems of its mining and transport, was first suggested by Sir William Siemens in 1868, and at various times since then trials have been made but without much success. To make the gas, a series of holes is drilled into a seam of coal, preferably one sloping regularly upwards. A controlled fire is lit within the seam, and air, oxygen, steam or some combination of these is passed through the holes and into the combustion area, where a kind of producer gas is formed and drawn off. This can be used directly, upgraded into town gas, or used as a feedstock for a methane-producing process.

The temperature and extent of combustion cannot be controlled with precision, yet these are critical in the formation of the gas. Variations in the quality of the coal further complicate the control problems. The output gas varies widely in its characteristics and, if air is used as feed, has a calorific value only about a tenth that of natural gas. Nevertheless, the attractions of underground coal gasification remain strong. It is probably the only practical way of gaining access to the energy stored in the earth's deeper and more-difficult-to-work coal deposits. Intermittent research has been carried out in a number of countries, including the USSR, and a joint Belgian and West German trial project was launched in 1986. But there is little expectation that a feasible method of underground coal gasification will be developed within the next few decades.

Oil from Coal

The conversion of coal to a liquid petroleum-like product, sometimes called syncrude, involves a number of complex processes. Petroleum-type fuels have a considerably higher hydrogen-carbon ratio than coal. Part of the liquefaction process therefore involves the addition of hydrogen, which must be obtained in a separate process. In addition, the oxygen, sulphur and other chemicals contained in the coal must be eliminated. The products of different liquefaction processes vary widely: some produce liquid hydrocarbons which can act as a direct replacement for today's petroleum fuels; others yield a product which is closer to bitumen or heavy fuel oil.

The main developments in coal liquefaction technology have taken place in Germany. There were commercial plants in operation in the 1920s using what was known as the Bergius–Pier catalytic hydrogenation process; two such plants were also built in the USA in the 1930s. During the Second World War twelve of these plants produced about 4 million tonnes of fuel per year in Germany, about a third of the country's liquid fuel requirements.

Another German development by which gas from coal was turned into a liquid fuel was called the Fischer–Tropsch process. By the end of the war there were nine of these plants operating in Germany and one in France; Japan had also adopted the process and had four plants operating, as well as a further one in Manchuria.

The 1970s saw considerable interest in a variety of coal liquefaction processes, particularly in the USA. Other research and pilot project work was carried out in West Germany, Japan and Australia. Major coal and oil companies, as well as governments, committed large sums of money to research and demonstration projects. The financial climate seemed right, with a virtually unanimous belief that oil prices were going to continue rising. The estimated production costs of liquid fuels tended to be anything from $70 per barrel upwards. With oil costing $35 per barrel and apparently set to reach $80–100 per barrel by the turn of the century, it looked as if plants could profitably come on stream in the 1990s. Long-range planning in the nascent synthetic fuels industry was geared to such a future.

Most of these hopes have now evaporated. Today, South Africa is the only country with a large-scale synfuels programme. It relies on the Fischer–Tropsch process at its massive Sasol coal liquefaction plant. A unit with an output of 240 000 tonnes per year has been in operation there since 1955. Two extensions to the plant, one in 1980 and the other in 1984, have brought the total output capacity to more than 3 million tonnes of liquid fuel per year.

A certain amount of research and development work is still being carried out in Japan and the USA. It is clear that, technically, coal liquefaction will be available to the industrial world when oil prices again begin to rise. But the difficulties also need to be borne in mind; the transition to liquid fuels from coal will not be a painless one. Net yields are unlikely to be much more than 2·5 barrels per tonne of coal. To produce the present oil consumption of the USA would require over 2 billion tonnes of coal per year, three times the present level of production. It is a daunting technical and environmental prospect. There are also fears that some of the complex hydrocarbon molecules formed in the liquefaction process may be potent carcinogens; controlling the emission of these could be difficult and costly.

Fluidized Bed Combustion of Coal

Fluidized bed combustion of coal had its technical beginnings in the 1920s but, as happened with so many of the initiatives of the early decades of the century, the Second World War and the arrival of cheap oil killed commercial interest. In recent years research has been resumed in the USA, the UK and West Germany.

In a fluidized bed combustion unit air is passed upwards through a layer, or bed, of fine incombustible material, causing it to behave as a fluid. Crushed coal is fed into this fluidized bed and burned there. The combustion temperature is about 850°C; this is just about half the temperature in a normal boiler. Boiler tubes run directly through the bed and absorb the heat required to generate high-pressure steam. Fluidized bed units can be designed to run at atmospheric or at elevated pressures.

Fluidized bed combustion units have some important advantages over conventional coal-burning boilers. The transfer of heat to the boiler tubes is more efficient than in a normal boiler where the tubes are in the walls and roof of the combustion chamber. This increased efficiency of heat transfer means that for any particular heat output the fluidized bed units can be smaller than the conventional boiler. It is hoped that units will be produced of the same size as oil-fired units of the same output; this would increase the possibility of replacing existing oil-fired boilers with fluidized bed installations.

The quantity of inert matter contained in the coal burned in a fluidized bed can be much higher than would be acceptable in other boilers. This permits the use of lower and cheaper grades of coal; in fact, much of the colliery waste piled in the slag heaps beside coalmines can be burned quite easily in fluidized beds. Another advantage is that when limestone or dolomite is added to the bed, up to 90 per cent of the sulphur contained in the coal is absorbed; this greatly reduces the problem of pollution.

A further bonus is provided by the fact that the lower combustion temperatures reduce the formation and emission of oxides of nitrogen. These oxides are the main cause of atmospheric smog, and there is increasing pressure to limit their emission. In conventional boilers, because of the high temperature at which they operate, atmospheric nitrogen is combined with oxygen, as happens in the engine of an automobile. In a fluidized bed unit, because of the lower operating temperature, no oxides of nitrogen are formed in this way.

Demonstration fluidized bed combustion units were built in the UK and the USA in the late 1970s. The technology is now available for small-scale units for industrial uses or electric power generation, but there are still problems to be solved before large generating stations can be built. Despite its many attractions, the deployment of fluidized bed combustion of coal on a significant scale appears to be several decades into the future.

Methane from Biomass

The production of energy from organic matter, or 'biomass' as it is commonly described, is another area of technology which was greatly stimulated during the 1970s. A variety of approaches were developed. One which received a great deal of attention was the production of methane, or 'biogas'.

When organic material decays under anaerobic conditions – that is, without oxygen, as for example in the mud at the bottom of a marsh – methane is produced. This is the marsh gas which produces the mysterious will o' the wisp if it ignites. In municipal sewage works where the organic material of sewage is digested in sludge digestion tanks, methane is also produced, and sometimes referred to as sludge gas. The technology of sludge digestion is well established and the gas is often used to produce power for the sewage works. Sometimes there is even a surplus which, as one authority on sewage plant design says, can be 'burnt in a burner at some distance from the tanks. This can be designed as an attractive ornamental feature.'[28] The term biogas is used in recognition of the fact that the gas produced by the biological digestion of organic matter is not pure methane, but rather a mixture of gases. It is about 60–70 per cent methane with the rest consisting of carbon dioxide, and some nitrogen, carbon monoxide, hydrogen and hydrogen sulphide.

In the late 1960s biogas production was very much in vogue. It was even referred to as the 'fuel of the future'. It became the subject of much earnest amateur experimentation which, luckily for the experimenters, was generally a failure. Air and methane form an explosive mixture. The only reason many of the leaky home-made digesters did not cause fatal accidents was that they rarely produced any methane. Effective operation demands fastidious care and control of the temperature and the mixture of materials used.

The idea of households in the industrial countries becoming self-sufficient in energy through the use of backyard methane digesters using domestic wastes is quite impractical. The yield from such small-scale units is tiny, and in cold climates keeping the digester working is likely to consume more energy than it produces. Even large-scale sewage works do not have a net surplus when all their energy consumption is taken into account.

Municipal rubbish dumps, however, are turning out to be an unexpectedly profitable source of biogas. The large quantities of organic matter which are compacted and buried deep below the surface are often in ideal conditions for anaerobic digestion to take place. The gas produced normally percolates to the surface and is lost to the atmosphere; occasionally, it causes fires. It has been found that, by covering the dump with an impermeable sheet, useful quantities of gas can be collected. If there is a nearby demand for a combustible gas which can be used for industrial heat-raising, it may be possible to justify the recovery of the gas on a commercial basis.

The production of biogas on farms is also promising, particularly if they use battery methods of animal rearing. The quantities of animal and vegetable waste are usually sufficient to justify a reasonably large digester, and their disposal by other means can be difficult and expensive. A well-designed digester could provide a useful amount of energy and financially justify its installation under favourable circumstances. As well as providing energy and solving a waste disposal problem, biogas digestion has the advantage of retaining the nutrients in the organic material in the residual sludge. This can then be used as a fertilizer by spraying it on crop lands.

In the developing world the pioneering nation is China. Experiments were carried out in the 1950s, but the 1970s saw a remarkable dissemination of the technology. Some 8 million digesters were built, mainly in Sichuan Province in the west of the country. Most of these digesters were built by individual farming families and were usually 5–10 cubic metres in volume. They utilized the manure from domestic animals, human wastes and agricultural residues. They were able to provide enough gas to supply the basic cooking and lighting needs of the families building them.

Although families were responsible for the costs of the digesters, a considerable subsidy was provided by the state in the form of transportation of materials, a high level of organization and training, and an allowance of communal work-points, on which people's share of the production from communes depends, for time spent on the construction of the digester. The construction of the digesters demands a high level of skill and great care. Here is a quotation from the training manual used in China:

The pits must be absolutely hermetically sealed so that the whole pit is watertight and the gas sections are airtight. This requires conscientious work and a strict scientific attitude throughout the process of construction . . . any slackening of attention to quality in the building of these pits will interfere with normal gas production, affect the durability of the pits, and may even require far more work to remedy defects . . . So before the pit is built there should be exhaustive study and discussion of its size, the model to be used, the location and the materials.[29]

Reports over the past few years have suggested that there have been considerable maintenance problems with the digesters. The level of enthusiasm for the technology seems to have fallen somewhat. The future of biogas development in China is thus unclear.

Efforts to promote biogas in other developing countries have been much less successful than in China. It is a cumbersome and demanding technology. It is not really suitable where the climate is arid. Where wood or agricultural residues are available, most rural families would prefer to use them directly. It is significant that the Chinese programme was not primarily based on energy production. Its main justifications were the sanitary disposal of human and animal wastes and the production of fertilizer. The only other country in which significant progress has been made is India, where about 120 000 digesters have been built. These rely on a digester which uses a steel cover; they have mainly been built by rich farmers as a supplementary source of energy and a means of fertilizer production.

Ethanol and Methanol from Biomass

The production of ethanol, or ethyl alcohol, is one of the oldest chemical processes known to humanity. The fermentation of vegetable matter through the action of yeasts produces beer or wine, but the maximum proportion of alcohol which can be obtained in this way is about 17 per cent. Higher concentrations are produced by distillation: commonly sold spirits such as whisky and gin are usually 35–40 per cent ethanol. The technology of brewing and distilling is well established and capable of producing ethanol in very large quantities.

Ethanol can be used in combination with petrol, or gasoline, as a motor vehicle fuel; the mixture is often referred to as gasohol. Ordinary internal combustion car engines can use a mixture of up to 20 per cent ethanol without modification. Relatively simple changes allow engines to burn pure ethanol. The use of ethanol as a motor vehicle fuel dates back to the early days of automotive engineering, before petroleum fuels were widely available. It was also used to supplement petrol supplies in the First and Second World Wars.

Brazil is the largest user of ethanol fuel at present. Because of the country's massive balance of payments problems as a result of the oil price rises in the 1970s, the Brazilian government launched a huge ethanol production programme, mainly using sugar cane, or cassava in areas where it was a more suitable crop, as feedstock. Technically, this has been a brilliant success. In 1985 over 7 million tonnes of ethanol were produced from around 400 distilleries. About 2 million cars, some 20 per cent of the total fleet, use pure ethanol as fuel; the remainder use a 20 per cent mixture with petrol.

The programme has, however, given rise to considerable controversy in Brazil. One of its objectives was to increase the spread of wealth in the rural areas by providing an opportunity for small farmers to produce sugar cane or cassava as a secure and profitable crop. Experience has shown that the benefits have gone mainly to the rich. There have also been problems with pollution as the ethanol production process creates large volumes of acidic waste.

The economics have also been doubtful. Even with oil at $30

per barrel, there were some economists who argued that the process was uneconomic. There is no question that at crude oil prices of $15–20 per barrel, ethanol production is a very much more expensive source of fuel than petrol. This is bound to restrict investment in the further expansion of ethanol production in the immediate future.

Much more limited ethanol production programmes have taken place in a number of other countries, including the USA, Kenya, Zimbabwe and South Africa. There have also been suggestions that some of the food mountains and wine lakes of the EEC should be turned into ethanol. But even the most ardent supporters of the Common Agricultural Policy tend to balk at the level of additional subsidies which would be required to make the ethanol saleable to European motorists.

Methanol has also been suggested as a possible candidate for production on a large scale to meet future fuel needs. It is also called methyl alcohol, or wood alcohol; it used to be obtained from the distillation of wood. It is a poisonous liquid which is used to make formaldehyde and other industrial chemicals, and is also used as an additive to make ethanol undrinkable in the form of methylated spirit. It is normally made using natural gas as a feedstock. In principle, it could be made from a variety of biomass feedstocks but a practical and economic technology for doing so remains to be developed.

There have been optimistic calculations which show that all of humanity's energy needs could be met from biomass sources. But this represents an ideal world in which biomass sources are readily accessible and easily harvested, conversion technologies are developed far beyond what they are today, and economics do not matter. The immediate future is much more constrained. It is certainly feasible, in principle, for countries with large fertile areas of land to use them for producing fuel. In most countries, however, there are competing uses for the same land. It would be surprising if biomass technologies were producing more than a small fraction of a per cent of world energy needs within the next couple of decades.

Small-scale Gasification by Partial Combustion

Gasification by partial combustion is a process by which wood, coal or charcoal is broken down to produce a combustible mixture of gases. The physical and chemical processes involved are essentially the same as those which take place in the manufacture of producer gas, with the main combustible component being carbon monoxide. The gas produced has a calorific value of about 10–15 per cent that of natural gas.

The operating principles of a gasifier are extremely simple. In essence, it consists of a container into which wood, charcoal or coal is fed. In the lower part of the container there is a combustion zone to which a limited supply of air is admitted. The heat of this combustion breaks down, or pyrolyses, the fuel above the fire, producing a combustible gas; but this does not burn because of the limited air supply. This gas contains 20–30 per cent carbon monoxide and 5–15 per cent hydrogen, depending on the feedstock and the type of gasifier.

The gas can be used as fuel for an internal combustion engine. The use of gas as an engine fuel in fact predates that of liquid fuels. Most of the early internal combustion engines were designed to be run on coal gas. The use of liquid fuel did not begin until the introduction of the spark ignition engine by Daimler in 1886.

There was a certain amount of interest in the use of gasifiers to power motor vehicles before the First World War. Towards its end some tests were carried out on gasifier powered trucks in France, and worries about the level of oil resources sparked further research during the 1920s and 1930s. One call for gasifier development in 1938 pointed out that proven oil reserves were sufficient to sustain prevailing consumption levels of 250 million tonnes per year for only another fourteen years.

In a vehicle-mounted gasifier the engine air intake is connected to the gas outlet by a piece of tubing. The gas is drawn from the gasifier through a cleaning and filtering system by the suction of the engine. In a spark ignition engine the gas can be used by itself; in the case of a diesel engine, a small proportion of diesel fuel is required to provide ignition.

The shortage of petroleum fuel during the Second World War

allowed gasifier technology to come into its own. Around 1 million gasifier-powered vehicles were in use by 1942, with 350 000 in Germany and about 100 000 each in Japan and France. Sweden relied on its fleet of 74 000 gasifier-powered vehicles for virtually the whole of its transport needs. All but a tiny proportion of these gasifiers used either wood or charcoal; petrol stations regularly carried a stock of chopped wood or charcoal. The role played by gasifiers in meeting transport needs was extremely important, and the technology clearly showed its practicability and versatility. But within a year of the ending of the war and the resumption of oil supplies, use ceased completely.

Interest in gasifiers for use in the developing world began in the late 1960s, some of the earliest work being carried out by Dr Ibarra Cruz at the University of the Philippines. During the 1970s work on reviving the technology was under way in Brazil, Europe and the USA.[30] By the early 1980s there were prototype or experimental programmes running in perhaps a score of developing countries. Most produced little or nothing in the way of tangible results: Brazil was the only country in which gasifiers came on the commercial market; several hundred were in use in 1983. A government-supported programme in the Philippines promised much, but failed to deliver many tangible achievements.

The apparent parallel between the oil-starved countries of Europe during the Second World War and the beleaguered economies of the Third World in the 1970s was a compelling one. But it was essentially misleading. Despite its apparent simplicity, gasifier technology is demanding in engineering and maintenance skills. When oil was scarce in Europe in the 1940s, the industrial might of the major automotive and engineering companies was there to make gasifier-powered road vehicles available as a last resort under emergency conditions; it was not for nothing that the technology was precipitately abandoned when the war ended. Most of the developing countries in which gasified programmes were launched had difficulties in obtaining the skilled labour and spare parts required for the maintenance of ordinary diesel and petrol engines; gasifier technology with its greater demands on skill and resources proved to be too difficult and unreliable for widespread use. It is therefore unlikely that gasifiers will find a useful role in motor vehicle transport in the developing world as long as normal petrol-engined or diesel-engined vehicles remain available. There are, however, possible niches which gasifiers might fill in pumping water and other applications in areas where conventional fuels are difficult to obtain. But such gasifier installations need to be chosen with care.

Part Three

Energy in the Developing World

The moment the first enamel pot or factory-woven cloth is imported into a self-sufficient rural society, the economic and social structure of that society receives its death blow. Afterwards, it is merely a question of time and whether the members of the community will be the participants or victims of the new economic order – PRESIDENT JULIUS NYRERE OF TANZANIA, 1973.

11

Energy Consumption and Supply

The benefits of high-energy society and the oil age are by no means universally enjoyed. They are still outside the reach of at least half the world's population, the people who live in the rural areas and the low-income quarters of the cities in the developing world. They continue to depend upon the same fuels which humanity began to use with the discovery of how to control fire.

These traditional fuels – wood, agricultural residues and dung – are all obtained directly from the biosphere, and are usually described as biomass fuels. The total consumption is probably in the range of 1·5–2·0 billion tonnes, ranking them fourth in the world hierarchy of fuel consumption. Their contribution to world energy needs is about five times that of nuclear power.

Dependence on traditional fuels is greatest in the rural areas. In most countries of the developing world virtually the whole rural population relies exclusively on these fuels for cooking, heating water and keeping warm. For many families, unable to obtain or afford kerosene or bottled gas, the open fire is also the only source of light available to them for the evenings and nights. Wherever it is available, wood is the preferred fuel for family use. About 2 billion people rely on it for all, or the most part, of their daily energy needs, making it the world's most widely used fuel. Industry, particularly in the rural areas, also relies heavily on wood. The heat required in the drying and processing of tea, coffee and other commercial crops is frequently supplied by wood-fired boilers. The myriads of small-scale commercial activities by which local needs are satisfied, such as brick and lime making, brewing, fish smoking, sugar making, copra drying and so on, almost universally depend on wood.

In the cities, too, wood is widely used as a fuel, particularly among the poor. Sometimes it is burned as firewood, in other places it is in the form of charcoal. It is a puzzle why this difference in fuel preferences exists. Historically, charcoal was associated with metal working and that may account for its use in some areas. Historians have also speculated that its use in Africa may have been spread by Arab traders and settlers. But for the most part there does not appear to be any immediately apparent reason why charcoal is popular in one place and virtually unknown under similar conditions elsewhere. Thus, charcoal is widely used in the towns in Ghana, yet in nearby Nigeria firewood is the main urban fuel, with charcoal being used mainly for small snacks and roasting. Across Asia there are also wide variations. Charcoal is used in the cities of Malaysia, Nepal and the Philippines. Yet in India, Pakistan and Bangladesh, despite long traditions of using charcoal for metal working, it is not used on a substantial scale as a domestic cooking fuel.

The generic term 'woodfuels' is generally used to refer to firewood and charcoal. Statistics on their consumption are generally poor. Woodfuels rarely figure in the energy balances drawn up by national statistical offices or international organizations. Nevertheless, the importance of woodfuels at both a family and a national level is clear. Among the poorest developing countries, wood accounts for over 90 per cent of the energy consumed for all purposes. Even in oil-rich Nigeria it supplies 80 per cent of the total national energy consumption. Table 23 gives a list of countries with their average incomes and the estimated proportion of national fuel needs supplied by wood. As a general rule, it can be seen that the lower the average level of wealth, the higher the dependence on woodfuels.

Most of the countries listed in the table are from Africa; it is the poorest continent by far. In Asia and Latin America the overall wealth is generally higher and the proportion of wood in the total national energy consumption is low. But in the rural areas of many of these countries – Indonesia, India, Brazil, Mexico and others – there are millions of people who still depend heavily, if not entirely, on wood and other traditional biomass fuels.

Table 23. Proportion of national energy needs supplied by wood in selected developing countries

	Wood as percentage of total energy consumption	GDP, $ per head (1984)
Mali	97	140
Rwanda	96	280
Tanzania	94	210
Burkina Faso	94	160
Ethiopia	93	110
Central African Republic	91	260
Somalia	90	260
Burundi	89	220
Niger	87	190
Benin	86	270
Sudan	81	360
Madagascar	80	260
Sierra Leone	76	310
Ghana	74	350
Guinea	74	330
Kenya	74	310
Senegal	63	380
Sri Lanka	54	360
Ivory Coast	46	610
Honduras	45	700
Tunisia	42	1270

Sources: Hall *et al.*, *Biomass for Energy in the Developing World*, 1982. World Bank, *World Development Report*, 1986.

Rural Energy Consumption

In the rural areas hardly any of the fuel that people use is purchased. People collect wood from trees on their own farms and around their houses. Others get their supplies from the trees and bushes on open grazing lands; from farmlands which are under fallow; from wastelands; or from nearby forests; in short, from anywhere trees are growing and to which they have reasonably free access.

People usually supplement their wood supplies with other burnable biomass when it is available. Hard, dry maize cobs make an excellent fuel and are widely used; so also are coconut shells. People may also use straw and the stalks of millet and sorghum for kindling or as an additional fuel when these are readily available after the harvest. In areas where wood is becoming scarce, people may be forced to switch to the use of such materials as a substitute for wood.

Dried animal dung is also widely used when wood is scarce. There are strong cultural objections to its use in areas where other fuels are available. But, in fact, it is an excellent cooking fuel which burns easily with a steady flame. In India, where it is very widely used, any unwillingness to burn dung 'does not usually stem from a feeling that dung is somehow "unclean". More often it is because dung is seen to have a variety of other more valuable uses, especially as a fertilizer.'[31] It is usually used in the form of dung cakes which are spread out to dry on the ground, or stuck to walls, trees or any available free space.

The quantities of woodfuel used vary extremely widely. Among families living in well-wooded areas in Tanzania and Central America, observers have measured consumption levels of up to 2·5 tonnes of wood per head per year. In areas such as the Sahel – that band of arid or semi-arid land immediately to the south of the Sahara – the barren uplands of South America or the more arid areas of India, consumption is more likely to average 300–400 kilograms per head per year. But there are also major differences within regions and even between adjacent families living in the same village.

Wood consumption is affected by the types of food cooked. Long-simmering stews of some countries require a great deal more cooking than quickly fried or braised dishes: it is said that the stir-fry traditions in Chinese cuisine come from areas where wood was scarce and cooking was done on hot, quick-burning straw fires. The climate can also be important. Even in some of the hot countries, night temperatures can fall sharply, making it necessary to use a fire for heating. The biggest factor, however, is the availability of wood. Where it is easy to obtain, consumption tends to be much higher than when it is scarce.

The collection of fuel for the family is usually the responsibility of women. This is particularly the case in the sub-Saharan African countries where the wood is generally carried home in headloads. These loads can be extremely heavy. An average of about 20 kilograms is common in many countries in Africa, but weights of up to nearly 40 kilograms have been measured in some places.

Carrying such weights over long distances can lead to severe spinal problems in later life.

The Three-stone Fire

In the majority of rural households the most common method of cooking is over an open fire. Usually the fire is enclosed by three stones or lumps of mud which act as supports for the cooking pot. There are many variations on this basic theme.

In Latin American homes the fire is usually on a raised adobe platform or it may be on a barrel filled with earth. In other areas the earth is scooped out between the stones so that the fire is slightly sunk into the ground. Inverted pots are used in parts of Burkina Faso; they are often installed in a bride's new home by her mother and filled with special charms. Sometimes the number of stones is increased to five so that two pots can be accommodated.

The open fire is generally dirty, dangerous and unpleasant to use. Small children are in constant danger of being burned by sparks or falling into it. When it is used indoors, the smoke and soot it produces make clothes, furniture, and wall and ceiling coverings difficult to keep clean. In Papua New Guinea it was found that progress in rural electrification was being hampered by the fouling of lamp fittings by smoke. Smoke can also be a major health hazard leading to chronic respiratory diseases and associated heart problems. Researchers have found that women cooking indoors over an open fire are subjected to a level of pollution equivalent to smoking twenty packets of cigarettes per day.

None the less, in the context in which it is used, the open fire has a number of extremely important advantages. It costs nothing and no special tools or materials are needed to construct it. It can be positioned wherever is most convenient for the cook, and changed without trouble as often as she wishes. It is also relatively easy to control the heat output from the fire in order to meet different cooking needs. Long sticks can be pushed in between the openings in the stones to increase the heat output, or pulled out when the heat is lowered for simmering. Where cutting tools are primitive or are not available to women, this may be the only practical way of using the branches of hard dry wood they collect for fuel.

Another important point is that the stones can be positioned to provide a stable support for different sizes and shapes of pots. Many traditional dishes are based on foods which are cooked in the form of a thick porridge which requires prolonged stirring when it is being cooked. This means the pot must be securely supported to prevent it from sliding about. Three stones embedded slightly in the ground provide what is required.

Even the smoke can have an important role to play. It is sometimes used as a means of curing and preserving food; it also helps to keep termites away from the walls and thatch of dwellings. In parts of Central America thick smoke from the cooking fire is relied upon to stick the straw of the roof together and make it waterproof. Another custom in this area is to hang ears of corn above the fire: the smoke eliminates parasites, enabling the corn to be kept for up to six or seven years.

Traditional designs of cooking stoves are also found in many parts of the developing world. In rural areas most of these stoves are made of mud or mixtures of sand and mud, and are constructed by their owners. In some cases they are built directly in their final shape; in other places a solid mud block may be formed into which the fire chamber, fuel opening and pot holes are cut. Few are fitted with chimneys. When built, they are often coated with cow dung to prevent them from cracking. In India a traditional domestic stove is often referred to as a *chula*; this is simply the Hindi word for a stove.

Woodfuel Consumption and Deforestation

It is widely believed that woodfuel collection is the main cause of the deforestation taking place in many parts of the developing world. There is a popular image of rural woodfuel collectors bringing an energy crisis on themselves by recklessly cutting the forest resources on which they depend for fuel. Such an impression is generally exaggerated, and is often grossly wrong. In most countries the major part of the wood used by rural domestic consumers does not come from forests; it comes from their immediate surroundings. Nor is it usual for people to cut whole trees to meet their woodfuel needs. They much prefer to collect dead wood because it is dry, lighter to carry and easy to burn.

Pressure comes on forest resources for a variety of reasons. Sometimes, as happened in the Sahel during the 1970s and 1980s, drought may ravage large areas of woodlands, killing all the trees. In the moist tropical countries logging for commercial timber can destroy large areas of forest. Around cities, too, there are often areas of concentrated cutting to supply the urban woodfuel market. But by far the most common cause of forest destruction is the clearing of land for growing food.

Population growth, migration, war and drought are driving impoverished people in many developing countries to move into woodlands and forest areas and clear them of trees in order to farm the land. Initially, there may even be a surplus of wood as a result of tree felling. But, inevitably, there comes a time when there is not sufficient fuel to meet everyone's needs. The women who remain responsible for supplying their families with fuel now have to walk further and search longer for what they need. In places they can be seen cutting branches from living trees. To the unwary outside observer, it may look as though they are causing the shortage that is afflicting them. In fact, they are its helpless victims.

Fuel for the Cities

Urban woodfuel consumers differ in one key respect from the majority of those in the rural areas. They pay cash for their woodfuels, buying them in markets or obtaining them from sellers who call at their homes. Usually it is only firewood and charcoal which are commercialized in this way. But in a number of countries – India in particular – dung and crop residues are also sold in some cities.

The fact that woodfuels are traded commercially means that they must compete in the market-place with other sources of fuel. If their relative price rises too high, customers will tend to other fuels which give them better value for their money. Equally importantly, expenditure on woodfuels has to be balanced against that required for other items in the household budget. Thus, a woman may decide that it is worth spending more money to purchase processed food which saves on cooking fuel or which has a shorter preparation time and allows her additional time for paid work.

In most Third World cities, the better-off urban dwellers tend to rely on bottled gas, kerosene (paraffin oil) or electricity – usually referred to as 'conventional fuels' – for a high proportion of their energy needs. In some cases, however, charcoal is used by even the richest families for grilling meat because of the flavour it gives; this, incidentally, comes mainly from the smoke of the burning fat dripping from the meat, rather than from the charcoal. The preference for conventional fuels among those who can afford them is easy to understand. They are cleaner, easier and more efficient to use than wood or charcoal, and most people would change to them if they had a chance. Wood is the fuel of the poor.

The proportion of people using conventional fuels varies greatly across the developing world. In some of the African cities the use of conventional fuels for cooking is confined to the top 5 per cent of the urban population, whereas in Asia and Latin America the proportion tends to be considerably higher. The barrier to a wider use of these fuels is generally their price; it is often several times that of woodfuels. There are cases, however, where conventional fuels would actually be cheaper for cooking, but the price of the stove is too high for the poor to afford.

When towns are small, their wood supplies come from their immediate surroundings. Wood-sellers collect the fuel and bring it into town for sale directly to customers or to wholesale dealers. The wood is carried by donkey or bullock carts, bicycles, or even headloads. People living on the fringe of the town may be able to obtain all the wood they need simply by collecting it from the nearby countryside. But as towns get bigger and woodfuel demand increases, the nearby wood resources become exhausted, and supplies have to come from further afield. Access to motorized transport becomes a critical factor and truck owners are often able to establish control over the urban wholesale market. Frequently these trucks are being used to distribute goods to distant parts of the country, and instead of returning empty they fill up with wood or charcoal for the urban market. The transport costs for this woodfuel are thus almost nil, enabling some Third World cities to draw their supplies from a surprisingly wide area. Some of the charcoal sold in Nairobi, for example, comes from the Sudanese border – 600 kilometres to the north.

Very little wood is grown for the urban market. Most of it comes from common lands and other areas where it can be obtained without payment. In many countries there is widespread evasion of forestry regulations and large quantities of wood are illegally removed from protected forests, sometimes with the connivance of corrupt forestry officials. In countries where new areas are being opened up for agriculture, clearing the land of trees can also provide new and cheap sources of woodfuel.

The concentrated demands of the urban market, and the incentives to cut trees created by a cash market for woodfuel, can dramatically increase the rate at which deforestation takes place in the urban hinterland. Charcoal production is particularly destructive because live trees are cut instead of the dead branches which rural people usually collect to supply their own needs. The opening up of new roads also has the effect of making the urban woodfuel market more accessible to remote areas. This spreads the deforestation further.

Although most countries have legislation covering the cutting and transport of wood for sale, practical control is very difficult to implement. In the majority of cases the forestry services which are responsible for guarding woodland resources do not have the means to carry out their task properly; they frequently lack vehicles, spare parts, fuel and adequate staff levels. Even ensuring that the large numbers of woodfuel transporters pay their dues and taxes is a difficult task.

When dealers from the cities start to buy wood in a new location, it imposes an additional pressure on the woodfuel resources of the area and can make it more difficult for the people living there to obtain their own fuel supplies. Usually it is the men who become interested in these commercial woodfuel dealings. As anthropologist Jacqueline Ki-Zerbo observed about men in West Africa, the emergence of a commercial market 'is the recognition of a new situation, that wood has become a rare and therefore valuable commodity deserving the attention of the male sex'.[32]

The result is that women gathering fuel for the family can find themselves in competition with men collecting it for sale.

But the woodfuel trade brings little real or enduring prosperity to the rural areas. The people who make a living cutting and selling wood to dealers are usually the landless or very poor farmers with little alternative means of earning a cash income. They have virtually no negotiating power against dealers or intermediaries who therefore get away with paying the absolute minimum necessary to obtain the wood they want.

One of the most fundamental problems is that the price paid is sufficient to encourage people to cut trees but is rarely enough to make it worthwhile for farmers to invest in growing wood for sale. But this does not concern the woodfuel dealers: when all the saleable wood in a particular place is depleted, they simply move on to another area and begin the process of resource depletion again.

Charcoal Making

Charcoal making is one of the oldest crafts in the world. It dates back to at least 5000 BC, when copper began to be used for making weapons and ornaments in Egypt. Charcoal not only provided the necessary high-temperature heat, it also acted as a reducing agent – combining with the oxygen in metallic ores to form carbon monoxide or carbon dioxide and leaving the metal behind. Charcoal held a key position in the rise of industrial society up to the late eighteenth century, when coal began to take over its role. But it was still important in Sweden until the 1940s, and in Brazil the charcoal industry provides almost the whole fuel needs of the country's steel industry: charcoal consumption in 1981 was over 4 million tonnes.

In some areas in the developing world there are long traditions of professional charcoal making, and those entering the trade have to serve a long apprenticeship. Elsewhere it is less formally organized and is carried out by individuals working on their own with varying degrees of skill. Often it is the last resort for the poorest in the community who have no other way of earning an income.

The most common manufacturing method is the earth kiln, or

clamp. This is simply a heap of wood covered with vegetation and a sealing layer of earth. There is an immense range of such kilns, varying in size from just a few cubic metres up to 150 cubic metres or more. The smaller mounds are usually made by one person, but the larger are generally built by a team of professional charcoal makers. In Zambia, monster kilns 8 metres wide, 2 metres high and up to 100 metres long are sometimes used; these can take months to build. Another common traditional method is to make the charcoal in a pit in the ground.

In charcoal making there are three distinct processes. The first is called the drying phase in which the water from the wood is driven off. Once this has happened, the temperature of the kiln rises quickly and what is called the pyrolysis reaction takes place. In this, the chemical structure of the wood breaks down. A complex mixture of substances known as the pyrolysis products are given off in gaseous form, leaving behind the charcoal. When the pyrolysis reaction is finished, the emission of gases ceases, and the kiln gradually cools down.

Charcoal has twice the energy content of wood: this is one of its principal attractions for consumers. A small amount of it provides an intense steady heat, and it also burns without much smoke. But just as in electricity production, there is an energy penalty paid for the advantages. When charcoal is being made, a high proportion of the original energy in the wood is lost. An unskilled maker may obtain a yield by weight of only 10 per cent of the original wood – an energy efficiency of just 20 per cent; even when made by the most skilled professionals, the energy yield is rarely more than 50 per cent.

In practice, the charcoal maker begins the process by igniting the kiln at one end or, in the case of circular kilns, at the centre. Initially, one or several openings are left in the kiln so that the fire draws properly. At this stage there is a copious emission of white smoke, which is mainly water vapour. When the fire has caught properly, the charcoal maker seals the kiln. In a short while, as the pyrolysis reaction begins, the colour of the smoke seeping from the kiln changes to a darker bluish colour. There is also a heavy characteristic smell of wood creosote. This is the beginning of the most critical stage in the operation of the kiln. During the pyrolysis, or carbonization as it is sometimes called, the kiln requires continual supervision both night and day. Cracks which appear in the cover have to be sealed; any sign of flames or a red glow are a sign that combustion rather than carbonization is taking place and the air supply to that spot must be blocked. In the case of a large kiln, the pyrolysis reaction must be steered through the charge of wood by opening and closing ventilation holes in the earth covering. If there is any lapse of attention, serious trouble can ensue.

The problem of keeping a kiln under control is a perennial one, as can be seen from a chronicle dating from 1457. It tells of Phillip the Good, Duke of Burgundy, who was upset after a row with his son one night and went wandering on his own in the woods. He saw a glimmer of light:

> The more he approached it, the more it seemed a hideous and frightful thing, for the fire came out of a mound in more than a thousand places with thick smoke and at that hour anyone would think it was the purgatory of some soul or some other illusion of the devil.[33]

The truth was more prosaic: he was witnessing a charcoal kiln burning out of control. When this happens, the operator must immediately attempt to seal all the openings through which air is getting into the kiln. The work is dangerous since he has to climb over the kiln, which can give way and plunge him into the fire.

Carbonization proceeds slowly in a kiln. Much depends on its size and the exact method of construction. In small mounds it may take about a week; in large kilns of 50–100 cubic metres it may be as long as a month. The kiln is then allowed to cool slowly, after which the earth covering is removed and the charcoal is spread out to season for a day or two. It can then be bagged for the market. It is very common to see bags of charcoal being offered for sale along the roads leading into the cities where charcoal is used in the developing world. This charcoal has usually been made in the bush or woodland nearby.

12

Addressing the Problem of Woodfuel Depletion

Woodfuel, which supplies the majority of the energy needs of the developing world, is a renewable energy source. The irony is that it is running out. Taking the developing world as a whole, there is no doubt that woodfuel resources are being depleted considerably faster than they are being renewed.

The first widespread recognition of this came in the mid-1970s. The environmental writer Erik Eckholm began to piece together the evidence of forest depletion and destruction of wood stocks throughout the developing world. His study, entitled *The Other Energy Crisis: Firewood*,[34] had an immense impact on thinking among governments, international organizations and technical assistance agencies concerned with Third World development.

It is certainly not true, as is sometimes believed, that the industrial countries have neglected this 'other energy crisis'. In the past decade there has been a flood of energy projects with considerable amounts of time and effort being invested in efforts to deal with the problem of depleting woodfuel resources. In the Sahel alone about $160 million were spent on tree-growing projects between 1975 and 1982. Nor has there been any lack of ideas, as the following comment on tree-growing efforts in the Sahel clearly reveals:

It would not be far from the truth to state that virtually every conceivable strategy has been proposed by someone at one time or another over the past decade – each strategy with its proponents, many of them with funding for at least a pilot effort. Fortunately, some of the more questionable and costly of these schemes have been avoided, the trans-

Sahel green belt for example, an idea that made neither technical, economic nor social sense, however compelling the visual image of a line of trees stopping the 'advancing desert'. Many of the other ideas have been tried with results ranging from excellent through questionable to downright counter-productive.[35]

Similar remarks could be made about the efforts made in other parts of the developing world. Countless tree-growing projects have been initiated by organizations ranging from huge international institutions such as the World Bank, through to small charities or groups of volunteers. But the successes have been far outnumbered by the failures. It is now becoming clear that one of the main reasons why so many programmes failed was that the method of analysis used to determine whether there was a woodfuel 'crisis' brewing in an area was far too simplified. It relied on a method of projecting trends forward which gave outsiders a view of events which was not shared by local people.

Figure 9 illustrates the general analytic approach that was taken in a great many studies. It can be taken to apply to a particular country or any region where people rely on woodfuel for their energy needs. The actual quantities involved and the dates will vary according to the particular circumstances being considered. But the basic form of the analysis is the same in each case.

The upward-curving line shows woodfuel consumption increasing with time as the population grows. The other line shows the yield of woodfuel which can be obtained on a sustainable basis from the existing stock of trees at any given time. To start with, the diagram shows the sustainable yield above the consumption level: this means that people in the country or the area concerned can obtain their woodfuel needs without cutting into the stock of trees. Eventually, however, consumption increases to a point where it is equal to the sustainable yield – shown on the diagram as the intersection of the two lines – and then rises above it. Now people can only meet their needs by cutting into the stock of trees: this means that the sustainable yield declines, thus increasing the rate at which the stock of trees must be cut. The deterioration in the position accelerates and the 'gap' between supply and demand rapidly widens.

At first sight this is quite a convincing model. When they were

Figure 9. Schematic representation of the woodfuel 'crisis'

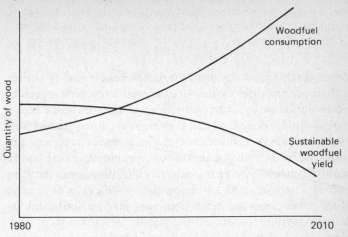

first carried out, such analyses caused widespread alarm and provoked a call for massive tree-growing programmes throughout the developing world to fill the future woodfuel gaps and prevent what appeared to be a rapidly approaching catastrophe. The amount of tree growing which was apparently required, however, was obviously far more than governments could manage with their limited resources, and there were campaigns to 'help people to help themselves' by promoting tree growing by farmers and local communities. For the most part, these were met by a resolute reluctance on the part of local people to invest land, time and effort into growing trees to fill the energy 'gaps' they were supposed to be facing.

Many of the 'experts' involved in these studies believed that local people were simply too ignorant or short-sighted to understand the dangers facing them. Governments launched programmes to educate people about the need to grow trees. International organizations supplied volunteers and educational materials. Free seedlings were provided to farmers. But still the forests failed to spring up – some farmers were found to be feeding the seedlings to their goats. Payments based on the number of seedlings were offered to farmers in some places, but a programme in Haiti found the local people dutifully planted their allocation of seedlings and then pulled them up so that they would be paid to plant them again the next year. It soon became clear that the 'gap' analysis was yielding results which did not correspond with reality as it was being experienced by the people most deeply concerned.

In fact, such 'gaps' have no physical meaning: they merely signal that previous trends cannot continue. They do not provide any information on what happens when the trends break down. In the real world, people do not continue consuming wood until the last tree has been cut. As wood begins to become scarce, they start to economize. When wood is freely available, there is little incentive for such economies, but as collection becomes more difficult and time-consuming, there is a trade-off in that extra care over the cooking fire reduces the amount of wood which has to be collected.

People also tend to increase their use of agricultural residues and dung for fuel as wood becomes harder to get. Some of these alternative fuels are more awkward or unpleasant to use than wood. The stalks of millet and sorghum, for example, are lighter and quicker-burning than wood and make cooking more difficult. But though there may be added inconvenience, the position is far from being one of desperation, and people are able to cook whatever they can grow. Moreover, these changes tend to take place gradually. People do not experience a sharply defined energy 'crisis'. Rather, there is a gradual transformation in the patterns of rural domestic energy consumption.

The switch towards dung and agricultural residues raises the question of the possible damage this may do to the agricultural system. The answer depends on local conditions. In some of the more humid and densely populated Asian countries where there are long traditions of composting and recycling organic residues, any diversion of these for fuel could indeed be damaging. But the harder, more woody residues such as millet and sorghum stalks have a low fertilizer value; moreover, they are difficult to recycle in the dry climates in which they grow. Using these as fuel is therefore unlikely to have any serious impact on the agricultural system. Even the use of dung need not be the disaster that is sometimes feared. Not all dung is automatically recycled for agricultural uses. That which is left to dry in the air loses much of its nitrogen and hence its value as a fertilizer. If the dung which is used for fuel is collected dry from waste lands and common grazing areas, then there is little loss to the agricultural system.

The difficulties of growing trees in the arid areas also need to be set against the benefits they are likely to provide. The work of planting and weeding the tree seedlings has to be carried out during the short crop cultivation season when the demands on labour are at their heaviest. The young trees then have to be watered during the long dry period of the year when the family may be hard pressed to meet even its own drinking water needs. Although woodfuel may be scarce, so also are most other things, particularly in the arid regions where the depletion of wood is at its most acute. If there are remotely adequate alternative fuels available, the onerous, time-consuming and uncertain business of growing trees to meet future woodfuel needs simply does not make sense for most rural families.

It has, however, been found in many areas that people who are not interested in growing trees for fuel are keen to grow them for other purposes. Fruit trees and those which provide fodder for animals provide very tangible benefits and, in fact, also provide fuel when they are trimmed and pruned. There has now been a switch in priorities in many places and assistance programmes are based on the promotion of these 'multi-purpose' trees. But, again, care must be taken to ensure that local conditions are properly understood before launching tree-growing programmes. The climate must be right for the trees being used. There tend to be waves of enthusiasm for new 'miracle' trees which grow rapidly and provide a multitude of benefits. The nitrogen-fixing leucaena tree was very much the rage some years ago, but experience has shown that it can be very disappointing if the conditions are not right for it. Before any new tree species can be promoted with confidence in an area, there have to be trials which demonstrate that it is suitable. Otherwise there is likely to be a lot of wasted effort and some angry and disillusioned local people.

The local land tenure system also needs to be taken into account. It is futile to try to persuade people to plant trees over which they have no rights of ownership. It seems an obvious point, but it is sometimes missed. It can arise in some areas because the land belongs to the community, and though people may farm it permanently, they do not have personal rights to any trees that grow on it. In other places, most of the land is by tradition unfenced and open to grazing animals once the harvest has been gathered. People cannot be expected to plant trees if they have no socially acceptable way of protecting them against marauding cattle and goats.

The success or failure of tree-growing programmes depends heavily on the extent to which programme planners are prepared to put themselves in the position of the people they are trying to help and accept that their point of view is valid. This human element, which is so easily submerged by generalized technical analysis of energy 'gaps', is crucial. No tree-growing programme will work unless the local men and women who have to implement it are convinced of its benefits and relevance to them.

Rising Urban Woodfuel Demands

Most of the cities in the developing world are growing rapidly. Driven by the shortage of agricultural land and the lack of economic opportunities in the rural areas, migrants are pouring into the urban areas in search of work. In some countries the cities are growing at 7 per cent per year, doubling in size every ten years. The question of how these cities will meet their future woodfuel needs is a cause of great concern for many planners.

Urban demographers are now beginning to question whether such rapid growth rates will be sustained. But no one doubts that there will be a substantial increase in the number of urban dwellers over the next few decades. This particularly applies in the poorer countries, in Africa especially, where the present proportion of urban dwellers tends to be in the range of 10–20 per cent, compared with the 80–90 per cent found in the richer industrial countries. Some observers have predicted that the woodfuel demands of these cities will increase in line with population growth and lead to a major crisis in the next twenty years or so. But just as in the case of the rural areas, it is unlikely that the worst of these projections will be realized. Because of the many social and economic changes which take place when a city grows, urban woodfuel consumption is unlikely to grow in parallel with population growth.

As a city increases in size, the arrangements for its administration, provisioning and maintenance become more complex. There is a steady growth in the numbers of administrators, professional people, wholesale and retailer traders, and providers of a continually widening and more sophisticated range of services. The number of middle and upper managers, as well as white-collar workers, rises. The provision of roads, office buildings, commercial buildings and urban infrastructure requirements provides a large amount of work for the construction industry.

The social structure reflects such changes, becoming increasingly stratified according to income. The poor become increasingly crammed together in small run-down accommodation in the older parts of the city; new arrivals from the country tend to go to shanty towns on the outskirts. Many of the new arrivals are young single men or married men without their families. In some cities which are growing rapidly, the number of men can be up to 25 per cent higher than that of women. Meanwhile, as their prosperity grows, the middle-income and upper-income classes adopt a distinctive style of life. They establish residential areas of their own in the suburbs and better parts of the city. They employ a considerable number of servants, many of whom eat and sleep in the accommodation provided by their employers.

These social changes are also reflected in the patterns of domestic energy use. As people become richer and rise in the social scale, they tend to shift away from woodfuels: they, and their servants, make increasing use of bottled gas and electricity for cooking. In the poorer quarters, poverty and overcrowding make it increasingly difficult to obtain and use woodfuel in the quantities possible when the city was smaller and more closely in touch with its rural surroundings.

Eating habits also change. Many single men do not cook for themselves but obtain their meals from small cafés and eating-houses. Working people also tend to take their midday meals in small cafés, or buy food from kiosks and street vendors. Breakfasts are often bought on the way to work instead of being cooked in the home. These wholesale food providers are generally much more economical in their fuel consumption than families cooking one meal at a time.

An increase in city size also brings about changes in the food supply system. The provision of fresh foods becomes more difficult and expensive because of the growing complexity and cost of storage and distribution. This results in a greater use of processed and packaged cereal and milk products and canned foods. Although people may not like them at first, the economies of scale brought about by the increasing market, together with their easier distribution and storage, make these more economical for consumers than traditional foods.

The use of foods which are quicker and easier to cook also makes the substitution of woodfuel by conventional fuels easier and more likely. Using a gas or kerosene stove for a stew which requires two hours' stirring and simmering is quite impractical; but this is not so if it is a case of quickly making a porridge from preprocessed cereals or dried milk products. In fact, the use of conventional fuels usually starts with the preparation of snacks and hot drinks, and in time it spreads to the preparation of other meals.

It is clear that the majority of these changes accompanying urban growth reduce both the number of people relying on woodfuel and the average consumption of those who do. The changes do not take place overnight, but over the years the cumulative effect is very large. The Indian city of Bangalore, for example, is set in an area in which the vast majority of local people use woodfuel for their cooking needs. Yet 65 per cent of the urban population rely solely on conventional fuels and do not use any woodfuel whatsoever. It is only among the poorest urban families that there is an exclusive use of woodfuel for cooking and water heating. Among these people, the average consumption is only a third of that in the villages in the surrounding area.

Future urban woodfuel demands in the developing world will therefore be considerably less than extrapolations based solely on population growth would indicate. But it is still difficult to be more specific than this. The broad outlines of the changes that take place are clear, but there have been few quantitative studies on how the social and economic changes accompanying urban growth affect energy consumption patterns. This is an area in which further research is urgently required. Energy policy formulation for the cities of the Third World is taking place in an almost total vacuum of reliable information.

Growing Trees to Meet Urban Woodfuel Needs

Whatever the exact levels of urban woodfuel demand, it is nevertheless clear that a substantial amount of wood is going to be needed to meet the energy needs of urban consumers in the Third World over the coming decades. The present methods by which these supplies are met are extremely destructive: they provoke tree cutting but provide no incentive for the renewal of wood resources. Much thought has been given to the possibility of creating woodfuel plantations which would enable urban woodfuel supplies to be met on a sustainable basis.

One of the most commonly suggested measures has been the creation of large plantations in the areas around cities – sometimes referred to as peri-urban plantations. An early success with this approach was achieved around the turn of the century by the Emperor Menelik of Ethiopia. His efforts to promote the growing of eucalyptus to supply the needs of Addis Ababa were so successful that a description of the city in 1920 said that 'the streets and paths of Addis Ababa began to look like clearings in a vast continuous forest'.[36]

By their nature, large-scale peri-urban plantations involve substantial investment costs. Ground must be prepared, seedlings planted, weeded and protected; as the trees mature, the plantation must be guarded against the depredations of wandering animals and illegal woodcutters; and all of this has to be done with paid labour. Peri-urban plantations are economical only if the price obtainable for the wood is sufficient to cover the costs. The key to the urban woodfuel problem is thus the price that woodfuel fetches in the market. One of the problems faced by programme planners is that, despite the worries about depletion, the price of woodfuel in most places is still far below the cost of producing wood in a plantation. This is because woodfuel supplies are being obtained from the natural tree cover. It costs nothing to grow these trees: the only costs incurred by woodfuel dealers are those of transport and the small amount paid to the poor villagers who collect or steal it.

With time and the continued depletion of natural woodland resources, however, woodfuel prices should rise, making tree growing for the market more attractive. Under these conditions, farmers would be willing to plant trees to supply the urban woodfuel market – always provided they had no more profitable use for their land. But, of course, there is also an upper boundary to prices. Once the price of woodfuel reaches a level where customers decide it is bad value in comparison with kerosene or bottled gas, they will switch away from it.

In a number of areas the precise set of conditions which makes tree growing for woodfuel a profitable exercise do exist. Much of the woodfuel supply for Madras, for example, comes from private plantations of casuarina trees. These are grown on saline soils near the coast for which alternative profitable uses are hard to find. The city of Bangalore also obtains a substantial proportion of its wood supplies from private plantations. Furthermore, a recent project in Haiti has shown that growing trees for charcoal making is financially attractive. But in areas where tree growing is slow and difficult, woodfuel plantations to supply the market are not yet – and may never be – economically viable.

Growing a small number of trees around the house or the boundaries of fields can, however, make sense to farmers even in areas where the price of woodfuel is too low to justify a larger-scale woodfuel plantation. Since the land and labour required for this is negligible, they have nothing to lose. Indeed, in some countries such as Peru and Ecuador this kind of tree growing is regarded as a type of long-term savings to pay for special events such as weddings. If carried out on a sufficiently large scale, the cumulative effect of such tree growing can be surprisingly large.

As woodfuel prices rise, these small-scale tree growing efforts will tend to become more common. It is therefore unlikely that Third World cities will completely run out of wood. But in many cases it seems inevitable that the position will have to become worse before it begins to get better.

Improving the Efficiency of Energy Use

At first sight, the case for trying to improve the efficiency of domestic energy consumption by persuading people to switch away from their traditional open fires and stoves appears unassailable. The open fire is obviously a pretty inefficient way of using the energy of wood.

When a large fire is built between stones which are relatively openly positioned around it, there is little to prevent the heat radiating laterally outwards from the burning fuel, with a considerable loss of heat to the surroundings. Hot gases from the fire also tend to pass straight up past the cooking pot without transferring any heat to it. When there is a wind, the heat losses are greatly increased. The extra air coming into the fire will also speed up the rate of combustion. At the same time, the wind blows the hot gases away from the pot. Thus an unshaded fire under windy or draughty conditions can have a heavily increased rate of fuel consumption together with a reduced ability to heat a pot.

Many of the inefficiencies of the open fire are shared by traditional stove designs. There is usually no control over the supply of air entering the fire box. The seating for the pot is often crudely designed so that the heat transfer is poor and there is a lot of wastage of hot gases from the fire. Therefore, designers working on improved stoves for the developing world usually focus on three main areas of concern: reducing the heat losses from the fire; controlling the flow of air through the fire; and improving the transfer of heat to the pot. Because these new stoves have to be used by extremely poor people, it has also been necessary to ensure that the costs of the stoves are kept to a minimum. Some types are designed to be built by the people using them.

Interest in promoting improved stoves dates back at least forty years. In India an improved stove design called the *magan chula* was introduced in 1947. After the country's independence further efforts were stimulated by the publication in 1953 of a famous paper called *Smokeless Kitchens for the Millions*.[37] There was further interest in the early 1960s when a consultant from the Food and Agricultural Organization of the UN (FAO) called Hans Singer produced a report for the government of Indonesia in which he made detailed recommendations on the introduction of more energy-efficient stoves in order to cut down on the country's woodfuel consumption.

Contemporary interest in improved stoves began in Guatemala in 1976, when a new stove design was introduced by volunteers working on reconstruction after the disastrous earthquake of that year. This was made from a mixture of mud and sand and was called the *Lorena* stove, from the Spanish words for mud and sand. These stoves were designed to be built by their owners. A variation on the Lorena stove was introduced into Senegal in 1980, where it was called the *Ban ak Suuf* stove, this being derived from the Wolof language words for sand and clay.

Further programmes were started in a number of other countries and enthusiasm for improved stoves began to mount. They were seen by many as the 'answer' to the problems of woodfuel scarcity and deforestation in the developing world. One rallying call issued in 1982 said: 'At the moment, 10 000 stoves have been built. To solve the problems of deforestation we should have 100 million stoves within twenty years.'[38]

It soon became clear, however, that all was not well with the programmes which were under way. People were building stoves in response to the urgings of government officials and foreign advisers, but many were simply not using them. The number of stories of disenchantment began to mount. A woman in Senegal, for example, was found to be using her *Ban ak Suuf* for storing dried fish. Many of the stoves which were in use were falling apart and were not being replaced. Finally, and dishearteningly, the savings in fuel were turning out to be much less than expected; in some cases they were using more than the open fire they replaced. As these conclusions began to sink in, a major review of thinking about improved stoves took place.

It was found that the open fire or traditional stove was not nearly as inefficient as had been thought. True, wood was used in large quantities when it was readily available. But where it was scarce one observer said: 'Economy is second nature to people.' Thus the people most likely to use improved stoves were already using wood economically.

The whole design philosophy of training people to build their own stoves from locally available materials also began to come into question. The initial reasoning behind this was sound. People in the rural areas did not buy their woodfuel. It was therefore unlikely that they would be prepared to pay for a stove which enabled them to reduce woodfuel consumption. One way round this was to offer them a stove which cost them nothing except the labour involved in building it. The problem in practice was that it was virtually impossible for people to construct a stove to the design tolerances necessary to ensure significant energy savings; and even if they managed to do so, the durability of the mud-and-sand mixture was so poor that its performance rapidly deteriorated.

Although some workers have continued to seek solutions to these problems, enthusiasm for promoting owner-built stoves in the rural areas has greatly waned in the past few years. The emphasis is now much more upon metal or ceramic stoves which can be made by local craftsmen and sold in urban markets. These can be produced to much more tightly controlled dimensional tolerances and are considerably more durable than those made of mud-and-sand mixtures. The fact that urban consumers have to pay for their woodfuel means that they are potential customers for a stove which offers them energy savings and a reasonably quick pay-back period for their investment.

The improved stove now being widely adopted in Nairobi is one such example. The design is based on that of an ingenious double-walled stove which is widely referred to as the Thai bucket. It appears to have originated in China and came into use in Thailand in the 1920s. It has a metal outer skin made from a bucket, often complete with the handle for carrying it. There is a prefabricated inner lining made of ceramic material, and the space between it and the bucket is filled with an insulating material such as the hard cellular ash obtained when rice husks are burned. The excellent insulation provided by the double skin reduces heat losses considerably and makes this a particularly energy-efficient stove. A version of this stove designed for Kenyan conditions was introduced to Nairobi in 1982. By mid-1985 total sales had reached 180 000 and were running at between 5000 and 8000 per month.

The main lesson from the efforts made to date to promote improved stoves in the developing world is one that is being learned in other areas too. It is that traditional methods are rarely irrational, no matter how they may seem at first sight; the poor are not generally frivolous about the resources on which they depend. That is not to say that technical improvements are not possible. But they must be designed so that they are matched to the needs, priorities and financial capabilities of the people for whom they are intended.

The same is true when programmes to improve the efficiency of charcoal making are being considered. The inefficiencies apparent in traditional charcoal-making methods have excited the reforming zeal of foresters and others for over a century. The first attempts to introduce more efficient portable steel kilns were made in India in the 1890s. Sporadic efforts have been made in a variety of countries ever since. But in most cases the permanent impact of these programmes has been negligible. Even where the new techniques have had an initial success, they have tended to be abandoned when the project promoters leave.

This need not be so. It is certainly possible to introduce improvements in traditional charcoal-making techniques. But any intervention, if it is to succeed, must be based on an understanding of the needs of local charcoal makers and the resources available to them. Most of the programmes up until now have concentrated on trying to improve the energy efficiency of production so that the charcoal makers would obtain a higher yield of charcoal per tonne of wood used. But this is of little concern to most traditional charcoal makers because they do not have to pay for the wood they use. It fails to take into account the fact that charcoal is made for money. Charcoal makers are not particularly interested in the yield of charcoal per tonne of wood as such; what concerns them is the financial return they obtain for their efforts. The only improved charcoal-making projects with a hope of success are those which will improve the income of charcoal makers.

Strategies for Action

The experience with the various types of woodfuel programmes carried out to date clearly reveals how difficult it is to devise a strategy for action to counter the depletion of woodfuel resources taking place across the developing world. A large part of the reason for this is that the Third World's energy problems have rarely been defined from a local point of view.

This focus will have to change if effective strategies for action are to be devised. Local people do not act to solve global problems; this is as true of woodfuel consumers as it was of motor-vehicle drivers in the industrial countries during the 1970s. Their behaviour may be affected to a certain extent by exhortations from on high and forecasts of doom and destruction, but the main determinants of what they do are the imperatives and economic realities of their daily lives.

At times it seems as if there is a kind of intellectual imperialism among even the best-intentioned outsiders, a determination to mould the energy problems of the Third World to the preconceptions of those observing it from the outside. It is often forgotten that energy is not the only or necessarily the most important issue facing people. Food, water, shelter, health and the need to make provision for the future all jostle for attention and a share of the available family resources. The luxury of specialization in any particular problem is not one that most Third World families can afford.

None of this is to minimize the appalling plight of millions of people in the developing world. The pictures on the world's television screens have made this abundantly clear in recent years. Nor is it to deny that there are serious dangers to the environment if the tree cover is stripped from vulnerable areas of land. It is to say that the onus is on outsiders proposing new initiatives to show that they actually will make life better for the people who have to take responsibility for implementing them.

If large-scale change is to be brought about at a local level, it cannot be imposed from the top downwards. No matter how grave the problems appear from the outside, if local people do not regard them as serious their response to external suggestions and government directives will be grudging and the practical results will be small. This is true not just in the domain of energy but elsewhere as well. People will not make serious efforts to resolve a problem they do not regard as serious.

There is no point in appealing to people who do not know if they will survive the next harvest to make sacrifices for the long term. The only feasible route to a satisfactory future must be through policies which make sense to local people on their present merits. This puts heavy demands on the skill and initiative of programme planners and technical assistance agencies. If it can be achieved, it may make it possible to turn some of today's woodfuel problems into opportunities for fruitful action and broadly based development.

13

Energy Projects and Programmes

The large-scale industrial and commercial sectors in the economies of the Third World are closely linked to those of the industrial countries. Most of the energy used is in the form of oil or electricity. Machinery, equipment, design standards, technical and administrative skills either come from abroad or are based on the models of the industrialized world. The path of technological change is therefore likely to follow the same lines as that in the industrial countries.

The position is very different outside this modern sector. In the rural areas, in particular, technology tends to be primitive or virtually non-existent. Power for tilling, pumping, lifting and carrying is supplied by animal or human muscles; in sub-Saharan Africa even the use of animal power is relatively rare. It is easy to romanticize this state of existence, characterizing it as harmony with nature. In fact, it is back-breaking, disease-ridden and almost defenceless against the manifold vagaries of nature. Life expectancy in the poorer countries of Africa is little better than it was in medieval Europe.

One theory of development which held sway in the 1950s and 1960s relied upon what was called the 'trickle-down' effect. According to this, investment in roadworks, power stations and large-scale industrial projects would set a process of development in motion, the benefits of which would eventually reach the poorest people. This was an optimistic time. Developing countries embarked on vast projects such as new capital cities. It was also the era of huge dam projects such as Aswan in Egypt, Cabora Bassa in Mozambique and Tarbela in Pakistan. As time passed, however, it became clear that the trickle-down was happening more slowly than expected, or was not happening at all. The urban middle classes benefited from the contacts with the industrial world. But the powerlines passed by the rural villages and over the shanty towns of the poor. Modern developments were found to be widening rather than narrowing the gap between rich and poor in many countries. Large-scale development projects came under increasing attack.

The debate on development shifted towards the problem of how to reach the 'poorest of the poor'. A profoundly influential book was *Small is Beautiful*, published in 1974, and written by E. F. Schumacher, a former economic adviser to the U K National Coal Board. It introduced the concept of 'intermediate technology' for developing countries. This was a technology which was supposed to bridge the gap between the modern capital-intensive technology of the industrial world and the traditional production methods of the developing world. He wrote:

Such an intermediate technology would be immensely more productive than the indigenous technology (which is often in a condition of decay), but it would also be immensely cheaper than the sophisticated, highly capital-intensive technology of modern industry. At such a level of capitalization, very large numbers of workplaces would be created within a fairly short time; and the creation of such workplaces would be 'within reach' for the more enterprising minority within the district, not only in financial terms but also in terms of their education, aptitude, organizing skill and so forth.[39]

An unexpected convert to the new view of development was the President of the World Bank, Robert McNamara. He had been the U S Secretary of State for Defense in the 1960s and was the architect of the 'electronic battlefield' approach to the Vietnam war. In the 1970s he applied his considerable talents to publicizing the cause of the rural poor in the developing world, and was undoubtedly responsible for a major shift in emphasis in development projects.

When the oil price rises of the 1970s came, they had a devastating effect on the economies of the developing world. Some of the poorer countries found their oil import bills were greater than their total export earnings. Renewable-energy technologies seemed to offer a way of reducing dependence on oil imports.

Their small scale and potential for decentralized applications fitted well with the new thinking on development. Many new energy projects were therefore launched but, as in the case of woodfuel programmes, the majority of these efforts were failures. The catalogue is dismal and seemingly endless. All over the developing world there are broken windmills and solar pumps, empty biogas pits, unused solar cookers, abandoned gasifiers and derelict small hydro installations.

In many cases the causes of these failures can easily be identified. They include difficulties in getting costs down to an acceptable level, a lack of local technical skills, unawareness of local customs – or indifference to them; as well as administrative incompetence or corruption. Far too frequently there were, in addition, basic flaws in the technologies being offered. Devices which would not meet the minimum standards of safety, durability and effectiveness required in the industrial world were optimistically offered to rural people in the developing world as a contribution to meeting their energy needs. It sometimes seemed as though the attitude of the donors was that people with nothing should be glad to have anything. Not surprisingly, such offerings found little favour; people on the edge of survival have little margin for experiment or error. As a recent book, *Africa in Crisis*, commented:

> Many of the 'renewable-energy' aid projects run by northern countries have much more to do with the donors' need to experiment than with what the recipients need or can afford. USAID (the US Agency for International Development) has a 'two phase' renewable-energy project in Mali. During 'Phase I', four photo-voltaic pumps and fifty-five woodstoves were installed in villages; stove dissemination activities were begun; a photo-voltaic refrigerator/freezer and seven lighting systems were installed in village schoolhouses and clinics; wind pumps and electrical generators, a Chinese-style dome biogas digester, solar thermal food driers and water heaters and distillers were all built, according to an official report.
>
> And what was Phase II? A socio-economic study is under way towards identifying village energy needs![40]

Many of the necessary lessons have now been learned. It is unlikely that the worst mistakes of the past will be repeated as frequently in the future. A great deal of the former naive enthusiasm has given way to a much more hard-headed realism; the difficulties of achieving anything worthwhile, let alone making a major impact on the most grievous areas of need, are more clearly recognized. Much valuable work has been done on understanding the social and cultural constraints on the introduction of energy innovations.

But a careful tailoring of solutions to local problems is only part of the battle. The crucial criterion, if a project is to be judged a success, is whether local people find it useful enough to repeat themselves and are able to do so without external assistance. Donations from outside will never be adequate to meet the energy needs of the rural Third World. Any energy innovation, if it is to have an impact, must be able to spread rapidly with a minimum of external support. To assess whether this is likely to happen in the case of any particular technology, it is useful to be able to fit it into a broad view of the rural energy economy and the different opportunities it offers for action.

The Rural Fuel Economy

A simple schematic categorization of rural energy uses in one of the poorer developing countries is shown in Figure 10. There is no pretence that this conveys anything of the social and cultural influences at work. Its purpose is to illustrate some of the key economic considerations which determine whether an energy innovation can be successfully introduced and whether it has any prospect of spreading spontaneously.

Figure 10. Schematic categorization of rural energy uses

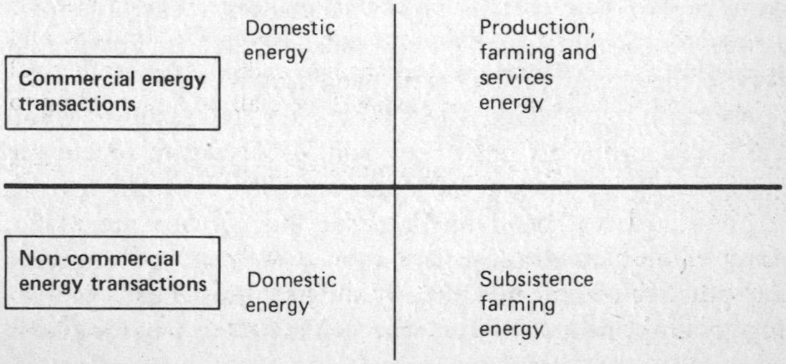

The heavy horizontal line marks the division between applications in which the energy used is obtained without any cash payments and those in which it is purchased. They are referred to as non-commercial and commercial energy transactions. The vertical line divides domestic uses from those involved in farming and the production of goods and services. These divisions are not meant to be rigidly exclusive; there is an income gradient from the very poorest at the bottom up to the high-income levels at the top.

In the bottom left-hand quadrant are found the domestic heating and cooking uses of biomass fuels which are collected without payment. The upper-left quadrant includes the domestic uses of purchased wood and conventional fuels. The energy uses of a very poor rural family would be 'located' entirely in the lower quadrant; those of a family which uses non-commercial woodfuel for cooking and heating but purchases some kerosene for lighting would straddle the horizontal line. Those of a fully modern household with a gas cooker and a variety of electrical appliances would be in the top portion of the upper quadrant. A similar set of distinctions can be made between the two right-hand quadrants. The use of unpaid family labour for subsistence farming fits in the lower quadrant. The energy uses of a modern mechanized farm or a tea factory would fit in the upper quadrant.

Given this kind of simple 'map' of rural energy uses, it is now possible to look at a number of energy technologies and see whether they can be matched to appropriate end-uses. If they are to 'fit', they must be suitable for both the energy and the economic characteristics of the 'location' for which they are intended. The exercise of matching technologies to their end-uses in this way helps to explain why there is no simple answer to such plaintive questions as: 'Surely, solar energy must be able to provide an answer to the energy problems of the Third World?'

Consider, in that context, the solar cooker, and assume that all the technical problems have been solved. Trying to locate the solar cooker in the bottom left quadrant will not work; there is no money there to spend on domestic energy. Moving to the upper left-hand quadrant where money is spent on domestic energy puts the cooker in competition with other means of providing cooking energy. No one who can afford to pay for fuel is likely to be willing to put up with the inconvenience and difficulty of using a solar cooker.

A flat-plate solar water heater is a different matter. A family or a business which is paying for its water heating may well find a flat-plate solar collector is economically attractive. But it is useless suggesting it to a poor family which relies on the woodfuel it collects to supply its hot water needs. The place for flat-plate solar collectors is in the upper right and left quadrants.

A solar photovoltaic water pump provides another interesting example. The peak power output is usually 0·25–0·50 kilowatts. This is roughly the range of power outputs of human beings and draught animals. From the energy point of view, solar photo-voltaic water pumps fit naturally into the energy patterns of subsistence existence, either the bottom right or left quadrants. The charities and technical assistance organizations which in-stalled them in various villages of the Third World have found this to be the case; villagers and small farmers are very glad of a device which removes the drudgery of drawing water from a well for domestic uses or irrigation. But solar pump installations cost up to $10 000. There is little hope of a subsistence community raising this amount of money, or, if it did, having a solar pump as its top priority. Thus, even when there is a successful de-monstration project in an area, the likelihood of other com-munities being willing to pay for their own solar pumps is small. The place for a solar pump, if it exists, is in the top part of the upper right-hand quadrant; there it has to justify itself technically and economically in competition with well-established power sources for pumping such as diesel or electricity.

Examining the case of improved cooking stoves is also in-formative. The initial instinct of programme promoters was to aim for subsistence households in the rural areas because their need appeared to be greatest. But because no money is spent on domestic energy, the stoves had to cost nothing. This meant that the stoves had to be home-made using locally available materials. The technical limitations imposed by these conditions meant that in practice the stoves were little, if any, improvement on the traditional methods already in use.

The upper left-hand quadrant where people pay for their wood offered much greater technical and economic freedom in the design of the stove. If the stove was able to offer a cash saving which paid off its purchase price reasonably quickly, there was a good chance of it being bought by woodfuel consumers. Well-designed new stoves which save fuel are, in fact, finding a market in the cities of the Third World.

The case of biogas can be used as a final example. When it was realized just how successful the Chinese programme had been, there was considerable interest in trying to replicate it elsewhere. One of the principal motivations was to use biogas as a substitute for woodfuel in order to take the pressure off wood resources. Attempts were therefore made to introduce it to rural families in Tanzania, Senegal and other countries, aiming it at the lower left quadrant. Little, if any, success was achieved. In fact, biogas was completely inappropriate for such energy consumers. Although it has been promoted as a fuel of the rural poor in China, it nevertheless, requires a fairly substantial cash investment. The system of communal effort and workpoints under which most of China's biogas digesters were installed makes it difficult to assess their real financial costs, but there is no doubt that it is beyond the reach of most subsistence families. It is also noticeable that in China itself biogas was frequently employed as a substitute for electricity used for lighting or small-scale farm uses. Its place is in the upper left or right quadrants.

Figure 10 also shows how the introduction of biogas can make life worse for the poor under certain circumstances. When, for example, a wealthy farmer installs a biogas digester, it will provide him with an additional source of fuel. If, however, some of the dung going into the digester would otherwise have been used as fuel by the poor, the digester becomes a means by which energy resources are transferred from the lower to the upper quadrants on the left-hand side.

Switching to Conventional Fuels

It is frequently assumed that a significant switch to conventional fuels by woodfuel consumers is not feasible for the poor countries of the developing world because of the constraints on world resources or the burden it would place on the balance of payments of these countries.

Any such switch would, of course, take place over a period of time. The lack of money and poor distribution facilities in the rural areas would also mean that it was mainly confined to urban dwellers. It is nevertheless informative to examine the implications for world energy consumption of a really major shift to conventional fuels by, say, half the world's present woodfuel consumers, some 1000 million people. The conventional fuel requirements of a family making such a switch cannot be estimated by simply taking the energy content of the present consumption of woodfuels and expressing this in terms of petroleum fuel. A gas or kerosene pressure stove is likely to be anything from three to five times as efficient as a wood fire or traditional stove. Preparing the same meal using conventional fuels will therefore use correspondingly less fuel.

The switch to conventional fuels also needs to be seen as part of a more general change in the economic and cooking habits of the household. It is highly unlikely that the family which now relies on a millet stew which simmers over a wood fire for three or four hours would attempt the same cooking task on a gas stove. If they make the switch to conventional fuels, they will almost inevitably change towards a more urban diet.

Assume therefore that each family shifting from woodfuel uses 300 kilograms of petroleum fuel (kerosene or bottled gas) per year on average. This is a fairly generous allowance: it is, for example, about twice the average annual fuel consumption for cooking by families in the UK. The total consumption by the 1000 million people switching from woodfuels is only 50 million tonnes. This is negligible in a global context: it is considerably less than 1 per cent of the world's total energy consumption in 1985.

Similarly surprising results are obtained when the effects at a national level are examined. Calculations based on 1980 data, when oil prices were considerably higher than today's, have shown that in countries such as Kenya, Zimbabwe, Sri Lanka and Nicaragua a shift away from woodfuels by 50 per cent of present consumers would increase total import bills by only 3–5 per cent. Such changes could obviously be accommodated without difficulty over a period of, say, a decade.[41]

Some governments, such as that in Senegal, have in fact

provided subsidies for conventional fuels to encourage a shift away from the use of charcoal. This, however, can be a dangerous path to tread. The Senegalese experience has shown that the rich, who are using bottled gas in any case, have been the main beneficiaries of the scheme and the effect on charcoal consumption has been undetectable. In other countries, where subsidies have been provided for kerosene, the problem is that the kerosene can be mixed with diesel fuel or used on its own as a transport fuel. Instead of helping families with their cooking bills and easing the pressure on woodfuel resources, the government finds itself subsidizing the transport industry.

Thus there are practical obstacles to a sudden shift away from woodfuels in the developing world. Nevertheless, the calculations reveal a policy dimension which has often been lacking in developing country energy planning in recent years. The energy demands of future domestic consumers do not necessarily have to be supplied by woodfuel. There is ample room for them to be shared or met completely by conventional fuels in the medium-term future.

When the total conventional fuel consumption of the developing world for all purposes is considered, there is also considerably more room for manoeuvre than is commonly believed. According to World Bank figures, the average energy consumption of conventional fuels in the world's thirty-six poorest countries in 1984 was 288 kilograms of oil equivalent per head; the total number of people was 2·4 billion. This was almost exactly half the world's population; their combined energy consumption was about 690 million tonnes, just over 9 per cent of the world total. Very large increases in conventional fuel use in these countries could therefore take place before there is any significant impact on total world energy consumption.

Future Strategies

The concept of another 'energy crisis' running parallel to that of the industrial world in the 1970s was extremely important in rallying attention to the problems of the Third World energy consumers. But it has also been counter-productive in that it has concentrated attention on a search for large-scale solutions which might be applied with maximum speed – the 'answers' to the energy problems of the developing world.

It has also unduly emphasized the technical aspects, tending to obscure the fact that, for the overwhelming majority of the poor in the Third World, energy shortage is not a technical issue which can be considered in isolation from the rest of their lives; it is simply another aspect of the general deprivation from which they suffer. Those living at or near subsistence level are unable to benefit from the majority of technical initiatives. Their problem is poverty.

A rural community is thus more likely to be short of energy because there is a lack of economic demand for it rather than because there is no supply. Shortages of finance, technical skills and access to markets for their produce prevent people from mobilizing the resources which are already available. The low levels of energy use in the low-income communities of the developing world are generally far more a symptom than a cause of their low productivity and vulnerability to climatic conditions and economic pressures. The only way out of this is through a process in which an economic demand is created for energy at the same time as the means of supplying it are provided.

Farmers were dying of hunger within a few kilometres of the River Niger because of the failure of their crops in the recent Sahel drought. The Niger is one of the largest rivers in the world. The technical problems of bringing sufficient groundwater up to the surface to irrigate subsistence crops like millet are negligible; they have been solved in hundreds of ways throughout history and in different parts of the world. The problem facing the drought victims was that they lacked the economic means to apply any kind of technology. Their position would not have been improved by offering them an even wider choice of technologies they could not afford.

In this context, the energy issue is a minor one. The rural poor primarily need a commitment by their own governments to the land reforms and social equity which will allow them to invest in their land and build up their own production capacities. Their countries need equity in international trade, and markets for their produce rather than competition with subsidized exports. The difficulty is not in seeing what needs to be done, but in getting it done. Once the conditions have been established in which there is a demand for energy technologies, there will be no problem in meeting it. But providing energy technologies to people who are unable to benefit from them will accomplish little, if anything.

Part Four

Choosing the Energy Future

Thoughts of economy and conservation will inevitably replace those of development and progress, and the hopes of the race will centre in the future on science. So far it has been a fair-weather friend. It has been generally misunderstood as creating the wealth that has followed the application of knowledge. Modern science, however, and its synonym, modern civilization, create nothing, except knowledge. After a hand-to-mouth period of existence it has come in for and has learned how to *spend* an inheritance it can never hope to restore. The utmost it can aspire to is to become the Chancellor of Nature's Exchequer, and to control for its own ends the immense reserves of energy which are at present in keeping for great cosmical schemes – FREDERICK SODDY, *Matter and Energy*, 1912

14

Approaches to Energy Forecasting

Futurology is one of the oldest professions. But from the Pythian priestesses of Delphi to Herman Kahn of the Hudson Institute no one has devised a method of forecasting, with certainty, what is actually going to happen.

The rise of an inspirational leader can transform the attitudes of a country or a continent; an accident, illness or assassin's bullet can make the difference between peace and war. No one can foretell the breakthrough in understanding which can revolutionize science or create a whole new technology. The rise in oil prices in 1973 took the forecasters and economists of the industrial world almost completely by surprise. So also did their collapse in 1986. Major social change is influenced by so many factors that it is almost impossible to predict the shape and attitudes of society twenty or thirty years in advance.

But the future is also unpredictable because so much of it is under human control. A great deal of forecasting goes wrong because it is too mechanistic. It assumes that in the future things must occur as they have done in the past. It ignores the possibility that people will alter their behaviour. The 'doom' literature of the early 1970s often extrapolated into the future past rates of growth in the consumption of resources or the emission of pollutants and reached quite absurd conclusions. A Victorian, seeing the growth of horse-drawn traffic, might have extrapolated a graph of manure deposition in the streets of London and concluded the city would be submerged by now.

The *Limits to Growth* study, which caused such a fuss when it was published in 1972, is a good example. It certainly did useful work in focusing attention on a number of important issues and forcing many people to begin to consider the implications of the undeniable fact that the earth is finite. But one serious objection to the study was its clear implication that humanity has little option but to smash itself against the limits to its own expansion. Here is a key quotation:

Although we have many reservations about the approximations and simplifications in the present world model, it has led us to one conclusion which seems to be justified under all the assumptions we have tested so far. *The basic behaviour mode of the world system is exponential growth of population and capital, followed by collapse* [italics in original].[42]

The study team obviously convinced themselves that the world had no option but to follow the mathematical recipe for disaster which was the basis of their computer model. According to this there must be an exponential rise in population, food consumption, pollution and industrial output matched by a corresponding decline in resources, with the system inevitably collapsing catastrophically some time next century.

This at least had the merit of being reasonably definite about things. The book's amazing popularity at the time may have had something to do with its air of pessimistic certainty. But it oversimplified the real world alarmingly. The world is not a homogeneous entity with evenly distributed resources. Neither is it correct to think of it as ineluctably committed to exponential growth of the kind described in the study. The future is not necessarily bound by the laws of the past. It is possible to behave in a different way provided a decision to do so is made. The *Limits to Growth* conclusions demonstrated the valid point that, *if* the world behaves in the way the model supposes it does, and continues to do so for the next hundred years or so, the whole system will collapse. But if, heeding such warnings, humanity decides to behave differently, then the results will be different.

The detailed forecast can thus easily become a source of gentle amusement for future generations. When Professor Stanley Jevons was writing just before the outbreak of the First World War, the future of Britain's coal trade was anything but a matter of amusement. Jevons was a perceptive and able analyst, steeped in knowledge of the British coal industry, and concerned, too, with wider economic and social issues. He produced the forecast shown in Table 24 which covers the population, home consumption and coal exports of Britain through until the year 2201. It is a fascinating mixture of hits and misses. Population and energy consumption (measured in tonnes of coal equivalent) for the 1970s are surprisingly close to reality. But he failed to see the importance of oil, completely misjudged exports, and missed the

Table 24. 1915 Forecasts of population, home consumption, exports and total output of coal in the UK, 1911–2201

Year	Population of Great Britain (× 10⁶)	Consumption per head (tons)	Annual home consumption (tons × 10⁶)	Exports (including bunkers) (tons × 10⁶)	Total annual output (tons × 10⁶)	Total output to date (tons × 10⁶)
1911	40·83	4·43	180·9	87·1	268·0	900*
21	44·77	4·52	202·5	125·0	327·5	4 175†
31	48·76	4·6	224·0	172·2	396·2	8 137
41	52·73	4·65	245·1	227·1	427·2	12 859
1951	56·62	4·7	266·1	272·0	538·1	18 340
61	60·38	4·75	286·8	314·0	600·8	24 248
71	63·94	4·8	306·9	347·0	653·9	30 787
81	67·25	4·8	322·7	375·2	697·9	37 766
91	70·27	4·8	337·3	394·8	732·1	45 087
2001	72·96	4·8	347·0	411·0	758·0	52 667
11	75·30	4·8	361·4	423·0	784·4	60 511
21	77·29	4·8	371·0	435·0	806·0	68 571
31	78·93	4·8	378·7	443·5	822·2	76 793
41	80·24	4·8	385·0	456·0	841·0	85 203
2051	81·26	4·8	390·0	468·0	858·0	93 783
61	82·03	4·8	393·7	479·5	873·2	102 515
71	82·58	4·8	396·4	488·0	884·4	111 359
81	82·95	4·8	398·2	497·0	895·2	120 311
91	83·19	4·76	395·0	505·0	901·0	129 321
2101	83·34	4·73	394·0	508·0	902·0	138 341
11	83·49	4·70	392·4	501·5	893·9	146 380
21	83·64	4·68	391·3	488·0	879·3	155 173
31	83·79	4·66	390·5	457·0	847·5	163 648
41	83·94	4·64	389·1	413·0	802·1	171 669
2151	84·09	4·61	387·7	355·0	742·7	179 096
61	84·24	4·58	385·7	294·0	697·7	185 893
71	84·39	4·55	384·0	208·0	592·0	191 813
81	84·50	4·50	380·2	132·0	512·3	196 935
91	84·50	4·45	376·0	72·0	448·0	201 415
2201	84·00	4·40	371·0	38·0	409·0	205 505

* Estimates for 1913 to 1915 inclusive.

† Estimates for 1916 to 1925 inclusive, and so on.

Source: H. S. Jevons, *The British Coal Trade*, first edition, 1915; David & Charles, 1972.

peak in British coal production by 188 years: it occurred in 1913, the very year he was writing, whereas he predicted output would continue to rise until 2101.

It is worth taking the cautionary tale of Professor Jevons further and follow him as he speculates about the time when the world's coal resources are finally exhausted:

'It will not be in the temperate regions of the earth that the great aggregates of population will be situated some four or five hundred years hence, but in the tropics. The population will tend to multiply more rapidly there in the era of peaceful government and with the extension of modern industrial methods ... there is likely to be, I believe, a progressive concentration of the cruder and coarser manufacturing processes, and also much of the production of bulky goods in tropical regions. As the natives of tropical countries progress under European guidance, and ultimately under their own government, in education, skill and enterprise, they will undertake in their own countries tasks which the more refined Europeans will only do for high wages. When the coal of northern countries is nearing exhaustion, and recourse is had to sun-heat ... it is the tropics which will have the advantage for manufactures requiring much power.[6]

This beautifully illustrates the perils of extrapolation. Jevons is stimulating when he looks at the implications of the decline in coal and predicts a society running on solar energy. But he is simply absurd when he begins to spell out the social and political details of life in the future based upon his assumptions about European benevolence, refinement and superior technical skills.

Nearer the present time, there have been many enthusiastic predictions about the changes that nuclear power would bring. One commentator writing in the late 1950s said: 'Nuclear propulsion for ships is not only a possibility; it will, by the sheer force of its advantages, become the normal form of marine propulsion within the next quarter of a century, at least for larger craft.' He also speculated about 'nuclear-powered windowless, delta-shaped transport planes travelling at speeds of up to 2000 mph between Europe and America and carrying at least 100 passengers.' At the same time, he had definite reservations about the professional prudence of nuclear engineers. He went on uneasily:

It is to be hoped that the designers and constructors of nuclear-powered ships will be aware of the special dangers in case of a collision or crash. If such a vessel happened to collide, say, with one of the piers of Tower Bridge, the entire Pool of London might become radioactive. This is an engineering problem that must be solved before the first commercial atom-powered ships put to sea.[1]

The forecaster must therefore remain humble. Detailed prediction is impossible. The task is, rather, to examine the implications of trends and to help present as clearly as possible the choices before society. Seen in this light, there is no disgrace if things turn out differently from how the forecaster predicted they would; having seen the direction in which it is heading, society may choose to go elsewhere.

All forecasts are thus conditional. The best that any forecaster can do is to say that such and such will be the energy requirements *if* trends evolve in a particular way. The most important skill required is not the gift of prophecy but an ability to pick apart the forecast and see what are its deeper implications. Certain courses of action may be self-limiting or constrained by external factors; others may have implications which would be unacceptable to society if they were spelled out in detail.

Figure 11 shows a set of estimates and projections of future world energy consumption assembled by the Institute for Fuel in the early 1970s. It was found that 'with very few exceptions, published forecasts lie within the areas enclosed by the dotted lines'. Events have shown that the expert consensus was rather badly wrong. World consumption in 1985 was about 7·4 billion tonnes of oil equivalent, which fell outside the predicted range of 8·2–10·2 billion; no one would now think even the lower bound of the predicted consumption for the year 2000 is remotely possible. Armed with the priceless gift of hindsight, it is possible to draw some lessons from such experiences.

One of the most important points to note is that up to the early 1970s energy planning had been carried out almost entirely on a national basis. The availability of petroleum fuels on the international market could be taken for granted. Economists debated the merits of coal, oil, gas and nuclear power on the basis of their costs of production and distribution. There was also discussion about the ways in which governmental actions through taxes and

Figure 11. Estimates of future world energy consumption

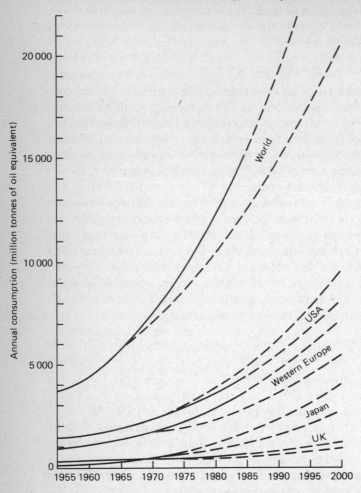

Note: The solid lines show historical figures and trend projections to 1985.
Source: Institute of Fuel, *Energy for the Future*, London, 1973.

import controls might be used to alter the competitive balance between these fuels in the furtherance of particular policy objectives. It was rare, and considered distinctly eccentric, for anyone to discuss overall questions of resource depletion. Nor were government energy planners encouraged to speculate about developments in the Middle East; such matters were for the diplomats and foreign ministries. As a result, there was no overall view of what was happening in world oil markets. Individual governments happily drew up their development plans on the basis of a continuation of past trends, with little concern for what others were doing. Virtually the only people who were aware of the implications of what was going on were the major oil companies. Their geologists were becoming increasingly convinced that there were no more oil provinces like the Middle East waiting to be discovered. It was becoming clear that the likely level of recoverable oil resources would not be able to sustain a doubling of consumption every decade for very much longer.

M. King Hubbert, a geologist who had spent twenty years with Shell, in a study published in 1969 by the US National Academy of Sciences said that the growth in oil consumption would have to slow down within about a decade and that production would reach its peak by the turn of the century. Harry Warman, BP's chief geologist, although taking a very different analytic approach to Hubbert arrived at almost precisely the same conclusions in a number of technical papers published soon after this. In 1972 Sir David Barron, the chairman of Shell, said in a speech:

A serious situation is facing the world ... and there are certain ineluctable facts which have to be faced ... If we go on using energy at the rate predicted, we shall use as much oil in the decade just begun as in the previous hundred years, and twice as much in the next decade. If this happens, then, unless the finding rate is greatly extended, we could by the turn of the century be looking down the barrel of a gun.[43]

Such words, remarkable though they were, coming from the chairman of one of the world's biggest companies, passed virtually unremarked among energy planners. Events soon proved Sir David Barron right, though considerably sooner than he had envisaged. By 1973 rapidly rising oil consumption in the industrial world had completely absorbed the production capacity of the oil industry. The OPEC nations were able to use their power to withhold oil supplies in order to raise prices massively and win political concessions from the industrial world.

Energy planning was thrown into complete disarray. The failure of the forecasters had been that they had taken too narrow a view of their subject. They had not seen that the individual pursuit of their national interests by the major industrial powers added up to an unrealizable totality. The lesson, however, was quickly learned. The OECD countries established the International Energy Agency (IEA) in 1974. It is based in Paris, despite the fact that France refuses to join it, and maintains a watch on energy at a global level. It analyses trends and their implications and makes policy recommendations to its member governments.

The failure to take account of the broad context in which energy developments take place was not confined to conventional energy planners in the 1970s. There was also a great deal of optimism about new energy sources and the role they might play in industrial society and the developing world. The United Nations even held a Conference on New and Renewable Sources of Energy in Nairobi in 1981. Its expectations were high, but it turned out to be one of the UN's least memorable of such global gatherings. The enthusiasts for new energy resources completely underestimated the difficulties of making them reliable and commercially attractive.

One way of dealing with the problem of energy planning is to construct alternative 'scenarios'. These are imagined pictures of the future which try to envisage the full implications of a particular course of action. Thus, a high-energy scenario would try to imagine how people would actually use extra energy and would examine the social, economic and environmental implications of providing it. In constructing a scenario in which society depended on renewable energy sources, it would be necessary to look at how this might be brought about and what changes would be required in employment patterns, urban life, transport and so forth.

In the early 1970s the Ford Foundation sponsored such a study of the energy choices facing the USA. It developed three widely differing scenarios for the country.[44] The first scenario was called the 'historical growth' model. This assumed that energy consumption would continue to rise along the same path as it has done historically. This would mean that US energy consumption would increase by about 2·3 times by the end of the century. The major implications of this would be that it would require very aggressive development of all our possible supplies – oil and gas onshore and offshore, coal, shale, nuclear power. If it proved feasible to increase oil imports on a large scale, then the pressure on domestic resources would relax somewhat. Still, the political, economic and environmental problems of getting that much energy out of the earth would be formidable.

Such a scenario, according to the study, implies that economic growth could continue without interruption and that no allocation of energy or energy conservation measures on a large scale would be required. But Americans would have to endure the consequences of a maximum development of indigenous resources and a heavy dependence on imports. And if there were any failure in any area of energy resource development, the scenario would be impossible to realize.

The second scenario considered was called the 'technical fix'. This 'reflects a determined, conscious national effort to reduce demand for energy through the application of energy-saving technologies'. Energy consumption increases by about 75 per cent by the turn of the century. In this scenario the main feature of society would be 'a market-place in which energy is priced to reflect its true costs to society'. It would require innovations like a 'Truth in Energy Law' which would compel manufacturers to provide a label for 'automobiles, appliances and even homes which clearly spells out average energy use and operating costs'. Society would be more energy-conscious but not markedly different from that of today. The pressure to develop energy resources would be much less than in the 'historical growth' scenario, but a major effort would nevertheless be required.

The third scenario was called 'zero energy growth' but was in fact, rather mistitled. It represents an increase in energy consumption of nearly 50 per cent. But

it represents a real break with our accustomed way of doing things. Yet it does not represent austerity . . . It would substitute for the idea that 'more is better' the ethic that 'enough is best' . . . Redesign of cities and transportation systems would be a must. Growth in energy-intensive industries like making plastics from petro-chemicals would be de-emphasized.

The 'zero energy growth' scenario thus envisaged a future in which energy consumption rises for a while and then levels out.

American society, in fact, was imagined to make the voluntary decision that it had reached the end of growth and that 'enough', indeed, 'is best'.

The study comments on its choice of scenarios:

> Of course, an infinite number of futures is possible; and it is most unlikely that the real energy future of the United States will conform closely to any of the three scenarios we have chosen to describe. They are not predictions, but a tool for rigorous thinking. We do not advocate one option over the others but present each for comparative analysis by the reader.

None of these scenarios was judged to be impossible to realize. In fact, they were explicitly described as 'three plausible but very different energy futures'. Looking at them now provides a measure of how greatly thinking has changed in the past fifteen years. No one in the USA would now regard the 'historical growth' scenario with its doubled energy consumption by the turn of the century as even worthy of serious discussion. The anticipated efforts required to hold energy consumption to an increase of 75 per cent have proved quite unnecessary. Indeed, the country has achieved zero energy growth between 1971 and 1985 without change in its ethics or need to redesign its cities.

The Ford Foundation example thus shows that even the most elaborate and expensively financed scenarios can miss the point. Those who work on them are part of the thinking of their time. This is particularly the case with representatives of energy utilities, industries and government departments. It is extremely easy for professional jealousies and self-protective attitudes to come to the fore. Vested interests may refuse to concede, even as an hypothesis, anything which they feel weakens their position. The preliminary report of the Ford Foundation's study, for example, contained strongly dissenting memoranda from senior members of the oil, aluminium, nuclear and electrical industries.

But this is not a reason for giving up the effort to think rationally, broadly and systematically about the energy future. It simply demonstrates the need to widen the basis of consultation and discussion. The press and television obviously have a crucial role to play in this. Ideally, the choice of the energy path followed should be made, and regularly reviewed, by a well-informed public and its political representatives. History, the present position, expectations, economics, jobs and a variety of other factors define the boundaries within which energy planning necessarily takes place. The true job of the 'forecaster' is to illuminate the real choices which any particular society has in determining its energy future.

15

Economic Growth and Energy

One of the reasons commonly advanced for increased energy consumption is that it is necessary for economic growth. If this is true, it has to be taken seriously by governments.

Continued economic growth into the indefinite future is clearly impossible. It is unfortunately equally true that industrial society has not yet learned how to cope with a lack of economic growth. If growth in the Gross National Product (GNP)* of an industrial country slows down seriously, or ceases, its economy runs into severe trouble. For example, the building industry and others which exist to provide for growth find themselves short of work. There is no need for extra roads, factories, offices and services; society can get by with what already exists. Construction workers, architects, engineers, surveyors and all those whose work is concerned with making provision for growth are left with little to do. Secondary effects follow as these people reduce their spending on cars, consumer durables, holidays, entertainment and consumption of all kinds. Unemployment begins to mount.

All this happens when growth merely slackens or ceases. Some economists talk of the 'steady unemployment' growth rate, the minimum growth rate required if unemployment is not to increase. An actual decline in the level of GNP has even more severe consequences. A major fear if this happens even for a

---

* Gross Domestic Product (GDP) and Gross National Product (GNP) seem to be used almost indiscriminately in this context. In UK official statistics, GNP is the total value of goods and services produced, together with property income from abroad. GDP omits the property income from abroad. The difference is small – about 1·5 per cent. Other definitions which differ slightly from these are sometimes used, but the differences are well within the margin of error of the correlations discussed here.

short period is that it may quickly spiral downwards into a full-scale recession with a loss of business confidence, falling share prices, reduced capital investment, massive unemployment and a government so short of revenue that it is unable to stimulate the economy or relieve hardship with welfare payments. Such worries are, indeed, legitimate.

Any connection between energy consumption and economic growth therefore has a wide political and social significance. Figure 12 shows GDP and energy consumption for a large number of countries. The broad relationship is clearly identifiable. The higher the energy consumption, the higher the GDP. The countries with the highest income levels, such as the USA, Canada and Sweden, are also among the top energy consumers. At the other end of the scale, the low-income countries, such as India, Ghana and Thailand, are also very low consumers of energy. The non-commercial energy used by subsistence farmers is excluded from the figures, but this makes little difference since their contribution to GDP is also small. There is no avoiding the general conclusion: the higher the GDP, the higher the consumption of energy. It would also seem to follow that if a country wishes to increase its GDP, it must consume more energy.

Closer examination of Figure 12, however, begins to reveal certain anomalies. Sweden and Canada have virtually the same GDP per head, but Sweden's energy consumption per head is only 65 per cent that of Canada; France has the same GDP per head as Norway with half the energy per head. There is an even more striking difference between the USSR and Switzerland; though they have the same energy consumption per head, the GDP per head in Switzerland is three times that in the USSR. One reason these differences are not immediately so obvious is that, because of the huge spread in the figures between the energy and income of the highest and lowest countries, such diagrams of GDP and energy consumption are normally drawn on a logarithmic scale, which tends to reduce the visual impact of such differences.

The study from which Figure 12 is taken was called *How Industrial Societies Use Energy*[45] and was published in 1977. It picked apart the energy consumption of nine major industrial countries in an attempt to see if there was any regular statistical relationship

Figure 12. Per head GDP and energy consumption – selected countries, 1972

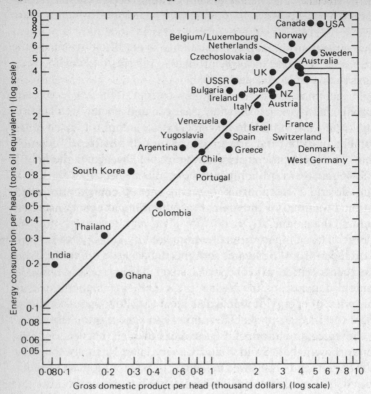

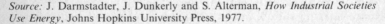

Gross domestic product per head (thousand dollars) (log scale)

Source: J. Darmstadter, J. Dunkerly and S. Alterman, *How Industrial Societies Use Energy*, Johns Hopkins University Press, 1977.

between the amount of energy consumed in a country and its level of wealth. It found that energy consumption and GDP production in the countries studied was so enmeshed in the geographical, industrial, economic, social and political character-istics of countries that useful generalizations were almost impossible to make. The authors concluded:

No tidy reckoning is possible on these questions. Our study points to complex and diverse reasons for intercountry differences in energy consumption. Variations in energy/output ratios should not in them-selves be viewed as indicators either of economic efficiency or even of energy efficiency . . . in numerous of its aspects, energy consumption is essentially a by-product or, at best, only one element within a wider framework of societal arrangements and choices.

This is not surprising. A country like the USSR which has a great deal of heavy industry producing relatively low-value products such as iron and steel will obviously tend to have a relatively high energy consumption per unit of GDP; another way of putting this is to say that the 'energy intensity' of its GDP is high. The energy intensity of the GDP in a country which relies on light industry and financial services will obviously be much lower. There is no mystery about the difference between the USSR and Switzerland; it is entirely to be expected. There is, in fact, no rigid relationship between energy consumption and national wealth; it is only remarkable that it was ever considered there might be one.

But making international comparisons has never been more than a peripheral academic interest for energy economists and forecasters. Their real concern has been the relationship between economic growth and energy consumption inside individual countries. Energy planning, particularly that relating to electricity production, began to become increasingly important in the 1960s. In the successful pursuit of economies of scale and energy efficiency, power stations had become very large. They took a long time to plan and build and they cost a lot of money. This brought a need to predict energy demand a considerable way into the future if shortfalls in supply or excess generating capacity were to be avoided.

One measure of the relationship between economic growth and energy consumption is what is called the 'energy coefficient'. This is the ratio between the change in GDP and the change in energy consumption in a particular year. An energy coefficient of + 1·0 means that if there is an increase, or decrease, of say 3 per cent in total GDP, there will be a corresponding 3 per cent change in energy consumption. A negative energy coefficient means that the changes move in opposite directions: a coefficient of − 1·0 would mean that a growth in GDP of 3 per cent was accompanied by a corresponding fall in energy consumption.

Study of past statistics showed that though there were fluctuations on a year-to-year basis, the average energy coefficient over a longer period was relatively stable. In the period 1952–69 in the UK, for example, the coefficient varied between 4·0 and 0·1, but over the period these variations were ironed out giving a long-term average of 0·6. In other industrial countries there were similar short-term variations around a rather higher long-term average of 0·8.

The energy coefficient was a boon to planners searching for a means of predicting future energy consumption levels. It appeared to offer a simple, objective and quantitative measure of the relationship between energy demand and economic growth. It was the basis of energy planning in most of the industrial countries in the 1960s and 1970s. Governments predicted whatever levels of economic growth appeared feasible or necessary for their political lives; the energy planners plugged in their latest refinement of the value of the energy coefficient and arrived at an energy demand. The chairmen of utilities and power corporations could then proclaim that their country's economic future depended on an immediate commitment of funds to the necessary programme of investment in the energy sector. Everything seemed to be in harmony and few questioned what appeared to be the natural order of energy matters.

Events since 1973 have, however, shown scant respect for the historical precedents established in the previous two decades. In the period 1973–84 the energy intensity of GDP fell by about 20 per cent among the OECD countries. In some countries the value of the energy coefficient not only fell sharply, but became negative. This was particularly the case in the years 1979–83, when some quite startling figures are recorded in the International Energy Agency's 1985 review. In Germany, for example, GDP grew by about $17 billion, at an average rate of roughly 0·4 per cent per year, but energy consumption fell by 2·9 per cent per year, to give an average energy coefficient of −5·5. The USA had an average energy coefficient of −3·53 for the same period, while that of Japan was −0·41.

It is easy to put this down to the exceptional energy circumstances of the 1970s and early 1980s, and assume that it is only a question of time until normality returns. The question is what is normality. The 1950s and 1960s were also rather special. It was a time when the pent-up consumer demand of war-time and the years of post-war austerity was suddenly released. Cheap oil was flowing in apparently limitless quantities into the industrial economies. Consumers went on a buying spree. The number of cars in use soared; in Britain car registrations rose from 3·5 million in 1955 to 11·5 million in 1970. At the same time, homes were being equipped with energy appliances at a previously unprecedented rate.

But such periods of growth in energy consumption do not continue indefinitely. The phenomenon of 'saturation' of energy demand in particular areas of consumption needs to be taken into account. Take, for example, the question of domestic heating. When a family is poor, heating standards are low. Perhaps only one room is heated to a level which people find comfortable. Improved heating therefore has a high priority, and when the family income increases some of the extra money is spent on it. The temperature is raised, more rooms are heated, and finally full central heating is installed. People take advantage of the freely available hot water to have more baths and showers. While this is happening, it will almost certainly be possible to identify a definite correlation between rising income and expenditure on energy for domestic heating. But beyond a certain level, no matter how rich they are, people do not want any increase in the temperature of their homes; and there is a limit to the amount of time they want to spend washing themselves.

Similarly, in the early stages of affluence families acquire washing machines, refrigerators, colour televisions, and clothes driers; somewhat later they may buy dish-washers and deep freezers. These are the heaviest consumers of domestic energy. The next purchases such as home computers, video recorders, electric carving knives and the other energy-using devices with which the better-off citizens of industrial society surround themselves use proportionally very much less energy. The increase in energy consumption therefore begins to level off as incomes continue to grow.

The same is true of transport. As incomes rose, families which had never had a car before used their new wealth to buy one. The previously low level of ownership meant there was a large demand waiting to be filled. But the rate of growth in ownership began to slow down eventually. The increase in car ownership in the UK between 1970 and 1984 was 4·7 million, compared with 8 million in the period 1955–70.

Technical change within industry in general works to increase the efficiency with which energy is used to produce materials and finished goods. As old equipment is replaced, the energy intensity of production therefore tends to fall. A spectacular example of this in the UK was the case of rail transport. In the period 1960–76 freight traffic fell by about a quarter and passenger traffic by 12·5 per cent; but energy consumption was cut to a sixth of what it was in 1960. This was done simply by eliminating the picturesque but appallingly inefficient steam locomotive.

With the maturing of an industrial society there is also a shift away from manufacturing industry towards the services, or 'tertiary' sector of the economy. An increasing proportion of the population is employed in sales, finance, insurance, professional activities and government. In the USA in 1956, 'the number of white-collar workers (professional, managerial, office and sales personnel) outnumbered the blue-collar workers (craftsmen, semi-skilled operatives, and labourers)' for the first time.[46]

Another distinctive feature of the mature industrial society is the amount of time which must be spent by its citizens in receiving the education necessary for them to be able to obtain and retain employment within an ever more complicated economic and social system. The 'learning force' – that is, all those 'in some form of continuing as well as formative education' – outnumbered those working at their jobs for the first time in the USA in 1965.[47]

Services and education obviously do not require as much energy as shipbuilding or the manufacture of steel. There is therefore a tendency for the average energy intensity of GDP production to fall as an industrial society matures and moves towards what is sometimes described as a 'post-industrial society'. In fact, it is not necessary to wait for the emergence of the post-industrial society to see the beginning of a reduction in the energy intensity of GDP. Historical research into energy and economic statistics for the eighteenth and nineteenth centuries in the UK and the USA have shown that the decline has been going on for a long time indeed in both these countries.

The pattern seems to be as follows. In the beginning of industrialization, large amounts of additional energy are required as industries are established and the physical infrastructure of the country is being built. Domestic energy consumption also rises rapidly as living standards and disposable incomes rise. It is easy to see why the energy intensity of nineteenth-century urbanized industrial Britain was considerably greater than the agricultural and small-scale craft-based society it succeeded. But once the basic structure of the industrial economy was established, further increases in GDP did not require as much energy as before. The average energy intensity of GDP therefore started to fall. The peak in the energy intensity of GDP was in fact reached in the UK as long ago as the 1880s; in the USA it came in 1910; in Italy, which industrialized much later, the peak was in the 1950s.

Moreover, as might be expected, the peak energy intensity was lower in each case. Victorian Britain relied on machinery which was extremely inefficient in its energy use. Its housing stock was certainly not built with any notion of economical fuel consumption in mind. The USA had the benefit of the engineering and industrial experience which had been accumulated before its main industrialization drive began. Italy's industrial growth in the middle of the twentieth century could rely on considerably more sophisticated and fuel-efficient machines. One has only to compare the massive beam engines used in early industrial Britain with a small Fiat car engine with the same power to see why there should be such a difference.

In picking the energy coefficients of the 1950s and 1960s as the basis of their long-term forecasts, energy planners appear to have made an unfortunate choice. The surge in energy consumption in those post-war decades now appears to be the result of quite unusual circumstances. If the oil price rises and economic disruption of the 1970s had not happened, it is arguable that saturation effects would, in any case, have begun to damp the growth in energy consumption in the domestic sector.

The energy forecasters of the industrial world now find themselves in somewhat of a quandary. There has been more than a decade in which the OECD countries have had virtually no growth in their total energy consumption, but this has persuaded none of the forecasters that the long-term energy coefficient should be zero. The tendency has been to treat the past decade as an aberration and assume that growth in demand must soon resume its upward path. Thus, while the International Energy Agency's 1985 review of energy policies and programmes shows that total energy demand among its members fell by 0·9 per cent per year in the period 1979–84, it assumes that growth will be 1·9 per cent per year in 1984–90, and 1·4 per cent per year in 1990–2000. This may indeed happen. But it will not be because normality has been restored after a period of malfunctioning of the energy-using and economic systems of the industrial world. It will be sheer coincidence.

There are few, if any, short-cuts available to the energy planner. The relationship between energy consumption and GDP is not pre-ordained by immutable laws; it is a specific product of the history, particular circumstances and pattern of development followed in each country. Nor is the future energy consumption in a country rigidly linked to what has happened in the past. It depends on the energy policies adopted by governments. It is true there is a high degree of inertia in the energy supply system in all the industrial countries; the methods of energy supply and consumption cannot be changed overnight. But the room for manoeuvre is far wider than most governments or official energy forecasters ever like to admit.

16

Conservation: Getting More from Less

Waste brings no benefits to those who pay for it. It is a leaking hot-water tap, a draughty house, lights burning in an empty building, or a 300-horsepower car crawling through city traffic. In the biosphere, any creature which does not make the most of what is available to it is eliminated by more efficient competitors. Wastefulness is an evolutionary dead-end.

Eliminating waste should be a priority in any rationally run society. It should not require an atmosphere of crisis to justify it. But prosperity has conditioned many people into believing that avoiding wastefulness is something which is done only in times of emergency. Viewed with any detachment, such an attitude is absurd: energy may be cheap and plentiful at the moment; the aim should be to keep it that way for as long as possible. All consumption depletes finite resources and ultimately brings scarcity. Waste brings the hard times sooner, makes them worse than they might have been, and ill equips people to deal with them.

Conservation, which is simply another name for cutting down on waste, tends to have negative connotations. It is often associated in the minds of politicians and the public with hardship, scarcity and imposed frugality. Properly understood, conservation is, of course, none of these. It means producing more with less; it is liberating rather than oppressive. Nowhere has energy use reached its theoretically possible efficiency. In all the myriads of ways in which energy is used, the same result could be achieved with less consumption.

One area in which great improvements are possible is the energy consumed in heating and cooling domestic and commercial buildings. Figures for 1984 show that it was about 45 per cent of the total in the UK; in Sweden, with its much harsher climate, it was just below 40 per cent; in the USA it was just over 30 per cent; and in Japan it was only 25 per cent. In domestic houses, heating and cooling normally account for about three quarters of the total consumption, the rest being used for heating water, cooking, lighting and domestic appliances. The amount of waste can be enormous.

Heat is lost from a building by conduction through its walls, roof and windows; by draughts; and by deliberate ventilation. The proportion of losses attributable to each will vary, depending on the particular building and how much ventilation those living in it choose to have. There is no way of 'eliminating' the losses which take place through the fabric of a building – in spite of what many of the purveyors of double glazing and insulations claim in their brochures. All the heat energy in a house is always lost; left to itself in cold weather, a house will cool down to the same temperature as outdoors, no matter how well sealed and insulated it is. The important issue is how quickly this happens, or, more practically, how much fuel must be used to keep it at a comfortable temperature in winter.

The rate of heat loss through the fabric of a building depends on the materials of its construction and the difference between inside and outside temperatures. The insulation characteristics of a building material are described by what is called its U value. This measures the rate at which energy flows through the material when there is a temperature difference of 1°C between inside and outside faces. Table 25 shows some typical U values for various materials and methods of construction – the higher the U value, the worse the performance as an insulant. It can be seen that a solid brick wall loses heat three times more quickly than an insulated cavity wall. A single-glazed window loses heat nearly six times as fast as the insulated cavity wall: the all-glazed wall facing the view can therefore be very costly in energy. The advantages of roof insulation are clearly shown in the table: 100 millimetres (4 inches) of glass fibre or similar insulation in the roof space can cut the rate of heat losses to a sixth those of an uninsulated roof; adding a further 100 millimetres reduces the rate by a further 45 per cent.

Insulation standards vary widely in Europe. Traditionally,

Table 25. Standard U values for typical elements of building construction

Construction	U value watts/metre² deg C
Solid 105 mm brick wall with 16 mm dense plaster	3·00
Cavity brick wall with 105 mm leaves and 16 mm dense plaster	1·50
Cavity wall with 105 mm brick outer leaf, 100 mm lightweight block inner leaf and 16 mm dense plaster	1·00
Ditto but with foam insulation in cavity	0·45
Single-glazed windows	5·60
Double-glazed windows	3·20
Pitched tile roof with felt, roof space and 10 mm plaster-board ceiling	2·00
Ditto with 25 mm glass fibre or mineral wool	0·70
Ditto with 50 mm glass fibre or mineral wool	0·50
Ditto with 75 mm glass fibre or mineral wool	0·40
Ditto with 100 mm glass fibre or mineral wool	0·33
Ditto with 200 mm glass fibre or mineral wool	0·18

those in the U K and the Netherlands have been among the worst; those in Sweden among the best. In 1981 about 25 per cent of U K dwellings had no loft insulation whatsoever. Among those which had such insulation, the vast majority had less than the recommended thickness of 100 millimetres (4 inches). Only about 10 per cent of houses had cavity-wall insulation.

A Dutch study carried out in the 1970s compared the thermal performance of its housing stock with that of Sweden.[48] Its survey of houses showed that the average heat loss with an external temperature of − 10°C was 12 kilowatts. In other words, maintaining a constant indoor temperature of about 21°C required the operation of the equivalent of twelve single-bar electric fires. In Stockholm the average heating loss from comparable dwellings, with a lower external temperature of − 18°C, was less than half this – just 5 kilowatts. And the loss from some especially well-designed apartments built around 1958 in the Ostberga district of Stockholm was only 2·2 kilowatts. In other words, these apartments could be kept warm with an external temperature of − 18°C using little more than the incidental heat from lights, cooking and the pilot lights from gas appliances.*

* Pilot lights are surprisingly heavy energy consumers. A large pilot light, such as that on a gas boiler, uses about 2000 kilowatt-hours per year, almost 10 per cent of the total annual energy consumption of a U K dwelling.

The poorly insulated houses of Britain and the Netherlands are a legacy of the past. It will be many decades before they can be replaced by new buildings constructed to higher insulation standards. Nevertheless, a considerable amount can still be done with these old houses. It is nearly always possible to install loft insulation. Draughts around doors and windows and through the cracks in suspended ground floors can be sealed. Houses with cavity walls can have them filled with insulating foam. Double glazing can be fitted, particularly in living rooms with large windows. Heavy curtains can be used at night. Provided it is done carefully and precautions are taken to prevent internal condensation, internal linings can be fitted to solid walls to improve their thermal performance.

A detailed study of the potential for saving energy by 'retrofitting' the UK housing stock was carried out in 1982.[49] It looked at the cost and energy-saving implications of a programme in which all lofts were brought up to a standard of 100 millimetres of insulation and cavity walls were also filled with foam insulation. The figures showed that this would reduce total domestic energy consumption by 17 per cent. It was also extremely cost-effective. The cost per unit of energy saved would be only about a quarter of the price to the consumer of gas, the cheapest domestic fuel.

There is no excuse for not building new houses to high standards of thermal performance. The financial costs of incorporating insulation in roof spaces and cavity walls are much smaller than those involved in trying to 'retrofit' them to existing buildings. This particularly applies to double glazing. The labour costs of taking out old windows and replacing them with double glazed units are usually so high that the change cannot be justified on energy-saving grounds under UK conditions. If the double-glazed units are installed when the building is being built, the economics are much more favourable.

In the UK a major step in the right direction was made with the publication of the 1982 Building Regulations, which laid down mandatory standards for building construction. The new U value for walls is 0·6 as opposed to 1·7 in 1965 and 1·0 in 1975; that for roofs is 0·35 compared with 1·4 in 1965 and 0·6 in 1975. The study commented:

Although the 1982 Building Regulations substantially improved the required minimum insulation standards ... these are well below the economically desirable standards ... For example, by including commercially available and cost-effective measures such as 200 millimetres of loft insulation, floor and cavity-wall insulation, and 'heat mirror' glazing, the annual total fuel consumption of a typical new semi-detached house built to 1982 standards could be reduced by 22–23 per cent ... Further reductions of about 6–8 per cent can be had for no extra cost by simple design measures such as correct window orientation to maximize 'passive' solar energy gains.

Programmes to upgrade the thermal performance of buildings can therefore be justified on the grounds of the savings to consumers. There is, however, a large measure of public ignorance of what kind of measures make economic sense; there is also a justifiable fear of being cheated by short-lived 'cowboy' firms which unscrupulously promote various forms of building insulation and double glazing. Moreover, the poor, the old and those living in rented accommodation are unlikely to have the means or the necessary incentives to make substantial investment in energy conservation measures with a relatively long pay-back period. There is therefore a major role to be played by any government which is serious about encouraging energy conservation by domestic consumers.

Another reason for considering energy conservation at a government level is that it is an alternative to increasing the supply of energy. If the costs of building a nuclear power station or opening a new coal-mine are compared with those of saving the same amount of energy, conservation usually wins by a very large margin. The insulation programme for the UK discussed above would produce an annual saving of electricity equal to that of a 1300-megawatt power station; but the capital investment costs of the conservation programme would be about half those of the power station and, unlike the power station, conservation has no running costs.

The scope for energy conservation is not, of course, restricted to domestic housing. Transport is one of the largest energy consumers in the industrial world. It accounts for about 21 per cent of total energy consumption for all purposes in the OECD region. In 1984 this was 736 million tonnes of oil. In the USA, where the total consumption by transport in 1984 was 450 million tonnes of oil, it accounts for about 25 per cent of the national total. It is a somewhat lower proportion in most of the other industrial countries. In the developing world, however, transport can be the dominant consumer of commercial fuels: in Mali, it accounts for over 60 per cent of the country's oil consumption.

Substantial improvements in the energy economy of motor vehicles have taken place throughout the industrial world over the past fifteen years. In the UK, for example, the figure for vehicle-kilometres travelled by cars has increased by 59 per cent, whereas the total consumption of petrol increased by 46 per cent. One of the main reasons for this is that energy efficiency became fashionable in the 1970s and motor companies found they were able to sell vehicles on the basis of their lower fuel consumption.

It was also brought about by government actions. The US government introduced legislation which compelled manufacturers to reduce the average fuel consumption of the vehicle fleets they were producing from 13 litres per 100 kilometres in 1978 – which was itself a considerable improvement on the 'gas guzzlers' of the 1960s – down to 8·4 litres per 100 kilometres by 1985; this target date was later moved to 1987. Assuming the regulations are not rescinded and the motor manufacturers meet them, the whole US car fleet will eventually consist of these more energy-efficient vehicles.

The European countries, Japan, Canada and Australia have also introduced voluntary or mandatory schemes to reduce fuel consumption. In the UK, motor manufacturers agreed a reduction of 10 per cent in the 1980 figure to a 1985 target of 9·1 litres per 100 kilometres. Somewhat lower consumption figures were set in Sweden, Canada and Australia. Japan was aiming at a figure of 7·8 litres per 100 kilometres in 1985.

The room for achieving further savings through improved engine design and the use of lighter materials is considerable. Automotive engineers, having accepted the challenge of improving efficiency, see further significant reductions in fuel consumption being made in the coming decades. Major savings could also be obtained by encouraging a shift towards smaller vehicles. Many of the smaller cars now being manufactured have a fuel consumption of 5 litres per 100 kilometres or less. Increasing the proportion of these in the total vehicle fleet would lower the average consumption without any further technical advances.

There are also many ways in which energy consumption in other sectors of the economy can be made more efficient. Technical improvements which lead to lower energy consumption are being made in virtually all areas of economic activity. The following selection of examples makes no pretence to being comprehensive; it is given merely to illustrate the range of possibilities.

Advances in coating glass or using thin plastic films enable the thermal performance of double glazing to be improved substantially for relatively low increases in the total cost of units. These work by reflecting long-wave infra-red radiation back into the building, effectively increasing the insulation value of the window. The increase in cost over a conventional double glazing unit is about a third; the insulation value approximately doubles. Such windows could have a dramatic effect on heat losses from offices and other commercial buildings with large glazed areas.

There also appears to be an almost limitless potential for saving energy in industry. Older industrial buildings were notoriously badly designed for energy-efficient operation. Many manufacturing processes are carried out in large thin-walled sheds with open doors and with no attempt to use energy efficiently. Steam pipes may be unlagged and leaking; skylights and windows may be broken or jammed open. Often the energy used for heating and ventilation is considerably in excess of that used in the manufacturing process. Major savings can be obtained by nothing more elaborate than simple good housekeeping measures.

Many industrial processes can be improved too. Demonstration projects carried out by the U K government's Energy Technology Support Unit (E T S U) in the ceramic tile and pottery industry in the past few years have shown that savings of 50–65 per cent in the energy required per kilogram of output could be achieved. They also brought a reduction in breakages and the amount of labour required. Another demonstration project in which heat was recovered from the exhaust gases at a brick kiln and recycled to the drying chambers showed a saving of 62 per cent. Furthermore, ETSU provided support for a project to demonstrate the potential for saving energy in the sulphuric acid industry. There is a stage in the manufacturing process when the hot acid has to be cooled down. This used to be done by passing the acid through a cast-iron heat exchanger and sprinkling cold water on it. The reason why no heat was recovered was the fear that acid might leak through any heat exchanger and find its way into the system where the recovered heat was used. This problem was overcome by using a two-stage heat exchanger, with the first loop containing an acid-meter which would sound an alarm if any acid leaked into the water. The second loop of the heat exchanger was used for preheating boiler-fed water, thereby cutting down on the fuel required for steam raising. The project proved very successful and saved 1250 tonnes of coal equivalent per year, with a pay-back period of seventeen months. Within the next few years a further six companies had adopted the system, saving a total of 26 500 tonnes of coal equivalent per year; the pay-back period in each of these cases was a year or less.

A device with immense scope for use in energy-saving projects is the heat pump. This machine performs the apparently magical feat of taking energy from a low-temperature source, sometimes a river or the atmosphere, and raising its temperature to a useful level. The 'coefficient of performance' is used to measure the amount of useful energy produced by a heat pump compared with that used to run it. In practical operation, using the atmosphere as a heat source and delivering heat at, say, 50°C, the coefficient of performance of an electrically driven heat pump would be in the range 2·0–2·5; this means that a heat pump consuming 1 kilowatt would be producing 2·0–2·5 kilowatts of useful heat. The performance of a heat pump declines the greater the temperature difference over which it has to 'pump' the heat, and preferably this should not exceed 50°C.

Heat pumps are familiar objects in another guise: they are used for cooling in air-conditioning systems. The cooling unit takes heat from inside a building and dumps it, at a higher temperature, into the outside air. In a refrigerator the same principle is used. Heat is extracted from the cabinet and given off at higher temperature in the condenser coil at the back. It is sometimes said that a heat pump is a refrigerator in reverse; this is not so. It is using exactly the same principle as the refrigerator.

When it was first opened, London's Royal Festival Hall had a large heat pump installation which used the Thames as its heat source, but there were operating problems and the system was replaced. Since then the use of heat pumps for heating buildings has continued to teeter on the edge of being technically and economically viable. They have been the subject of innumerable publications and conferences and there is no doubt that they offer vast scope for saving energy. The fact that they are produced in small numbers means that they are still expensive and operating experience is limited; this in turn means that it has been difficult to find applications where they are reliable and cost-effective enough to be attractive to purchasers. But there are signs that the position is at last changing. A number of firms are now supplying heat pumps commercially in the UK. Around 150 have been installed in swimming-pool buildings; the heat is recovered from the moist warm air extracted by the ventilation system and is used in the heating system. Slow but steady progress can be expected in the development and wider use of heat pumps, but they are still a considerable way from being routinely installed in commercial and industrial buildings; their use in domestic heating systems lies even further into the future.

One of the simplest and most ingenious heat-recovery devices is the 'heat wheel'. It is widely used in Sweden, where it was invented and developed, but it is not as well known and widely used elsewhere as it deserves to be. It consists of a wheel, perhaps half a metre thick and a metre in diameter, made of wire mesh or some other material with good heat-absorbent qualities. If warm air is blown through the mesh, heat is absorbed; if cold air is then blown through, it is warmed by the stored heat. In practice the heat wheel is installed so that it intersects the inlet and outlet ducts of an air-ventilation system where, by rotating slowly, it absorbs heat from the outgoing hot air and transfers it to the incoming cold air. The efficiency of heat recovery can be as high as 80 per cent.

Although heat wheels and other heat-recovery systems can often be installed for less than the savings that they would bring in a single year, they are still surprisingly rarely used. The reason for this is partly ignorance. In many industries energy use has been taken as a cost element about which it was impossible to do anything much. The major costs have tended to be in the amount of labour used, and improved economic performance has tended to be associated with measures which reduce the amounts of labour required. Only in some of the modern heavy industries with high-energy use, such as chemicals and petroleum refining, has engineering expertise been deployed in a major way to reduce losses and recover waste heat. In Sweden, however, where keeping industrial buildings warm is a major problem, and can be cripplingly expensive unless it is done properly, heat-recovery systems are widely used.

No review of the potential for energy conservation can afford to ignore the electricity industry, the largest single consumer of energy in most of the industrial countries. Typically, it accounts for about a third of a country's total energy consumption. When electricity is generated from fossil fuels, 60–70 per cent of the energy must be sacrificed as waste heat. There is nothing culpable about this; it is not a result of incompetent engineering, but an ineluctable consequence of the laws of thermodynamics. It is the price that has to be paid for the convenience, flexibility and unique usefulness of electricity. It also highlights the energy advantages of 'thermodynamic matching' of energy supplies to their end-uses.

Poor-quality coal is an ideal power station fuel because it cannot be used elsewhere. The same is true of hydro or nuclear power: using them to generate electricity is the only practical way of using them to contribute to energy supplies. The use of natural gas for electricity generation, on the other hand, is thermodynamic nonsense, whatever its cash economics. In the USA, however, this is still done on a large scale: the total consumption of gas for electricity generation in 1984 was 74 million tonnes of oil equivalent. By contrast, almost the whole of the UK supply of natural gas is piped directly to consumers, thus providing domestic energy supplies roughly twice as efficiently as if the gas had been turned into electricity first.

The development of ways of using the vast quantities of waste heat from power stations seems an obvious objective in any campaign to reduce energy wastage. Unfortunately, this heat is at a very low temperature. That of the cooling water in a water cooled station will be perhaps 30°C. It is very difficult to find a use for such heat; a certain amount may be useful for winter heating of greenhouses or fish farming, but there is an obvious limit to such enterprises. The fact that large power stations are now usually built far away from centres of population adds to the difficulty of finding a use for the heat even if it were to be upgraded by employing heat pumps.

There is, however, a considerable potential in the use of power stations deliberately designed to produce both heat and electric power – they are usually called combined heat and power (CHP) stations. In these, instead of being cooled to the lowest temperature possible, the steam is drawn off at a usefully high temperature. There is a consequent fall in the efficiency of electricity generation to perhaps 20 per cent, but because the steam can be used for heating or other purposes, the overall efficiency of the system may be 70–80 per cent, twice that of a large modern power station. Alternatively, a CHP station may rely on a diesel engine to drive the generator with the waste heat in the exhaust gases being recovered in a heat exchanger.

The increased overall efficiency of operation of a CHP installation does not, however, mean that the energy consumption is reduced by a half if one is installed. The mathematics are deceptive, as can be seen in the schematic diagram in Figure 13. Case A shows the original position in which 40 units of electricity are provided at an efficiency of 40 per cent and an independent boiler supplies 120 units of heat at an efficiency of 75 per cent. The total energy input is 160 units. Case B shows the position when the CHP scheme has been installed. Now, 200 heat units are required to provide the electricity at a generating efficiency of 20 per cent. It is assumed that the waste heat is recovered at an efficiency of 75 per cent. The total fuel input to provide the same electricity and heat output is therefore 200 units and the total energy saving is 23 per cent.

The figure also illustrates another aspect of CHP installations: for the maximum energy benefit to be obtained, they need an appropriate and relatively stable balance between the heat and electricity loads. Any major deviations from this will lead to a substantially lower overall operating efficiency. They are there-

Figure 13. Comparison between energy inputs to separate and combined heating and electric power generation systems

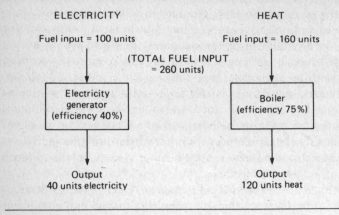

Case A: Separate Heat and Power

ELECTRICITY   HEAT

Fuel input = 100 units   Fuel input = 160 units

(TOTAL FUEL INPUT
= 260 units)

Electricity generator (efficiency 40%)   Boiler (efficiency 75%)

Output
40 units electricity

Output
120 units heat

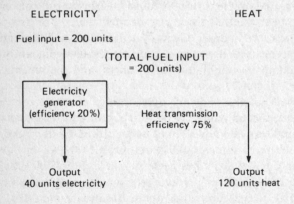

Case B: Combined Heat and Power

ELECTRICITY   HEAT

Fuel input = 200 units

(TOTAL FUEL INPUT
= 200 units)

Electricity generator (efficiency 20%)

Heat transmission efficiency 75%

Output
40 units electricity

Output
120 units heat

fore not particularly flexible in responding to changing heat and electricity requirements. They are most suited to industrial applications where the balance between heat and electricity consumption is fixed. When they are used for public supply, it is usually best if they are used to provide a fixed-base load of heating and electricity during winter, with the fluctuations and summer electricity load being supplied by other methods.

In spite of such problems, CHP schemes which generate

Conservation: Getting More from Less 269

electricity for the public supply and provide heat to dwellings and commercial buildings in urban areas – district heating schemes – are well established in some European and Scandinavian countries. They include Sweden, Germany and Denmark. One of the reasons for the success of the technology in these countries is the tradition of high-density urban areas in which people live in centrally heated apartment buildings. This reduces the costs of laying insulated hot water pipes. And as far as individual families are concerned, as long as the price is right, it is a matter of indifference whether the hot water in their taps and radiators comes from a boiler in the basement or a CHP plant a couple of kilometres away. It is a very different matter bringing individual pipes and installing new central-heating systems in the terraced rows of a typical British city.

The technical problems and costs of CHP have so far prevented any major schemes to supply domestic buildings from being implemented in the UK. Over the past decade major studies have been carried out into the feasibility of installing CHP schemes in nine different British cities. One envisaged converting an older power station which was nearing the end of its operational life to CHP in order to supply heat for part of Birmingham. The initial heat load unfortunately declined significantly because of companies going out of business, and the scheme was shelved.

The list of possible ways of saving energy could be continued indefinitely. A clear indication of the potential of those already available was provided by a study published by the International Institute for Environment and Development (IIED) in 1979. It was called *A Low Energy Strategy for the UK*.[50] It looked at how energy consumption might evolve over the fifty-year period between 1975, which was taken as the base year, and 2025. Two economic growth hypotheses were considered: a high case, in which the country's total GDP was assumed to treble by the year 2025; and a low case, in which it doubled by the same date. The economy was divided into four consumption sectors: industry, domestic, transport and commercial. Each was then examined to identify the most efficient methods of using energy already in use or likely to come into use in the near future. It was then assumed that these would gradually spread to the whole of each sector as equipment and buildings were replaced over the coming decades. No especially vigorous conservation campaigns or actions were assumed, though the government was expected to introduce legislation for higher building insulation standards and energy performance standards in cars and domestic appliances.

It used what forecasting jargon describes as 'surprise-free' projections. No new or exotic technical or social developments were assumed:

> One of our fundamental assumptions is that Britain's economy grows healthily along conventional lines: there is business as usual but more of it. This may be dismaying to those who are opposed to such growth – there are strong feelings, for example, against large increases in car ownership on both social and environmental grounds.

Standards of comfort and material welfare were assumed to increase:

> . . . houses become warmer so that everyone enjoys the amenities of the better-off today. Most families come to own freezers, dishwashers, clothes driers, colour TV, and other heavy users of electricity. Car ownership grows rapidly so that 72–75 per cent of households in 2000 have at least one car, compared with 58 per cent today . . . Air traffic grows 2·4–3·0 times . . . total industrial output increases by a factor of 1·7–2·2. The areas of offices, schools, hospitals, shops and restaurants increase by anything from 30–80 per cent.

The official view was that such increased living standards necessarily involved a massive increase in energy consumption. In the UK Department of Energy forecasts of energy demand produced at around the same time, the economic growth assumptions were almost identical to those in the IIED study. The energy projections, however, were essentially based on the idea of a fixed link between economic growth and energy consumption. Total UK energy consumption in the base year of 1975 was 330 million tonnes of coal equivalent (mtce). The official forecast demand figures for the year 2000 were 460 mtce for the low case and 570 mtce for the high case.

The results of the IIED study were startlingly different. In the high case, where GDP trebled over the fifty-year projection period, energy consumption increased by about 10 per cent up to the turn of the century and then fell back to its 1975 level of about 330 mtce by 2025. In the lower case, where GDP doubled, the total energy consumption fell by 14 per cent.

This study clearly demonstrates the potential for energy conservation which is already within the grasp of the industrial nations. To a degree virtually unimaginable a decade ago, energy conservation opens a possibility of sustaining economic growth and increasing material standards of living without significantly increasing total energy consumption. Indeed, a commitment to a truly vigorous energy conservation campaign could achieve significant reductions in energy consumption while maintaining a steady increase in living standards.

17

Reorganizing Society

Schemes for organizing society along more rational lines than humanity has hitherto managed are as old as Plato. Perhaps the first person to think the guiding principles should be those of thermodynamics was Frederick Soddy. He was a brilliant chemist who collaborated with Rutherford in the development of the theory of radioactivity, which they published in 1903; in 1913 he made the discovery of isotopes for which he was awarded the Nobel Prize in 1921. He was fascinated by the relationship between energy use and the evolution of human society. In the years immediately before the First World War he began to put forward the idea that it was necessary to go beyond economic theory and take into account the energy implications of industrial society. He pointed out that a crucial change had been made when society shifted from the use of constantly renewed or replaceable energy resources to dependence on the accumulated energy in the earth's reserves of coal. The economic chaos which followed the war convinced Soddy that society was deluding itself dangerously. He began to search for an energy theory of society. He wrote in 1922:

The laws of energy under which men live furnish an intellectual foundation for sociology and economics, and make crystal-clear some of the chief causes of failure not only our own but, I think also, of every preceding great civilization. They do not give the whole truth, but, in so far as they are correct to physics and chemistry, they cannot possibly be false.[51]

In a slightly later work he said of human history that

progress in the material sphere appeared not so much as a successive mastery over the materials employed for making weapons – as the succession of ages of stone, bronze and iron honoured by tradition – but rather as a successive mastery over the sources of energy in Nature and their subjugation to meet the requirements of life.[52]

He is also well worth quoting for the clarity of his description of the relationship between the flow of energy and materials and the activity of social and economic systems:

A continuous stream of fresh energy is necessary for the continuous working of any working system, whether animate or inanimate. Life is cyclic as regards the materials consumed and the same materials are used over and over again in metabolism. But as regards energy it is uni-directional and no continuous cyclic use of energy is even conceivable. If we have available energy we may maintain life and produce every material requisite necessary. That is why the flow of energy should be the primary concern of economics.[52]

His observations on the energy costs of industrial activities have a distinctly contemporary ring. Discussing the energy costs of a car, he looks at the tyres and says:

. . . If we pursue the tyres to their origin we shall find out how much of their cost is due to expenditure of energy. They call for a flow of the solar energy of a particular climate, physical labour in the rubber plantations, coal for the railways and ships that transport the raw materials from the tropics, as well as for the factories where it is made into tyres. These railways and ships, again, and all the buildings and equipment necessary for their manufacture, no less than the materials they use – the iron and metals and the coal which have to be mined – are the results of the expenditure of physical energy.[52]

He also saw the potential of nuclear power at a very early stage. In 1912 he wrote:

When coal is exhausted and the other physical resources of the earth have been squandered, when expanding civilization is met by a dwindling supply of energy, either science or the atom will have been tested to destruction and one or the other will be the arbiter of the future.[53]

H. G. Wells wrote his novel *The World Set Free*,[3] which deals with a society which has harnessed nuclear power, after hearing Soddy lecture. But apart from that, little attention appears to have been paid to his views on energy and society, and he himself failed to develop them. During the 1920s he became increasingly embittered and embroiled himself in ever more eccentric controversy on a wide variety of issues. In 1950, for example, he published a tract called *Frederick Soddy Calling All Taxpayers*.

In the 1960s, however, an increasing unease about economic growth and its consequences, particularly environmental pollution, began to be felt in the USA. The limitations on the availability of resources, including energy, also became a cause of worry. One of the people involved in this questioning of industrial society was the ecologist Howard T. Odum. He and his brother Eugene Odum had specialized in analysing the flows of energy through natural ecological systems. This painstaking and meticulous work requires a measurement of all the energy entering and leaving the system as well as a chart of the many pathways it follows within the system.

Howard Odum came to believe that the same basic analysis could be applied to the various activities of industrial society. The process of food production, for example, requires a sequence of energy-using steps. The ground is tilled by machines and fertilized with chemical products which have been manufactured in an energy-using factory. Harvesting requires further inputs of energy, as do the packing, distribution and final preparation of the food. He analyses a variety of systems in this way and claims that the 'energetics' provide some interesting insights. In monsoon farming, for example, the oxen or buffaloes seem to consume an inordinate amount of food considering the actual amount of work they do. Superficially, they appear to be a drain on the system. In fact, the animals act as an energy store for the farmer. They enable him to start cultivation immediately the climatic conditions are suitable. Stored energy then 'flows' from the animal into the cultivation process. This energy subsidy, applied at precisely the right time, enables the food crop to outdistance its weed competitors and exclude them from the tilled land.

A similar analysis of the role of the sacred cow in India also shows how they fit logically into the energy systems of society. They are not the parasites people sometimes take them to be. They glean their fodder from a wide variety of sources, many of them outside the farming system, and make it available as milk. Their dung provides cooking fuel in areas where wood is scarce.

They consume resources, but can also play a critically important role within the total energy system.

As a way of preparing for the future, Odum believes it is necessary to try to understand the whole of society in such energy terms. In his book *Environment, Power and Society* [54] he says:

> . . . energy language is used to consider the pressing problem of survival in our time – the partnership of man in nature. An effort is made to show that energy analysis can help answer many of the questions of economics, law and religion already stated in other languages.

He sees the control of energy flows as being the basis of all social organization and warns against the illusion that industrial society is permanent or self-sustaining. He says:

> Most people think that man has progressed in the modern industrial era because his knowledge and ingenuity have no limits – a dangerous partial truth. All progress is due to special power subsidies, and progress evaporates whenever and wherever they are removed.

He goes on to warn that the techniques of modern farming have not removed the basic constraints on food production.

> A very cruel illusion was generated because the citizen, his teachers and his leaders did not understand the energetics involved . . . A whole generation of citizens thought that . . . higher efficiencies in using the energy of the sun had arrived. This is a sad hoax, for industrial man no longer eats potatoes made from solar energy; now he eats potatoes partly made of oil.

The point is a valid one. Modern agriculture undoubtedly produces more food than primitive agriculture, but at a high energy cost. The beef and milk production of the fat cow in the battery farm are enormously higher than that of the scrawny animal of the peasant cultivator. This is achieved by virtue of the very large energy subsidies used by farming in the industrial world.

In a free-ranging state a cow has to devote a high proportion of its energy intake to the tasks of keeping warm or cool, finding food, fighting off the attacks of insects and other predators, and all the other necessities of survival. The surplus left over for producing flesh and milk is therefore relatively small. So the trick in intensive animal rearing is to remove as many energy-consuming tasks as possible from the cow so that it is free to turn a higher proportion of its food intake into flesh. It does not mean that the other jobs required for its survival do not need to be done. They are performed instead by machines and people: the atmosphere in the battery farm is controlled by heating and ventilation equipment; machines bring in food and remove waste; teams of vets, scientists, genetic engineers and technologists devise ways of optimizing usable flesh production and fighting off disease; tractors, harvesters and lorries sow, reap and transport the fodder. Some of Europe's most 'efficient' farmers use powdered milk from the surplus food mountain as a cattle feed supplement.

It is certainly useful to draw attention, as Odum does, to such energy-using aspects of life in a modern industrial society. Increasing energy use has made a great deal possible, but it has also created a new kind of dependency. If there were a really serious breakdown in energy supplies to the industrial countries, there would be a rapid and more or less total collapse of food production and distribution.

The case for using energy wisely and economically is overwhelming, particularly if a long-term view is taken. Finite resources cannot be mined indefinitely. Substitutes will eventually have to be found and the present energy appetite of industrial society will no doubt have to be curbed. This, however, is a long way from accepting that energy efficiency should be the basis of morality or that human society should seek for models of behaviour in the implacable competitiveness of the biosphere.

An extremely ambitious proposal for the total reorganization of society came from the *Ecologist* magazine in Britain. In January 1972 it produced a document called 'A Blueprint for Survival'.[13] This was supported by the signatures of thirty-three prominent academics among whom were Sir Julian Huxley, Sir Frank Fraser Darling, Peter Scott and seventeen university professors; five of the signatories were Fellows of the Royal Society. A letter written to 'welcome the document as a major contribution to current debate' and signed by another fifty scientists was published in *The Times*. The 'Blueprint' attracted immense national and international attention. One commentator wrote:

The 'Blueprint' for me is nightmarishly convincing. For those who like myself have regarded environmental considerations as a respectable, but not particularly arresting, type of cosmetic surgery on Industrial Society, it is mind-blowing. After reading it nothing seems quite the same again.[55]

The 'Blueprint', and the response to it, must be seen not as isolated events, but as the culmination of a number of trends of rising public concern about pollution and resource depletion. Rachel Carson's *Silent Spring*,[56] published a decade earlier in the USA, had played a major part in awakening the awareness of Americans, and others, to the dangers of carelessly applied technology. The writings of the Erlichs, Barry Commoner and others during the 1960s had heightened such anxieties; and Hubbert in *Resources and Man*,[10] published in 1969, had predicted a peak in world oil production in the 1990s. The 'Blueprint' therefore brought together in a succinct form many of the worries of the preceding years. It took a wide view of the perils the world was facing: energy scarcity was just one of the elements in its diagnosis of the plight of humanity. It said the only hope lay in a complete restructuring of industrial society, and proposed a detailed programme of population control, decentralization of industry, de-industrialization, de-urbanization, revision of energy-intensive practices in agriculture, and the development of non-depleting energy sources. It called for a comprehensive and 'orchestrated' change in the whole style and structure of society which would lead, over a period of about a hundred years, to the 'stable society' which was defined as 'one that, to all intents and purposes, can be sustained indefinitely while giving optimum satisfaction to all its members'.

The initial excitement of the launch was not, of course, sustained. The practical details of the proposals proved impossibly difficult to work out. No one, for example, could suggest a practical way of persuading industry to begin to close itself down in the interests of ecological stability. The only recourse was to withdraw to the sidelines, while continuing to issue warnings, and wait until events forced industrial society to its senses.

The 'Blueprint for Survival' was not the only voice calling for radical change in the early 1970s. There were many others who believed that the case for abandoning the centralized, polluting, heavy resource-consuming, urban-centred patterns of industrial society was irresistible. This inspired what came to be widely known as the 'alternative technology' movement. Other names used to describe it include 'soft technology', 'low-impact technology' and 'eco-technology'. In the words of one commentator, David Dickson:

> The approach of each group usually contains some combination of a set of common elements. These include the minimum use of non-renewable resources, minimum environmental interference, regional or sub-regional self-sufficiency.[57]

The movement concerned itself, at a practical level, with the development of small energy-capturing devices: solar heaters, windmills, waterwheels, methane digesters for domestic houses or small communities, and methods of growing food in urban locations. The emphasis in all of this was on home, or craft, methods of operation rather than factory production. The objective was to free people from the domination of large-scale centralized systems. The ultimate extension of this was the 'autonomous eco-house', a totally self-contained dwelling relying entirely on 'ambient' energy sources and recycling all its own waste products.

Although it focused heavily on small-scale energy technologies, the basic drive behind alternative technology was political. To quote from Dickson again: '. . . from the political perspective, any discussion of alternative technology must be necessarily utopian . . . and the various tools, machines and techniques described will be given the label "utopian technology".' He says of 'utopian technology': 'It forms a framework that is designed to eliminate the alienation and exploitation of the individual, and the domination of the environment by the activities of man.'

In a book called *Living on the Sun* another proponent of alternative technology wrote:

> The inexhaustible energies inherent in sunlight, in wind and water, in plants, in the earth's geothermal heat, and in the ebb and flow of the tides, provide a far firmer foundation for liberty, equality and fraternity among Mankind than the energy *products* purveyed by the present oligopolistic cartels, both capitalist and state-capitalist.[58]

Both these authors consider that the utopian vision of society is prior to and more important than that of technology. They are idealists with ideas about how society should function, rather than technologists. The technology they discuss is a hypothetical one and essentially derived from their idea of society. Their prescriptions, with their emphasis on personal liberty and social harmony, are based far more on the utopian anarchism of writers like Kropotkin than on the realities of trying to use small-scale energy technologies to provide life's necessities.

Alternative energy technology has turned out to be a fairly unmitigated disappointment to the enthusiasts of the 1970s. For the most part it has not worked very well, if it has worked at all. Where there have been successes, they have tended to be because of the application of modern engineering and advanced production methods, and considerable amounts of money. Nevertheless, the dream of a more free and decentralized society persists. Nuclear power remains a focus of a great deal of passionate opposition on the grounds that it epitomizes the technocratic and freedom-threatening aspects of modern society. In this view, it would still be unacceptable even if all doubts about its safety were completely resolved. The fear is that a society based on large, centralized technologies inevitably imposes an authoritarian rule on its people. It is interesting how well Aldous Huxley, writing in 1946, before there had been any significant development of civilian nuclear power, expressed this present-day fear:

... it may be assumed that nuclear energy will be harnessed to industrial uses. The result, pretty obviously, will be a series of economic and social changes unprecedented in rapidity and completeness. All the existing patterns of human life will be disrupted and new patterns will have to be improvised to conform with the non-human fact of atomic power. Procrustes in modern dress, the nuclear scientist will prepare the bed on which mankind must lie; and if mankind doesn't fit – well, that will be just too bad for mankind ... It is probable that all the world's governments will be more or less completely totalitarian even before the harnessing of atomic energy; that they will be totalitarian during and after the harnessing seems almost certain.[59]

This fear of the social implications of nuclear power has

received perhaps its most eloquent expression in the work of the American writer Amory Lovins, who coined the evocative term 'soft energy'. His book *Soft Energy Paths*, published in 1977, contrasts two energy futures between which he feels humanity has to choose. The 'hard' path relies on nuclear power, coal, large-scale developments of shale oil, solar power stations and the whole panoply of large-scale energy technology. He analyses what he believes are the consequences of such developments and concludes that they would lead to a nightmare society in which the worst of Aldous Huxley's fears would be realized. In contrast with this is the 'soft' path to a society in which conservation is given priority and energy sources are matched to their end-uses so that waste is minimized. Energy supplies are provided by small-scale, renewable, non-polluting, 'benign' energy sources. At the end of the 'soft path' lie:

. . . jobs for the unemployed, capital for business people, environmental protection for conservationists, enhanced national security for the military, opportunities for small business to innovate and for big business to recycle itself, exciting technologies for the secular, a rebirth of spiritual values for the religious, traditional values for the old, radical reforms for the young, world order and equity for globalists, energy independence for isolationists, civil rights for liberals, states' rights for conservatives.[60]

Alas, the case that he makes for the feasibility of the soft path is less than fully convincing. His book is crammed with calculations, but it is far from being a detached piece of technical analysis; numbers are used as part of a polemic in favour of his social vision. His optimism about the potential of small-scale energy technologies and, above all, about the social changes which would be required if they were to become the basis of society's energy supplies is not supported by dispassionate observation of the contemporary world. There is little sign yet of a major resurgence of 'such values as thrift, simplicity, diversity, neighbourliness, humility and craftsmanship' on which he relies for the creation of this new society.

At present, discussion of alternative technology and soft energy paths is muted. Much of the crusading spirit of the 1970s has disappeared. Partly this is because the energy scare is over; there are no longer worries about the security of oil supplies or the imminent depletion of energy resources. But it is also because of the amount of progress that has been made in getting environmental and energy issues taken seriously.

The 'green' political parties have become an important part of the European political scene and their influence on energy policy is undoubtedly real. Official attitudes towards conservation and pollution control have changed to an extent which would have seemed incredible fifteen years ago. The extraordinarily high energy-demand forecasts of the 1970s have been quietly buried by governments and energy utilities. Among the major political parties, nuclear power and energy in general have become issues on which they know they must tread warily.

A large amount of the credit for such changes in attitudes towards energy is undoubtedly due to the alternative technologists and writers like Lovins. Their radical visions remain unfulfilled; nuclear power stations are still being built. But it is a real measure of their success that so many of the bitterly contested energy issues of the 1970s are no longer in dispute.

18

From Crisis to Complacency?

Capture and control of energy made it possible for human beings to emerge from an insignificant niche in the biosphere to become the planet's dominant species. Coal fuelled the Industrial Revolution; oil carried society beyond it and enabled it to reach the furthest planets; nuclear energy has made it possible to make the world uninhabitable. The balance of military terror is the background against which society must evolve the strategies for its continued survival. Assuming it is possible to avoid a nuclear suicide, the future of human society depends, finally, on the availability of energy. It is worth reviewing the position as it now appears.

As Part Two showed, there is a large measure of uncertainty about the quantities of resources actually in place. There are even greater doubts about the amounts that it will be practicable to extract. But there is no question that the quantities involved are very large. History, moreover, has shown that with technological developments more resources tend to be discovered, and a higher proportion of those found can be extracted. There is no reason to suppose that the end has been reached in either of these trends.

Coal resources are truly immense. They are certainly large enough to sustain any likely level of world consumption for at least a couple of centuries. The worries about the use of coal are not about depletion, but about its environmental effects. It is heavily implicated in the problem of acid rain. As the full enormity of what is happening across the woods and lakes of Europe is gradually revealed, it becomes increasingly likely that the acid rain issue will grow in importance in the eyes of governments and the public.

The other polluting effects of coal are also likely to come under increasing scrutiny. Environmental monitoring of the effects of energy use has come of age because of worries about nuclear power to which the majority of attention has so far been devoted. The same sophisticated techniques are available to study the effects of coal burning; it is only a matter of time until they are applied. In particular, there is the unresolved question of the release of carbon dioxide from coal combustion and its contribution to a possible global greenhouse effect. There is as yet no conclusive evidence which would justify a major alarm about coal burning, but the threat is awesome. There is no doubt that if coal were now being considered as a new energy source and subjected to the same scrutiny as nuclear power, it would be deemed utterly unacceptable.

Coal, however, has far too important a role as an industrial fuel in countries like the USA, USSR, China and the UK for it to be possible to dispense with it without major difficulties over the next few decades. Moreover, it provides an alternative to dependence on oil for electricity generation, which keeps the power of OPEC in check. It is therefore probable that it will retain its position as the world's second most important fuel for a considerable time to come; and consumption is particularly likely to grow in Third World countries with coal reserves. But the possibility of a severe backlash developing against the use of coal as the public becomes more informed about its dangers cannot be entirely discounted.

The world oil position is that the firmly identified oil resources are sufficient to maintain the present level of consumption for a further thirty-four years. In this respect, the position is better than it was in 1973, when the ratio of proven reserves to production was thirty years. Ultimate reserves appear to be sufficient to sustain the present level of consumption for about a hundred years. Long before reserves are exhausted, however, the price of oil will start to rise and consumption will gradually start to fall as it is gradually priced out of its lower-value uses. Oil will therefore be available in large quantities for high-value uses for centuries to come.

Once conventional oil prices have passed the levels they reached in the late 1970s, it will also begin to become economical to produce oil in increasing quantities from the tar sands and heavy oil deposits of the world. At somewhat higher prices, as the research and development work of the 1970s has shown, the production of oil from shale and the production of syncrude from coal begin to become economical. South Africa demonstrates that, even today, a substantial industrial economy can supply a high proportion of its liquid fuel needs with syncrude.

There is also considerable room for shifting oil out of uses which can be served by other fuels and reserving it for those applications for which it is uniquely suited. Oil-fired power stations which are replaced by coal, hydro or nuclear plants release heavy fuel oil which can then be cracked in a refinery to provide the higher fractions which are required for transport, motive power, lubricants and other uses for which petroleum products are more or less essential.

If a breakthrough can be made in storage battery technology, it will open the way to electric cars suitable for urban use at least. This would also help to cut down the demand for petroleum fuels for transport. The pressure to move in this direction will undoubtedly be intensified by growing public awareness of the connection between the oxides of nitrogen produced in car exhausts and acid rain. If adequate electric vehicles can be developed, there will be rapidly mounting pressure on governments to create the necessary legal and tax framework to facilitate their introduction.

Natural gas reserves are estimated to be roughly equivalent to those of oil, though there is some evidence that they may be very much greater. At present rates of consumption, the estimated total ultimate reserves are sufficient to last for around another two hundred years. There is therefore room for considerable growth in natural gas consumption before resource constraints begin to become an issue.

Within this global picture, hydro and nuclear power are still minor energy sources. Hydro supplies just under 7 per cent of the world total consumption. The share of nuclear power is just about 4·5 per cent. Both hydro and nuclear are, of course, extremely important in their local context. If the nuclear industry were to close down in France, the country would lose over 60 per cent of its electricity generating capacity. But in the broad sweep of global energy consumption, nuclear power is almost irrelevant. Its present total contribution is no more than the growth which took place in coal and gas consumption between 1983 and 1985.

The energy picture is thus very different from that of 1976, when the first edition of this book was published. The atmosphere at that time was one of crisis. Now the anxiety seems to have completely disappeared. A decade ago there were worries about whether industrial society would reach the year 2000 without a major upheaval in its ways of obtaining and using energy; now the consensus is that the turn of the century will see business very much as usual. It is instructive to examine how the transition from crisis to complacency has taken place.

When the 'oil crisis' arrived in 1973, there was a widespread misapprehension that it was connected with resource depletion. In fact, it was almost entirely a matter of economics and world politics – and where the industrial world's oil came from. The most important basic factor was that in the late 1960s the USA had moved from being a major exporter of oil to being a heavy importer. Up till then the USA had always had vast surpluses of oil literally on tap, but now the balance of supply had shifted to the Middle East. The countries there had a different economic and political agenda to the USA. There was no spare production capacity in the world to replace the shortfall if any of these major producers decided to withhold supplies.

This was in complete contrast with the position during the 1956 Suez invasion, when the oil-exporting Arab states had no leverage on the world oil system. They were powerless as far as cutting off European oil supplies were concerned. The USA dominated the international oil scene, and any oil shortage in Europe could be dealt with by bringing some of its surplus capacity into production. In 1973, however, the Arab nations of OPEC were able to play a major part in enforcing a settlement in the war between Egypt and Israel. They were also able to increase the price of oil by a factor of four, pushing prices up from $2·50 to $10 per barrel. After the Iranian revolution in 1979, they were able to do the same again and prices went up to $40 per barrel. Again, however, this was as a result not of resource scarcities, but of control of production and markets.

This control has now been broken by disagreements between OPEC members about production levels, the rise of oil production by other countries, and the diversification of the energy supply systems of the industrial world. The price of oil at the end of 1986 was about $15 per barrel. In real terms that is about what it was at the beginning of the 1970s. At one point in 1986 it even dropped below $10 per barrel. There is so much spare production capacity that even the cutback of nearly 50 per cent by OPEC since 1979 has failed to prevent the world market being flooded with oil. It could, however, have been very different.

In 1973 the world's total energy consumption was about 5·9 billion tonnes of oil equivalent. By the end of 1985 it had increased by about 1·5 billion tonnes. If the bulk of that had been supplied by oil, as most planners were assuming in the late 1960s and early 1970s, oil consumption would now be about 5 billion tonnes per year. Production would almost certainly be running far in advance of the rate of discovery, the prospects of serious constraints as a result of resources depletion would be much closer, and the problem of finding alternatives to oil would be very much more difficult.

One of the major consequences of the OPEC actions of 1973 was to make other energy sources appear much more attractive on the grounds of price and reliability of supply. Instead of there being a continued growth in oil consumption, the whole of the world's extra energy consumption came from sources other than oil. The shares taken were 40 per cent by coal; 30 per cent by natural gas; 19 per cent by nuclear; and 11 per cent by hydro. The overall effect was to reduce the proportion of oil in total world energy consumption from 47 per cent to 38 per cent. Moreover, there was significant progress in conservation. The total economic growth in the OECD countries in the period 1973–85 was about 30 per cent, whereas energy consumption grew by only 2·6 per cent.

The industrial world has thus proved itself to be far more resilient and flexible than almost anyone believed possible a decade ago. Those who believed in a rigid connection between economic growth and energy consumption grimly forecast the end of industrial civilization if there were any break in the upward climb of energy consumption. Hence came the clamour for massive programmes of nuclear power, synfuels and other sources of energy. In retrospect, it is clear that the 'energy crisis' was to a very large extent a creation of the major energy interests.

Their opponents saw such economic growth and increasing energy consumption leading to intolerable pollution and a destruction of all the humane values of society. They saw radical change as necessary: bicycles instead of cars; villages instead of cities; handicrafts instead of mass production; wood instead of plastic. The emphasis was on changing social values and restructuring society on more frugal and energy-efficient lines. They too were convinced that a cessation of growth meant the end of industrial society, but they welcomed it.

The 'energy crisis' of the 1970s was, in fact, never as bad as it was popularly portrayed. There was no question of the world running out of oil or any of its major energy sources. The only real point at issue was whether the previous rate of growth in oil consumption could be sustained. When it was said that oil consumption was going to reach a peak in the year 2000, this was widely construed to mean that all the world's oil would be depleted by then. But, in fact, the most pessimistic forecasts still envisaged the world using as much oil in 2030 as in 1970.

Today the energy prospect is comparatively bright for the industrial world. Its energy supply sources are considerably more diversified than they were fifteen years ago. The technological possibilities of conservation have been demonstrated and are becoming widely accepted. Old habits die hard among governments and energy utilities, but even the most conservative of spirits no longer believe in the growth rates in energy consumption which were deemed essential a decade ago. There is also a much greater sensitivity to the issue of pollution. Now, all but the most irresponsible commercial and governmental enterprises recognize that preserving the biosphere is not an optional extra; it is a condition of the continued existence of the human race. Oil spills, land dereliction, poisoning of the lakes and seas, contamination of ground water, acid rain, disruption of the earth's thermal balance – these are no longer the whimsical concerns of eccentric environmentalists. Energy planning has to take place within the constraints imposed by the need to keep the earth habitable.

The prospects for the developing world are also brighter. It is now clear that there is no immediate resource constraint on its use of oil and coal. The energy resources are there for any country which can pay for them. Moreover, as vehicles, industrial machinery, commercial equipment and domestic appliances are made to higher standards of energy efficiency, their use in developing countries will bring the same savings as they do to consumers in the industrial world. As economic and industrial development take place in Third World countries, they will therefore tend to do so at lower energy intensities than in the past.

This is the bright side of the picture. It also needs to be borne in mind that it is possible to undo the progress that has been made in the last decade. Because oil prices are now low, there will be pressure to revert to the energy consumption standards of a decade ago. Energy conservation standards may be lowered again. In a pervasive climate of complacency about energy, consumption may start to climb again, leading to a repetition of the problems of the 1970s.

Any indefinitely prolonged growth in energy consumption is obviously absurd. If world energy consumption were to continue growing at 5 per cent per year, as it did through the 1950s and 1960s, it would double every fourteen years and increase eightfold in just over half a century. Such a process has to end relatively soon; it is automatically self-limiting. If resource limitations do not restrict the growth in consumption, it will eventually reach a level where the biosphere or the heat balance of the earth are disrupted with catastrophic consequences. Energy consumption would then fall because of the disappearance of energy consumers.

At the moment, it appears as if a few decades of precious time have been bought. It would be very easy to squander them. They provide the time to weigh the choices; to look again at nuclear power in a fundamental way and decide if there is not a better route to harnessing it as a major long-term resource; or, if it is rejected, to be sure about what should go in its place. The study of how society can and should obtain and use its energy resources has occupied a place in the centre of the world's concerns for the past fifteen years. Now that the spotlight of public attention is switching away from it, that does not mean it has become irrelevant.

As the human population inexorably mounts, and standards of living continue to rise, energy consumption is bound to increase. The effects on the environment will become more severe and resources will continue to deplete. Prudence dictates that the growth in energy consumption should be kept as low as possible. The last fifteen years have provided the industrial world with a salutary shock and some valuable lessons. The task now is to build upon what has been learned and ensure that lack of foresight, ignorance or carelessness do not lead the world into another energy crisis. The next time, it would almost certainly be very much worse than anything experienced up to now.

Appendix

LENGTH

1 inch = 2·5400 centimetres	1 centimetre = 0·3937 inches
1 foot = 0·3048 metres	1 metre = 3·3281 feet
1 statute mile = 1·6093 kilometres	1 kilometre = 0·6214 miles

AREA

1 acre = 0·407 hectares	1 hectare = 2·4710 acres
1 hectare = 10 000 square metres	1 square kilometre = 100 hectares

1 square mile = 2·5899 square kilometres = 640 acres
1 square kilometre = 0·3861 square miles = 247·1 acres

WEIGHT

1 lb = 0·4536 kilograms	1 kilogram = 2·2046 lb

1 tonne = 1000 kilograms = 2204·6 lb
1 Imperial ton = 2240 lb = 1·0161 tonnes
1 short (US) ton = 2000 lb = 0·9072 tonnes

VOLUME

1 cubic foot = 0·0283 cubic metres	1 cubic metre = 35·3147 cubic feet
1 Imperial pint = 0·5682 litres	1 litre = 1·7600 Imperial pints

1 Imperial gallon = 1·2009 US gallons = 4·5461 litres
1 US gallon = 0·8327 Imperial gallons = 3·7854 litres
1 barrel = 42 US gallons = 34·97 Imperial gallons = 159·0 litres

ENERGY

1 kilowatt-hour (kWh) = 1·34 horsepower hours = $1·98 \times 10^6$ foot pounds = 3·412 British thermal units (Btu) = 859·845 kilocalories = 3·6 megajoules (MJ) = 0·034 therms

1 terawatt-hour (TWh) = 1×10^3 gigawatt-hours (GWh) = 1×10^6 megawatt-hours (MWh) = 1×10^9 kilowatt-hours (kWh)

1 gigajoule (GJ) = 277·78 kilowatt-hours

POWER

1 kilowatt (kW) = 1·34 horsepower

1 gigawatt (GW) = 1×10^3 megawatt (MW) = 1×10^6 kilowatt (kW)

TEMPERATURE

1 Kelvin = 1 degree Celsius = 1·8 degrees Fahrenheit

For conversion:

$$°C = (°F - 32) \times \frac{5}{9}$$

$$°F = \left(°C \times \frac{9}{5}\right) + 32$$

0 K ('absolute zero') = $-273·15°C$

OIL INDUSTRY UNITS

1 tonne crude oil	= 7·3 barrels (average)
	= 256 Imperial gallons
	= 301 US gallons
1 barrel per day	= 50 tonnes per year (average)
1 tonne motor spirit	= 8·45 barrels (average)
1 tonne fuel oil	= 6·70 barrels (average)

CONVERSIONS BETWEEN FUELS

Conversion factors between different fuels vary widely between sources. The following conventions have been used in the statistics compiled by British Petroleum and have been generally used in this book.

1 tonne of oil = 1·5 tonnes coal = 3·0 tonnes lignite = 1·11 cubic metres natural gas = 12 000 kWh = 400 therms = 40×10^{12} Btu = 10×10^6 kilocalories = 43 000 MJ

(*Note:* The figures have been slightly rounded for simplicity.)

The output of hydro, nuclear and geothermal stations is usually expressed in terms of the fuel which would be required to produce the same amount of electricity in a modern power station. One million tonnes of oil produces about 4×10 kWh of electricity.

The following are approximate calorific values for domestic fuels:

1 kg kerosene (paraffin)	= 11·94 kWh/kg	= 43 MJ/kg
1 kg natural gas	= 12·50 kWh/kg	= 45 MJ/kg
1 kg coal	= 7·78 kWh/kg	= 28 MJ/kg
1 kg wood (oven dry)	= 5·55 kWh/kg	= 20 MJ/kg
1 kg wood (air dry)	= 4·16 kWh/kg	= 15 MJ/kg
1 kg dung or agricultural residue (air dry) =	3·30 kWh/kg	= 12 MJ/kg

References

Sources of tables and figures are noted where they occur. The following are the sources referred to by superscript numbers in the text.

1 Egon Larsen, *Atomic Energy: The First Hundred Years*, Pan, 1958.
2 Thomas Robert Malthus, *An Essay on the Principle of Population*, first edition, 1789; Penguin, 1970.
3 H. G. Wells, *The World Set Free*, first edition, 1914; Collins, 1956.
4 K. Marx, *Capital*, quoted in T. B. Bottomore and Maximilien Rubel, eds., *Selected Writings in Sociology and Social Philosophy*, Penguin, 1967.
5 J. Stanley Clark, *The Oil Century: From the Drake Well to the Conservation Era*, University of Oklahoma Press, 1968.
6 Herbert S. Jevons, *The British Coal Trade*, first edition, 1915; David & Charles, 1972.
7 Frederick Alderson, *Bicycling: A History*, David & Charles, 1972.
8 J. D. Bernal, *Science in History*, Volume 2, Penguin, 1969.
9 A. C. Walshaw, *Heat Engines*, Longmans Green and Co., 1956.
10 M. K. Hubbert, chapter on energy resources in Committee on Resources and Man, National Academy of Sciences National Research Council, *Resources and Man*, W. H. Freeman, 1969.
11 M. J. Chadwick and Nils Lindman, *Environmental Implications of Expanded Coal Utilization*, Pergamon Press, 1982.
12 T. Gold, 'Oil from the Centre of the Earth', *New Scientist*, 26 June 1986.
13 'A Blueprint for Survival', *Ecologist*, January 1972.
14 P. R. Odell, 'The Future of Oil: A Rejoinder', *Geographical Journal*, June 1973.
15 S. C. Ells, *Recollections of the Athabasca Tar Sands*, Department of Mines and Technical Surveys, Ottawa, 1962.
16 *An Energy Policy for Canada*, Volumes I and II, Ministry of Energy, Mines and Resources, Ottawa, 1973.

294 *References*

17 *Ionizing Radiation: Sources and Biological Effects*, UN Scientific Committee on the Effects of Atomic Radiation, 1982 Report to the General Assembly.
18 *Nuclear Power and the Environment*, Sixth Report of the Royal Commission on Environmental Pollution, HMSO, 1976.
19 Quoted in Irvin C. Bupp and Jean-Claude Derian, *Light Water: How the Nuclear Dream Dissolved*, Basic Books Inc., 1978.
20 Lawrence M. Lidsky, 'The Quest for Fusion Power', *MIT Technology Review*, January 1972.
21 J. C. Emmett, J. Nucknolls and L. Ward, 'Fusion Power by Laser Implosion', *Scientific American*, June 1974.
22 G. L. Kulchinski, 'Fusion Power – An assessment of its impact on the USA', *Energy Policy*, June 1974.
23 H. C. Hottel and J. B. Howard, *New Energy Technology: Some facts and assessments*, Massachusetts Institute of Technology Press, 1971.
24 *Energy Conservation: A Study by the Central Policy Review Staff*, Her Majesty's Stationery Office, 1974.
25 S. H. Salter, 'Wave Power', *Nature*, 21 June 1974.
26 R. F. Post and S. F. Post, 'Flywheels', *Scientific American*, December 1972.
27 J. K. Dawson, 'The Prospects for Hydrogen as a Fuel in the UK', *Atom*, May 1974.
28 L. B. Escritt, *Sewage Treatment: Design and Specification*, Contractors Record, London, 1950.
29 Ariane van Buren (ed.), *A Chinese Biogas Manual*, ITDG Publications, London, 1979.
30 G. Foley and G. W. Barnard, *Biomass Gasification in Developing Countries*, Earthscan, 1983.
31 Geoffrey Barnard and Lars Kristofferson, *Agricultural Residues as Fuel in the Third World*, Earthscan, 1985.
32 Jacqueline Ki-Zerbo, 'Women and the Energy Crisis in the Sahel', *Unasylva*, vol. 33, no. 133, 1980.
33 J. Huizinga, *The Waning of the Middle Ages*, 1924; Penguin, 1955.
34 Erik P. Eckholm, *The Other Energy Crisis: Firewood*, Worldwatch Institute, 1975.
35 G. F. Taylor and M. Soumare, *Strategies for Forest Development in the Semi-Arid Tropics: Lessons from the Sahel*, symposium at Wageningen University, Netherlands, 1983.
36 Quoted in *Firewood Crops – Shrubs and Tree Species for Energy Production*, National Academy of Sciences, 1983.
37 S. P. Raju, *Smokeless Kitchens for the Millions*, Christian Literature Society of Madras, 1953.
38 M. Christaaens, *Report on the Final Discussion about Dissemination*

of Woodstoves, Woodstove Seminar, Catholic University of Louvain, 1982.

39 E. F. Schumacher, *Small is Beautiful*, Sphere Books, 1974.

40 Lloyd Timberlake, *Africa in Crisis*, Earthscan, 1985.

41 G. Foley, *Exploring the Impact of Conventional Fuel Substitution on Woodfuel Demand*, Earthscan, 1985.

42 D. H. Meadows *et al., The Limits to Growth*, Universe, 1972.

43 *Times* report, 22 April 1972.

44 'Exploring Energy Choices' (a preliminary report of the Ford Foundation's Energy Policy Project), Washington, 1974.

45 J. Darmstadter, J. Dunkerly and S. Alterman, *How Industrial Societies Use Energy*, Johns Hopkins University, 1977.

46 Daniel Bell, 'Notes on the Post-Industrial Society', quoted in Nigel Cross, David Elliot and Robin Roy, eds., *Man-Made Futures: Readings in Society, Technology and Design*, Hutchinson Educational in conjunction with the Open University, 1974.

47 E. L. Trist, 'The Structural Presence of the Post-Industrial Society', quoted in *Man-Made Futures* (see Source 43).

48 *Energy Conservation: Ways and Means*, Future Shape of Technology Foundation, The Hague, 1974.

49 G. Leach and S. Pellew, *Energy Conservation in Housing*, International Institute for Environment and Development, 1982.

50 G. Leach, C. Lewis, F. Romig, A. van Buren and G. Foley, *A Low Energy Strategy for the United Kingdom*, IIED, 1979.

51 Frederick Soddy, *Cartesian Economics*, Henderson, 1922.

52 Frederick Soddy, *Wealth, Virtual Wealth and Debt*, Allen & Unwin, 1926.

53 Frederick Soddy, *Matter and Energy*, Williams & Norgate, 1912.

54 Howard T. Odum, *Environment, Power and Society*, Wiley-Interscience, 1971.

55 Lewis Chester, *Sunday Times*, 6 January 1972.

56 Rachel Carson, *Silent Spring*, Houghton-Mifflin, 1962; Penguin, 1965.

57 David Dickson, *Alternative Technology*, Fontana/Collins, 1974.

58 Godfrey Boyle, *Living on the Sun*, Calder & Boyars, 1975.

59 Aldous Huxley, Foreword to *Brave New World*, Triad, 1946.

60 Amory B. Lovins, *Soft Energy Paths*, Penguin, 1977.

Index